FRED WHITSEY'S
GARDEN FOR ALL SEASONS

Fred Whitsey's

Garden for all Seasons

HAMLYN

Acknowledgements

Colour photographs: Derek Gould, page 36; Jerry Harpur, pages 35, 121 (Heslington Manor), 139 (M. Bell); Photos Horticultural, pages 17, 70, 140; The Harry Smith Horticultural Photographic Collection, pages 18, 69, 87, 88, 122.

The publisher would like to thank the BBC for giving their permission to publish *New Vistas in Gardens*. This chapter is derived from a talk by Fred Whitsey broadcasted on BBC Radio 4 on 12 November 1981.

Published 1986 by
Hamlyn Publishing,
a division of the Hamlyn Publishing Group Limited,
Bridge House, London Road,
Twickenham, Middlesex, England

Copyright © original articles IPC Magazines Ltd 1986
Copyright © this compilation Hamlyn Publishing 1986

The material in this book derives from articles
previously published in *Popular Gardening* magazine.

ISBN 0 600 30604 6

Printed in Great Britain by
Butler & Tanner Ltd, Frome and London

Contents

Introduction

If a garden is an attempt to put order upon the unruliness of nature and tame it nearer to the heart's (or the eye's) desire, this book is like a garden. It is an anthology of articles that have appeared in the weekly magazine *Popular Gardening* over some years as season has followed season, cut from the pages with scissors and brought together to give them some sort of permanency, much in the way that you might cut a bunch of flowers and dry them so that their life may not be quite spent with the passing moment.

The origin of these articles is like a garden too. Just as the gardener responds to the inspiration that comes in a sudden flash or to the urgencies of the fine weekend, these pieces of writing sprang from some idea that came to us in the office, sometimes when a particularly appealing photograph arrived – from a justly proud reader as often as from a professional. Or they may have been occasioned by an event in my own garden that set the spirit soaring and made me want to take the reader by the lapel and tell him about it in the way that gardeners always do. Or again, it may have been something I saw in the course of garden visiting. And then, I admit, some were undeniably written out of disciplined necessity because it was the week either when this was in flower or that had to be done. Whatever the source it accounts for the somewhat random, though I hope not rambling, nature that is akin to the way gardens themselves are created.

In the way that we do plant our gardens, acting on impulse rather than principle, inspired by a touch of insight or freshly acquired knowledge rather than following plans, this book has grown rather than been compiled. With the help of Barbara Haynes, Hamlyn's Gardening Editor who combines the skill of a book editor with a profound knowledge of gardening, we have brought together a sheaf of articles that might offer the armchair reader still more inspiration to set his fingers itching for the

7

trowel or reaching for his own notebook of garden jottings, perhaps even to get up and drive straight to the nearest garden centre.

As a race gardeners may be calculating but they are not very objective. They are as full of prejudices as they are of passions. They can stand rapt with admiration for something that others may find looks just ordinary or not worth remarking about. They have theories and ideas that seem crackpot to their fellow men. They delight in things others wouldn't notice. They worry about the seemingly ridiculous. They harbour wild fears, though on the other hand they know that what nature takes from them with one hand she gives back with the other, that whatever trials she may subject him to her gifts will be munificent. They're an irrational lot. And that explains why the tidy-minded would find a little imbalance in the character of this book, perhaps a heavy emphasis here, a light touch there. It is the gardener's character, his prepossessions, which of course change with the seasons, that it represents.

Nature is constantly teaching us lessons. Some we learn, some we ignore. But our gardens are a schoolroom where all is done with the fun children find in working on projects. What I have learned repeatedly through contact with other home gardeners and visiting many gardens is that more gardening is really done in the mind than on the ground. This conclusion forced upon me is supported by the proliferation of gardening books and then reinforced by the number of times that at *Popular Gardening* we had been asked for such ruminative a book as this. Perhaps by sharing experiences and ideas it may contribute to the delight of that cerebral horticulture.

1
New Vistas in Gardens

Growing plants is easy compared with placing them in gardens. Placing them, that is, in such a way that they make the best use of the site and themselves, and allowing for the fashion in which they develop, the silhouettes they eventually form. I have known the gardener of deep knowledge and long experience who sat and confessed that no plant in his garden had stayed in the same spot where he had first put it. A better idea had always occurred to him at some time later and he had moved it. I suspect it is something to which many others would confess, as I do myself. Or else they would sometimes sit and look at what they had created and mutter 'If only I'd put that further to the left' . . . 'I ought to have had the foresight to put in three times as many of those' . . . 'That's just grown too big for that spot but I can't bring myself to take it out now, after all these years' . . . The problems never get less.

One way of coming to terms with them is to use mockups of the trees and bushes you put in, perhaps a sheaf of branches tied to a broom handle to resemble a tree, some prunings to serve as what a bush will look like in time, and then move these about until the right spot is found. Not in a morning, though, but over several days; perhaps even a succession of weekends. It's one of the royal roads towards successful garden making, which after all is largely a matter of placing plants as well as choosing them. And here in the pages that follow are some more thoughts on this perplexing matter.

Fashions in garden styles

If you hold, as many people do, that the making of gardens is something of an art form, then you'll agree it can't stand still. It must always find new methods of expression. The art of garden-making has always moved on under the impact of changing social and economic patterns, influenced by the materials available to the garden artist. And, of course, the most potent of these are the plants.

There was a time when garden plants were banished from gardens altogether, as those who led the 18th-century landscape movement tore up the elegant gardens of the past. Then the only plants that the designers were interested in were grass and a very limited number of species of hardwooded trees. Their parks – you can hardly call them gardens – are regarded by some as one of the glories of our inheritance, an artistic triumph to rank with our literature and our church music. Others don't agree. They see 18th-century landscapists as vandals who despoiled beautiful gardens and deprived them of Renaissance features inspired by noble Italian models – their elegant balustrades, perfectly proportioned flights of steps and intimate gazebos. The only trysting places the 18th-century landscapists provided were clumps of trees on top of draughty hills.

Perhaps, though, this reaction was one of those historical movements nothing can stop. For those elaborate gardens which the landscapists replaced had themselves grown out of earlier enclosures – mediaeval gardens created for the cultivation of medicinal plants or herbs, both to make foods palatable and to overcome human stenches. In the pre-landscape garden, design had become everything. It had an existence independent of nature. All was artifice. It was neither horticultural nor sylvan. It was due for a change.

Plant collecting

But when the next reaction came early in the 19th century it struck like a tempest. There was a dynamic man around named John Claudius Loudon, a man of superhuman energy and the most violent Victorian zeal, who went about not only making gardens but telling everyone else how they should garden. Loudon was passionate about plants and collected and distributed everything he could lay hands on.

It was also the great era of voyaging and exploration, when every expedition had a botanist, and everyone who went abroad wanted to bring home some of the strange and wonderful plants he saw, like the first fuchsias, and the first sprig of winter jasmine. The greenhouse was invented. Fuel was cheap and so was labour. The cultivation of exotic plants either kept in conservatories or put out for the summer, had everything going for it.

But it didn't last. Social change, and the rivalry of a different kind of planting, each took a hand in putting an end to it. Another type of plant, or rather two types, were weaving a new spell – conifers from North America and shrubs, the rhododendron in particular, from the Far East. Together they helped to create the woodland or at least the informal garden, a style which seemed at one time one that gardeners would follow for ever. No matter what the size of the canvas, castle or cottage garden, the informal garden of trees and shrubs, where no one need be ashamed of a few weeds, was what we were told we should all aim at. Indeed, if old William Robinson, that thunderer who was the scold of early 20th-century gardeners, had anything to do with it, we should actually be growing weeds. Plants, according to Robinson, must decide the character of the garden. And his influence dominated gardening fashion through the first half of this century.

But brambles eventually grew over the wild garden – and so came the next revolution. The ideal of the romantic English garden was realised – and realised by thousands of ordinary people. Of course, it had long existed in water colours and on calendars and it was a spirit that had always been waiting in the wings. But the same leisure, prosperity and mobility that in the 1960s enabled ordinary people to visit great country houses for the first time also took them into gardens they had never seen before.

The romantic English garden

By then, Hidcote, that National Trust garden up on the Cotswolds, one of the greatest flights of gardening imagination ever to take off, had been refurbished and was attracting thousands of visitors. Sissinghurst, Vita Sackville-West's garden in Kent, became everyone's province – and everyone's inspiration. She had been inspired by Hidcote. These two truly represented the romantic English garden, tumbling with roses, perfumed with lilies, fragrant with herbs, built upon a broad structure of shrubs, making a tapestry of rich colourings. At last the teachings of Gertrude Jekyll, who was a contemporary of Robinson but had her gardening boots more firmly on the ground, were heeded by a wide public, and gleaning much from her influence on Hidcote and Sissinghurst there were dozens who tried to copy them.

White gardens began to be made wherever 'colour supplement man' dwelt. Borders had to be composed of subtle blends of colour, never sharp contrasts. Contrasts were only permissible with foliage, which had become almost as important as flowers. By then, of course, the flower-arrangers had spread their influence across the land, and we'd talk always learnedly, if not with understanding, of 'texture' and 'accents'.

Underlying all the sophistication was the notion – only the notion, not the reality – of the English cottage garden, a tousled mass of pretty flowers all set off by beautiful leaves of Pre-Raphaelite intricacy and perfection. Today the gardens that make the greatest impact on those who go to see them seem to have been made by flower-arrangers. But where do we go from here? We can't stay on a plateau of perfection. Decadence and disillusion must set in as perfection becomes commonplace, and we say we've seen it all before.

What of the future?

I can see two vistas opening up here. The first is determined by the size of everyday gardens. I can't foresee garden plots of any size being available in the future. Nor can I see jumbled cottage gardens, however sophisticated, being in the least appropriate to new housing developments. In fact, the tiny plots seem to offer little scope for the gentle pursuit of gardening at all. That is, without a greenhouse. A greenhouse can create horticultural opportunity where none exists. An old-fashioned lean-to borrows heat from the house and helps insulate it at the same time. It doesn't need to be heated and it isn't wildly expensive – not if you adapt your plants to the limited protection you offer them. There are countless plants from the temperature regions of the earth that will flourish in an unheated conservatory.

The other vista I see opening up before us is the composition of our borders. I think we shall go on growing plants collected together in borders. We've tried the other extreme – growing them free-standing in grass. It doesn't create the kind of garden scene you always want to look out at, if only because it doesn't change enough. We've also tried the so-called 'close-boskage' system, in which you plant a lot of shrubs closely, so that they interlace and form thickets. We've gone through mixed borders, too. More often than not they become mixed-up borders, and you find they yield sporadic bursts of colour only here and there.

The next stage could be what I've called the transformation-scene border. For this you choose half a dozen different plants – shrubs, bulbs, hardy perennials – that flower successively at different seasons, and then, using as many of each as the border will take, you interplant them to follow one another. It's a simple system but full of possibilities and permutations. There are several things to be said in favour of it.

The first is that your border always seems full of colour. The bursts come in measured succession. I'm assuming, of course, that your borders lead away from the main point of vantage, so that the garden – by perspective – is made to seem larger than it really is. Another merit is that the borders make a really bold effect, not a spotty, hesitant one. And you're not tied to one colour scheme.

It can change several times over the course of a year, a bit like Versailles during Louis XIV's time. Armies of gardeners would descend on the formal flowerbeds when the Court had gone in to lunch and swap all the plants over. When they came out again, it all looked different. I'm not suggesting that we can make such dramatic transformations with perennial plants and shrubs, but certainly with this method of planting it's possible to surprise visitors who come to you often. The same border looks quite different from one month to another.

Successional planting

Let me recount one or two ways in which I've tried to apply it in our garden. In April one of our borders, no more than 12 m (40 ft) long, looks from one end full of pink trumpet daffodils. Next month paeonies dominate in pink and crimson. These are followed by the magenta Armenian geraniums, and then it's the turn of the Mock Orange – only four bushes – and succeeding these comes a repeated planting of 'Garnet' penstemons. These take you almost into autumn, but meanwhile, weaving its way in and about between everything, is that remarkable, creeping hardy geranium, 'Buxton's Blue'. So whenever you go down there, that part of the garden in the growing season has something worth seeing. That makes six plants to take us through the season.

The season opens in our main twin borders with the yellow shrubby spurge and white daffodils in bloom together. In late spring these will be followed by a series of green-flowered tulips with beautiful markings of white, amber and terra-cotta in their flowers. We mark midsummer with pale to deep-rose colourings from a few shrub roses and perennials, and when these moments are done a lavender and violet theme comes into being, using simply repeated plants of *Salvia superba* and that finest of all Michaelmas daisies, *Aster × frikartii*. The important thing always is that each plant is repeated several times over throughout the border, so that from one end it appears to dominate where it's in flower. That it fades is no worry, for there'll always be a partner to supplant it.

'All art', said that precious Victorian writer Walter Pater, 'constantly aspires towards the condition of music.' Gardening – evanescent, fleeting, full of moments that can never be held – is certainly very close to music already. And I'm inclined to compare a garden planted on this principle to that old dance form, the passacaglia, in which new themes and embellishments, one after another, are worked upon the same ground.

Starting a new garden

Anyone taking over a raw new garden today has an immense advantage over all the new gardeners that have gone before. Glyphosate (Tumbleweed). No matter how daunting the site, how deeply smothered in weeds it may be, at least you know you can kill them all off at a stroke now. And without poisoning the soil. That's the first consideration. If glyphosate has one shortcoming it is that you can't see where you have been with it for a month. Only then do the weeds show that they have received the poison and are on their way to eternity. But what you should really know about the stuff is that within days of its reaching the leaves on which you spray it the effective agent in the

13

solution travels down to the roots to start work. This means that a week after applying the spray you can slice off the top growth with a sharp spade, in the way that navvies always do – and your humble author with them – and know that you will see that particular crop no more.

Thus the site will be clear and then you can begin visualising. But at this point I would advise you to plant a tree. Nothing could possibly be better for your morale. Nothing else would give you the same sense of having made a tangible stake in the future. You will feel your garden really is beginning.

Where? Just to one side so that it will not overshadow either the whole garden or just your sitting out place. Not so that it will cast all its shade on your neighbour's garden. Don't worry about your own projected flower borders. They will be better for having some shade part of the day. It will widen the range of plants you can grow in them.

What tree? Not a flowering cherry, for the birds are too fond of the buds. Certainly not a weeping willow. Too big inside three seasons. Not even a birch whose hungry roots spread too far sideways. I would settle for one of the flowering crab apples. Their pink or red blossom is dependable, they are not too dense, and you can thin them very easily to control them without even making them look mutilated.

Next you need to pave your sitting-out place. It must be of ample proportions, so try the deck chairs first for size and for moving about between them. And it should get the sun. If the back of the house doesn't get enough you may have to make it at the other end of the garden. A sitting-out place will get much more use if it has a hard surface. You will be able to use it immediately after rain.

Crab apple in flower; *Malus* 'Katherine' bears semi-double pink flowers which fade to white

Now for your path. You must have a firm path to the rubbish tip, to the shed and to the sitting-out place if it's away from the house. But at this stage I wouldn't make it sound. Better just to put down some paving slabs where you have been walking most. Then you can move them later if you have to. Get the biggest slabs you can manage, about $60 \times 60\,\text{cm}$ ($2 \times 2\,\text{ft}$), but the lightest and therefore the thinnest. Later you will find that you can build up your design on your path.

It is now the moment to look at your levels. The slightest change in level is something to preserve, no matter how small the garden. It makes for a much more interesting mini-landscape, and an undulation is something to emphasise, perhaps with a low wall or even a row of big stones to mark it and with which to retain the soil.

By now ideas will have been gestating in your mind and you will have something of a picture forming. This is the time to keep looking at the site from the windows. After all, it is from these that you will most often see the garden. All new houses today have far bigger windows than ever before, thanks to double glazing, central heating and building techniques and materials. The result is that such windows cry out to look upon outdoor living pictures. And this is exactly what you should aim at making, a picture set in the frame of the window.

2
Plan before you Plant

The seductions of the garden centre are hard to resist; all those strong, healthy-looking plants just waiting to be transplanted to our own gardens, promising great riches in seasons to come – and not too far off either from the look of the plants. But wait a moment: are you sure of your ground, that you know how to plant them to best effect? Top gardeners all say 'there's a plant for every place'. Of course they mean that the wettest bit of ground, the driest patch, has a community of plants appropriate to it and that you have to find them. It's no good putting silver-leaved shrubs on sodden land, any more than you can get rhododendrons to thrive on chalk. And again, most daisy-flowered plants like the sun. They sulk in the shade. But there are equally important rules about building up a garden composition when you've found the right plants for your site and your soil.

You must first know whether your soil is acid or alkaline, whether it contains lime or not. You can find out with a simple soil testing outfit from the garden shop. If it has no lime in it and is therefore acid, then you can grow rhododendrons, heathers, azaleas and other lime-hating plants there, at once widening the range open to you. If there is lime, then forget about them. If you were to plant them you would find yourself running a home for debilitated bushes.

Next thing. Is it heavy and clayey, or is it light and lets the moisture run away quickly after rain? Well, you don't need chemical help to find this out. Don't despair of clay. Your results once you have planted will in fact be much quicker than those achieved on light soil that is much easier to work. You have finally to decide for yourself whether it's a sunny garden most of the year or a shady one, remembering that the angle of the sun is much lower in spring and autumn than in summer and therefore more likely to be obstructed by trees or buildings. Some shrubs will flower reasonably well in shade, others just won't. And it is worth knowing that those which won't usually enjoy light soil. If truth really were told, in the everyday garden it's almost impossible to offer plants exactly what they like. It's more a matter of discovering what will put up with what.

Optical illusion Somehow we all want to push back the boundaries of our gardens and make them look bigger than they really are – the landscaping urge. There are several ways in which this can be done. The first is by the use of false perspective. If you actually make the lines of your flower borders and your paths converge as they recede they really will seem to mark longer vistas than really exist. Another is the stratagem of curling the lines. Assuming you are intent on making pictures with your plantings, to be seen from the windows (which indeed they mostly are), if your lawn not only tapers as it recedes but curls away to one side as though leading somewhere out of sight, it will be perennially intriguing to the eye.

The same stratagem can be used to make you wonder what happened on the way. If there are bays to each side of the main vista which you can just discern but can't see fully, again it will arouse curiosity. A friend of mine once had a garden with several such incidents. When you got to one opening you found that it was a setting for some big architectural plant. Another enshrined a bird table, and another still an urn with plantings that were changed with the seasons. You were never sure what you would find there. You couldn't quite see until you reached each little 'side chapel' because the plantings had been so cunningly arranged.

Another element of composition is always to put your bulky plants close to your viewpoint, more slender kinds in the distance. By bulky plants I mean those of bold proportions either individually or in groups. For instance the skimmia bush, evergreen and rounded, makes a good foreground plant. So do the hostas that have large leaves. It is a mistake always to put the big stuff in the background. By the same token, a plant set at the end of a vista is advisedly a slender, pale one. I find the ideal evergreen bush to make such an incident is *Rhamnus alaterna* 'Argenteovariegata', now in most good garden centres, an upright evergreen whose foliage is heavily marked with silver. The disposal of colour can also help to extend the limits of a garden by illusion. Never put strong bright colours in the distance, always in the foreground, with the softer colour further out. Try to grade them through part of the spectrum.

A good resolve to make for the opening of a new garden season is to start with a brand new exercise book and jot down each weekend the changes in the garden that could be made and which are revealed as the year goes on. Some changes could be made on the spot there and then, particularly during showery weather, the ideal moment. But others have to be pondered on for quite a while, even mock-ups made of bushes whose position could be changed for the better. Keep changing until just the right spot is found. This is where planting technique itself can help. If you plant anything, whether it's a rose, a bush or a herbaceous plant, in a little pocket of damp peat or composted bark worked round the roots, the root system it will be encouraged to make will be a compact tight network of fibres. When you want to make changes you will find that such a plant will come up readily and not notice the move.

Of course, it's better to think long and hard before you plant, working to sound and well-tried rules of composition. Not the least of these is to resist the allurements of the garden centre if you can and instead of planting a wide miscellany of different kinds make bold groups each of one kind. Then the contrasts you make between rounded kinds of plants and those of slender spire-like form will be all the more telling but the garden will also have the sense of harmony, surely one of the things we need to find most in our gardens today.

First turn to the soil

No soil, no life: it's as fundamental as water to plants as well as animals, yet we take it for granted – unless, that is, one has learned to be a true gardener. His respect for it is so great that under certain circumstances he won't even tread on it. So to make plants grow with anything like the success one reasonably expects of them in a garden you will have to acquire something of this attitude to the soil and better still will be your results if you know a little about what it's made of.

How big individually the particles of the bedrock have been milled by nature determines its texture, whether it is gritty like sand or plastic like clay. The mid-point between these extremes is what gardeners dub as loam when it's got the other constituents in it. Clay may seem to be a curse that lies upon most people who do gardening, but most of us have reason to grumble about our soil at some time, even if for different reasons. You can hardly stand up in wet weather on a clay soil, let alone work it or plant in it satisfactorily. On the other hand it's not such a problem in summer weather as sand. You may be able to work a sandy soil comfortably on most days of the year but in hot spells plants growing in it fall limp and lawns made on it turn brown quickly simply because it doesn't hold enough moisture to keep them comfortable. Moreover, plants can make swift progress in clay that has been only moderately improved when they are slow to put on new growth in light soils.

The key is the other main element – humus, a word that skilled gardeners mouth like a sorcerer's incantation, a substance that does seem to have magic properties for any soil. And what is it? The product of corruption. It's a mass of decaying plant remains and the relics of the creatures that have inhabited the earth, those teeming masses of insects that fly, walk or even hardly move from the spot in the course of their lifetimes. It is the chief constituent of the shallow black layer that lies at the surface of uncultivated soils; the substance in which dwell most of the vitalising agencies in the soil, especially those unnumbered multitudes of bacteria that work constantly on the decaying refuse of the earth, converting it from something beastly to something benign. It is humus that, peopled by its lowly population, puts life into the inert rock. It holds the very essence of fertility; you could almost say, 'No humus, no life'.

Since it is already present to some degree in all soils it also benefits all soils when it is applied artificially. Due to its physical structure it both absorbs and holds moisture, so increasing the moisture-retaining capacity of the sandy soils. Equally it becomes interwoven with the particles that go to make up clay, causing them to become crumbs separated from one another instead of lying closely packed. Then it is that air can penetrate, another of the essential constituents of a fertile soil, while excess moisture can drain away. No wonder, then, that there are societies of gardeners dedicated to proclaiming the wonders of this magic stuff, that any gardener of experience always makes sure that his soil gets every bit he can lay hands on and that its main source, the compost heap, has a place in the corner of every well-run garden. Here everything that has grown and is no longer wanted in its characteristic form has a new and welcome role. Here it is that treasure grows from rotting remains. Not only from the relics of cultivation does garden-worthy humus come, however. The fallen leaves, the bark that would otherwise be wasted in sawmills and the relics of the hops that the breweries have done with, the seaweed left on the seashore by the tides, the excreta of animals and birds, the medium in which mushrooms have been grown commercially, even yesterday's newspapers crumbled up – all can be turned into humus.

A well made compost heap

All gardening is intensive cultivation as plants are constantly taking from the soil the nutrients on which they feed. It is not enough to leave it to nature to return this, as it would if ground were left fallow for a few seasons. You have to make your own artificial contribution. Artificial – that's something that strikes a chill into many hearts. But the treatment of soil with fertilisers of organic origin is an artificial process, is it not? The humus-bearing substances do contain some nutrients, though in varying and often very small degrees, which will need supplementing. This can be done as well by one of the concentrated organic fertilisers available today as by the chemical mixtures, which in fact are usually derived from natural rock of some kind! Most fertilisers these days are universal, contributing the three basic elements plants require – nitrogen for leaf growth, phosphates for roots, potash for flowering and tough health – together with those so-called trace elements of which only very small quantities are ever needed.

The other main constituent you have to worry about is lime. Soils can contain it naturally and irreversibly, or they can lack it, which in much gardening is a good thing. If the ground lacks lime there is a whole world of plants, of which rhododendrons, heathers and camellias are the chief members, open to you. But if the stuff is present, then it is best to eschew all this group of plants and settle for those that either like lime or will put up with it. How do you know which of the two categories your soil belongs to? A simple soil-testing kit will tell you.

Many successful gardeners never use lime at all. They mainly grow flowers and grass, both of which are generally happy with a fairly acid soil if there is no natural lime there. But to get good crops of vegetables that are healthy you need to add lime to the ground about every three years under average circumstances. Not only does this help release plant nutrients but it encourages the bacteria to work all the harder, when in acid soil they are on the sluggish side. Moreover on clay, lime has a role to play in helping that valuable crumb structure to develop. However, if clay is to be made a home for lime haters this crumb-making process can be encouraged by adding gypsum to the soil, which though a chalk derivative has no influence on the acid–alkaline ratio of the ground but simply performs its refining work.

Dealing with clay

To some gardeners, no worse four-letter word exists in the vocabulary than clay. It is the enemy which stands defiant, ready to outdo all your endeavours, try your patience and reduce you to impotent teeth-gnashing whenever the weather's wet. But somehow you've got to learn to live with it, which is what I've done these thirty seasons now. And smug though it may seem I've learned to love it too because of its potential. For clay is rich. Accept it, treat it kindly, nourish it the right way, and it really makes things grow. When others on light soil, heathland and chalk, are frustrated by the slow progress made by the plants for which they pay good money and watch over tenderly, those who plant on clay – the right way – can almost watch the result taking place. Look how the weeds flourish on clay! That ought to show you what it can do for cultivated plants.

Paths are vital The first thing you want to think of installing in a clay garden, however, is paths. You must provide yourself with dry walking, as much for your own temper and safety as for the soil itself, which of course must not be walked on when it's damp for fear of compacting it more firmly than it is already. First, paths must be laid wherever you want to tread often in the garden. And where you want to go only occasionally you must have stepping stones, in borders as well as in turf. The ideal is to be able to circulate the whole of your garden dryshod on any day of the year.

To roughly the same end you want to keep yourself supplied with plenty of coarse organic refuse. For in this lies your best hope of making the clay workable. It is the only thing that can really change it. To keep a tidy garden you must work in your borders at least twice a year, weeding, staking, cutting down, and for this you must walk on the soil itself, if indirectly. This means mulching the surface with the refuse, which will reduce the need for the weeding and at the same time make it possible to tread on the soil while carrying out other jobs. As well as this, the mulch will gradually unite with the soil and make its stickiness spongy. As I work I spread the mulch in front of me and stand on this as I go. Until quite recently I had always used rough, coarse peat. But they've stopped selling it now, so far as I can discover. So I am on to composted bark and find it a first-class substitute. I would not say it is cheap to buy but its action on the soil lasts so long and it opens up clay so securely that it amply pays for itself.

All this goes for flower borders and rose beds. One must never overlook the effect of weathering when ground is being prepared for these, and for lawns as well, and on vegetable plots left vacant during the winter. Dig as carelessly and roughly as you can – you will leave the soil horribly lumpy but with the greatest possible area vulnerable to the refining influence of freezing and thawing in alternation. The effect of this is miraculous, as you quickly discover when you work at it with a fork in the late spring.

The process is only equalled by burning lumps of clay on a bonfire. You get a fire going with plenty of material that will keep it in and then you cover it with the lumps like an igloo. It will slowly burn for at least a week, after which you have the sort of ash that added to the surface of clay and lightly pricked in will have an astonishing effect on it. Best to follow this method where you are going to sow seeds. Liming with coarse ground chalk has a not dissimilar effect on clay soil, causing it to 'crumb', as they say. You can scatter the lime – taking care the day is still and none blows into your face – at the rate of about 200 g per m² (6 oz per sq yd).

When you sow on clay you always want to make trenches for the seeds deeper than usual and line these first with damp peat. Similarly when you plant anything you always want to surround the roots of the new plant, whether it has come from a container or the open ground, with liberal helpings of damp peat or composted bark, but with the latter it is wise to mix in a little general fertiliser in case the process of decomposition has temporarily depressed the nitrogen content. This is always low while the early stages of decay are going on.

Save compost Never waste a potful of potting compost. Save it all for the more important bits of your garden, such as when you are planting bulbs. It will be useful to put underneath them for their roots to strike into readily. No gardener of experience lets what he calls old potting soil go to waste. He stores it up in an old dustbin. In the same way no fragment of organic refuse, anything that has come from a plant, should be allowed to go to waste. Compost means just as much to the clay gardener as it does to anyone trying to garden on gravel. The only difference is that the clay man can safely use it in the half-ripened state. It doesn't matter, either, if you chop up rotting bits of wood into it. In fact if I've any brushwood lying around I chop it up and scatter it on our shrub beds. In time it all goes down and in the meantime makes for drier standing when you are doing jobs there, like pruning. At one time, before we got round to laying stepping stones everywhere, I used to cover the paths with brushwood during sodden spells.

There is a lot to be said for covering clay soil lawns with sheets of coarse-mesh Netlon and letting the grass grow up through this. You will find walking much easier, and much less harm will come to the turf, while pushing a barrow on it will become possible when it would have been otherwise out of the question.

At one time we used to get heaps of leaves in the autumn from the council, and it did not matter if they contained a good deal of grit. Nowadays, when so much salt is used on the roads in winter I'm not so keen, but if you can ever get a load of grit grab it and scatter it, leaving it to nature to integrate with your soil. And never let a spent bonfire disappear. Barrow this to your flower borders and scatter.

Gradually, by applying all these suggestions, you might end up by enjoying gardening on clay, as you watch the results instead of letting the frustration get you down.

The value of peat

Like oil and coal, peat is running out. Another half century and we shall have to look for something else to do what peat has done so ably for us these past 20 years or so. Of course, gardeners have used the stuff for much longer than that, but it's only in the past couple of decades that it has been fully exploited.

Sometimes I have asked old gardeners what they did before the days when you could go into every local garden shop and buy a bag of peat. They prevaricate. 'Well, there was plenty of old manure, and I suppose we made leafmould', they say hesitatingly. They had time to cultivate soil thoroughly, too, and could choose their day for it, unlike those of us who have to do our gardening at the weekends when, more often that not it seems, the ground is wet.

Peat has become so much part of our gardening lives that I cannot imagine how they did manage without it, any more than one can conceive what life was like without polythene. Like all forms of humus peat benefits good and bad land equally, giving body to light soil, opening up and refining heavy wet, clay land, with its spongy structure. Then it holds the moisture in just the right degree, again with equally good effect on light soil and heavy – to the benefit of the plants which grow upon it. They are advantaged in another way, since it encourages all plants to make a more fibrous root system than they would otherwise.

They grow better as a result, and for the home gardener it has the immense bonus that when you want to move them about – and who doesn't want to change the positions of his plants? – they can be transferred much more readily. Not only is it easy to get them up from such soil but they hardly seem to notice any change. I never plant anything today except in an envelope of peat around the roots before any soil is returned to the hole.

Of course, it must be used damp, for peat takes unto itself any moisture going if it is dry. This is one of the reasons why it is so valuable to the home gardener for mulching. Not only does it insulate the ground against the drying effects of wind and sun, but it also keeps the roots of plants cool but moist below. When you get one of those long rainy spells that keeps you off the ground for so long, you can soak it up with peat.

You have a living testimony of the value of peat to roots in the way plants grow in the peat-filled growing bags now in universal use. Growing bags have revolutionised home tomato growing. Personally I would not consider growing them any other way in my greenhouse now and have paved the whole floor of the house. Soil-borne diseases are avoided, the plants need less watering and you don't have the tedious business of changing soil or lifting those great heavy pots in and out.

Peat, in fact, is the main ingredient of several of the most used potting composts. Such composts are clean as well as light to handle and you don't have to worry about the pH factor going down if you keep a bag on hand. Think of all the time those old gardeners spent mixing up their favourite recipe, all the measuring, all the sifting. May the forecasts be wrong, and the peat last and last for ever!

Avoid confusion

So you've studied the soil and discovered what you have to deal with and now you've dug over the ground and are ready to get on with the layout and planting. This is the point where you have to determine the kind of effect you want.

Some of the most vividly striking gardens I have ever seen were on a new housing estate in Germany, where a group of garden designers had been invited to produce schemes side by side. You went through the little houses whose rooms were all fresh and stark, and the designers had each produced something completely in harmony with the character of the buildings. Firm lines, masonry with a texture, broad planes of turf and the compelling silhouettes of what we would call 'architectural' plants made up the medium in which they had worked, each producing an individual scheme within the narrow limitations.

Sometimes, though I am a rapacious collector of plants myself, I think it is a pity that the variety of plants available to us in nurseries is so great. It puts us in the way of temptation – to over-fill our gardens with too much variety. One is much more struck by a scheme where there is reticence than where this vast range is exploited. Borders where one plant is repeated and complemented by its immediate neighbours are always much more memorable, and therefore impressive, than those where you just don't know what to look at next, like a badly hung picture gallery. There must be focus. And there must be simplicity. At its simplest this principle is seen in both heather gardens and rose gardens, plots filled with totally dissimilar plants, but which both make the point equally strongly. A heather garden that has only a very few cultivars out of the great number available, each planted in bold patches, makes its point by creating its individual atmosphere far more strongly than a more varied jumble does. So should roses be planted individually, one cultivar to a bed, and repeated as many times as the patch will hold them. This is why rock gardens are so often displeasing places: quite often they have too many individual plants pressing for attention.

It's the same with colour. One-colour borders can be boring, but if two are used in the one area, or if many tones of the same colour are used together they can be striking. You remember the scene much more clearly than you do a jumbled one. When I am driving through North London in the summer I always keep an eye cocked for the little front garden full of soft yellow roses that are entirely under-planted with some pale blue creeping plant. Driving north of Oxford I am always on the look out for the small garden that has a great bank of arum lilies. Both are distinctive when you hardly notice the other surrounding gardens which simply take their place in the urban landscape. The distinctive touch also comes with emphasising the architectural character that some plants have. At its simplest it means isolating, say, a

Looking after your lawn

Edging Regular care will ensure a healthy-looking lawn. Edging will keep the outline sharp and neat.

Mowing There is a wide choice of mowers around nowadays. Rotary mowers are excellent for surfaces which are less than even and for steep banks where hover mowers are especially manoeuvrable. Both types will cope with long or wet grass but will not give such a fine result as a cylinder mower for the desirable striped effect. In dry weather, if the lawn is cut frequently it will do no harm to allow the clippings to lie, unless the mower is of a type that leaves the grass cuttings behind in hanks, in which case they should be removed.

Feeding and watering Specially formulated lawn fertilisers are widely available. Always check the manufacturer's instructions for the correct rate of application. In general, feed lawns in March or April, and again in June at a lower rate. An autumn feed is beneficial in September or October. In dry weather, grass can suffer badly, so don't wait until it turns brown but give it thorough and regular soakings with a spinkler until it rains again.

Weeding Selective weedkillers for lawns should be used with care, so, again, always follow the manufacturer's instructions. They will have maximum effect when growth is at its strongest at the beginning of summer. Large weeds, such as dandelion or plantain can be spot weeded.

Raking and aerating Dead material and old grass cuttings accumulate to form an impermeable thatch. This should be removed periodically, especially in autumn. A spring-toothed rake or powered lawn raker or scarifyer does the job. Spiking or hollow tining will also improve drainage and ease the compaction caused by summer use. So after scarifying, spike the lawn over with a fork to the depth of about 13 cm (4 in) or use a hollow tiner which removes plugs of turf – a valuable addition to the compost heap. Follow up with a top dressing of autumn fertiliser. These operations will also help keep the lawn clear of moss. For the same reason fallen leaves should be swept up regularly in autumn.

pampas or a red-hot poker that would be lost in a border with other plants. But I have seen some telling borders planted with such plants, or with tall grasses, and given a flat groundwork of creeping plants, set out boldly to make abstract patterns over the ground.

As gardeners we tend to be avid collectors, lured by plants we see in gardens, by pictures in books, by descriptions in catalogues – those most seductive of horticultural spellbinders. Once I was lured by flowering cherries. Each one was more alluring than the last. Now I would rather have six of a kind, than half a dozen all different. It's not just the flowers being different but the shapes of the trees themselves. Contrasting shapes can be used to effect but not an assortment of the same type. You can't make an arboretum on a small plot – better just an avenue. Now the lure to which I have succumbed in camellias. They are different in flower but similar enough in leaf and form to give a bold structure to the borders in which they grow. One day I hope they will grow up to give a distinctive touch to the whole garden for they are now planted throughout.

Start with a tree

Trees and shrubs have one of the most important roles of all plants to play in furnishing a garden. You can't do without them. They bring – some of them from their very first days in the garden – a third dimension to a flat plot, providing contours and form. Carefully sited, they can become the structure on which the whole garden is built up. In the case of trees careful siting means sparse planting. You need them, but only in the barest minimum number. It also means siting them where they will not eventually cast shade across areas of garden that are selected to remain in the sun, or stand close to houses where they will 'take the light' and eventually have to be scrapped in an embittered furious moment on a dreary day.

It also means positioning them where they will strike across the views of other buildings beyond the garden so that by illusion these are made to seem further away. Yet another consideration is bringing the trees to the fore of flower beds so that not only does their blossom fall on turf and give a further few days of delight lying there but also the beauty of their trunks, their colouring and their texture, can be enjoyed at close quarters.

Carefully siting shrubs implies long and careful thought. Besides bringing form and a third dimension to the garden every shrub has a distinctive silhouette. Some are gaunt, others are rounded, and others still arch their branches. Some remain small and bun-like, others grow swiftly and turn eventually into multi-trunked trees. This character is only revealed where each is growing in a fairly isolated position where they are not going to run into each other and their individual nature becomes dissolved into the whole.

This is the consideration which should always be borne in mind when one is making a so-called mixed border of which the components are trees and shrubs, herbaceous plants and bulbs, with perhaps the odd patch of annuals added here and there. It is also the underlying consideration when shrubs are planted free-standing on grass to form a miniature park. The former is doubtless the most satisfactory way for home gardeners to use shrubs. But don't underestimate the value of grass. As in music, where the pertinent pause enhances the melody to come, so in landscaping the use of open space underlines the value of the colour and shape of the shrubs and plants in the border, besides providing the perfect backcloth to a specimen tree or shrub whose beauty is best appreciated in isolation.

There is another fashion however, in which shrubs can be used satisfactorily if somewhat expensively. This is to plant them deliberately closely so that in time they will form a tight thicket that both marks the boundaries of a garden and conceals it from the common gaze. Bulbs can still be grown underneath them, as they would in woodland, and in time ferns can be added to thrive there and spread. Then as time goes on it will become a little bird-sanctuary as they find they can nest there away from possible marauders. This is one of the classic stratagems for making a garden seem bigger than it really is, provided there is an open clearing and the shrub plantings have an outline that takes a broad sweeping curve. This is especially effective if this curve is indented at infrequent intervals so that by illusion it seems that there are paths going off into what might be deeper woodland.

There is also one way of reducing the noise of mowers and play in neighbouring gardens. Perhaps silence is never attainable now, but at least a thicket of shrubs will subdue sounds beyond the garden to some extent. Especially if an ample proportion of the shrubs you choose are evergreen.

Evergreens This is a term to be approached with some wariness. It is tempting to think that a garden composed of evergreens is lively throughout the year. In reality it can be a very dull garden, hardly changing through the four seasons. Evergreens are best planted sparsely, though not quite so much as trees, to achieve their strongest effect. They have a most important part to play in the contrasts they make possible with deciduous species, which are usually more elegant in form and therefore are set off well by the heavier evergreen foliage. Particularly in winter, when the evergreens will emphasise the bare tracery of branch and twig and make a setting for the fresh, spring foliage as the days lengthen again.

In winter, too, the odd evergreen shrub that has variegated foliage integrated into the garden, preferably in an isolated position against a background of dark-leaved kinds, can make it seem that from somewhere there are shafts of sunlight appearing on the dullest day.

The following is a check list of shrubs for the foundation furnishings of a new or reconstructed garden. I have chosen those basic kinds which will tolerate the kind of soil and site given in each heading.

The following shrubs will grow anywhere, whatever the nature of the soil and the aspect, but will give most flowers when they get some sun during the day:

Berberis Yellow flowers, red or black berries, foliage often evergreen.

Chaenomeles (japonica) Red or pink flowers.

Cotoneaster White flowers, red berries, often evergreen.

Deutzia White or pink flowers.

Forsythia Yellow flowers.

Kerria Yellow flowers.

Magnolia × soulangiana White and pink flowers.

Osmarea Scented white flowers, evergreen foliage.

Philadelphus (Mock Orange) White scented flowers.

Pyracantha White flower, red or orange berries, evergreen foliage.

Spiraea White or pink flowers.

Symphoricarpos (snowberry) White or pink berries.

Viburnum White scented flowers, often evergreen foliage.

Weigela Red or pink flowers.

These will thrive on light poor soil in full sun:

Caryopteris Blue flowers.

Cistus White or pink flowers, evergreen foliage.

Cytisus White, yellow, bronze or red flowers.

Hebe Mauve flowers, evergreen foliage.

Hibiscus Pink, mauve or white flowers.

Lavender Mauve flowers.

Phlomis Yellow flowers, evergreen foliage.

Sage Purple flowers, evergreen foliage.

Santolina Yellow flowers, eversilver foliage.

Senecio 'Sunshine' Yellow flowers, evergrey foliage.

Spartium Yellow flowers.

Tamarix Pink flowers, evergreen foliage.

Here are the lime haters, flourishing only on acid soil:

Calluna and Erica (heathers) Many colourings.

Camellias Pink, red or white flowers.

Hydrangea Will tolerate other soil, but flower colour only blue on acid land.

Kalmia Pink flowers.

Pernettya Red or pink berries.

Pieris Red shoots, white flowers.

Skimmia Red berries.

Rhododendrons and Azaleas Many colourings.

Make the most of your tree By planting a tree in your garden you will have made a mark on the landscape likely to last well beyond your own time. Think what a responsibility that can be – especially if you plant it in your front garden for all who pass to see! In the residential areas round our towns and cities home gardeners have created an entirely individual landscape whose ingredients have originated from the four corners of the earth and can turn spring into a festival of blossom. Plant a tree, just one, and it can make you feel your garden has taken on a new shape, even a fresh character. Where though? And what tree?

First consider the role for which the tree is cast. To plant something for the blossom it is going to bear in the spring is only a small part of the story, two or three weeks of its entire year. What will be its effect the rest of the twelve months? You won't be able to ignore it, so it had better be doing the right thing.

Now, we had better take it that the tree you get from the nursery or garden centre is ready-grown when you buy it, with a 2 m (6 ft) trunk and a rudimentary head consisting of three or four main branches and a complex system of roots. The British Standards Institution has set specifications that the nursery trade adheres to pretty closely. If you ask for a standard tree, that's what you get. And our nurseries can offer these in many different kinds.

Some trees can only be planted small, as they dislike being moved. These you have to train up yourself. They include some greatly prized sorts, like the pink-flowered Judas tree (*Cercis siliquastrum*), but we are not concerned with them at the moment.

One of the most useful roles a tree has to play is to make the houses beyond your garden seem much less dominant. As the tree grows the smaller they will seem. This effect will be the greater the closer the tree is to your main viewpoint – generally the windows of your house. At the same time you have to remember that the closer it is to the house the more likely it will take light from the windows and its roots will get into drains or undermine the foundations.

The next most important function is to direct attention to a major point of focus in your garden or to divert it from some impediment to the beautiful view you hope to create on the site. When we started our garden we found when we looked out of the main windows our eyes were drawn to the gable end of another house a little to the right. We had to correct this and draw the eye straight in front by planting standard trees in that area where you looked involuntarily. Within two or three years it was amazing how that building became less dominant. For this purpose you do need striking, rather upright trees, which will soar rather than make round silhouettes.

Many flowering shrubs are happier when they get a bit of shade during the day, as the shadow of trees in leaf passes over them, and others will put up with it. So a few trees will greatly widen the scope of your plantings. This takes you into the field of woodland gardening. Do the

Planting a tree or shrub

How can you get the best from your tree or shrub in the least possible time? By following four basic rules of planting and aftercare.

The first is to surround the roots of a new shrub or tree with a planting mixture composed of either damp peat or composted bark, into which is mixed some basic general fertiliser, one with a high potash content, like Phostrogen or one of the rose or tomato fertilisers, and some coarse bonemeal or super-phosphate of lime to provide a slow-release reserve of root promoting phosphates. The new roots of new plants ramify readily into this, which enables them to take hold speedily.

When the plant is first released from its container, it is important to scratch at the ball of roots to turn the root ends outward (1).

Once it is in its hole it should be trodden really firmly in position (3). This is the third cardinal point. It may seem rough treatment but somehow even the roots seem to appreciate it, for besides making the plants safer against wind rock, it prods the roots into grasping their new environment. A tree or a tall shrub needs a stake from the start to support it, for when it is full of leaves and the soil is wet from heavy rain it can put up considerable wind resistance and is therefore easily moved in the sodden ground.

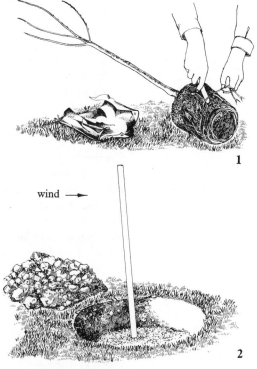

wind ⟶

1

2

An oblique stake pointing towards the prevailing wind (2) is more effective than an upright one in holding the tree firm against wind rock, which can hinder its establishment. Make sure to keep all weeds or grass from growing over the rooting area for the first three seasons (4); cover the rooting area with a mulch of peat, composted bark or half rotted leaves.

The fourth important point is spraying with nothing but clear water. This applies especially to evergreens but in any case should be carried out in the growing season after planting whenever the weather is dry – for the best results quickly, that is. For evergreens and especially conifers it is even more important than watering at the roots, though of course in a period of drought following planting in spring this is necessary too. Speed of growth in the early stages can also be aided by spraying the new plant over its leaves with one of the foliar feeds several times during the growing season. It is surprising what this can accomplish.

3

4

roots of trees run through the ground gobbling up all the nutrients, leaving none for other plants? Think of our native woodlands. Enough vegetation flourishes beneath them, doesn't it? Besides, assuming you have flower beds abutting on to grass, I'm sure that garden trees are best sited fairly close to where the two join. Then half the roots will run under the turf, on heavy soil, helping to drain it.

The following trees are specially recommended to help make a plot into a garden:

Round-headed growers for focal points:

Crataegus prunifolia (White-flowered thorn) Crimson berries, autumn leaf colour.
Prunus 'Accolade' Pink Japanese cherry.
P. 'Shimidsu Zakura' White-flowered Japanese cherry.

Pyrus salicifolia 'Pendula' Silver Willow-leaved Pear.
Sorbus vilmorinii (Red-berried mountain ash) Autumn leaf colour.

Upright-headed trees for creating false perspectives:

Betula pendula (Silver Birch) Light canopy, attractive bark.
Gleditsia 'Sunburst' Golden fern-like foliage.
Laburnum × **watereri 'Vossii'** Trails of golden flowers.
Malus 'Golden Hornet' Yellow flowering crab.
M. 'Katherine' Deep pink flowering crab.
M. tschonoskii Fine autumn colour.

Robinia 'Frisia' (False Acacia) Yellow foliage.
Sorbus aucuparia cvs (Red-berried mountain ash) Fine autumn colour.
S. hupehensis (White berried mountain ash) Autumn colour.
Prunus padus (Bird Cherry) White flowers.
P. × **hillieri 'Spire'** Column-like pale pink flowering cherry.
P. 'Tai Haku' Large flowering white cherry.

Provide some shelter

Save for rain, nothing spoils the gentle craft of gardening so much as wind. I've no sympathy myself with those famous lines about 'there's the wind on the heath, brother', put forward as one of the delights of life. Give me a calm spot in which to garden, and I'll garden all day. It's not only the gardener himself who can be prevented from following his pursuit by this element: plants hate it. If they're not distorted in their growth by it, sometimes they hardly grow at all in its teeth. My advice to anyone starting a garden would certainly be to make providing shelter from the wind one of the very first priorities.

The quickest way of providing shelter, of course, would be with 2 m (6 ft) high panels of interwoven fencing. If the place is very exposed you would have to be more than usually careful about the strength of the posts and about treating them with wood preservative before you set them in the ground. The cheapest way would be to fix coarse wire or plastic netting between similar posts and train ivy over the whole lot to make a tall 'fedge'. I say ivy and not that so called Mile-a-minute Vine, *Polygonum baldschuanicum* (Russian Vine), because this is deciduous, losing its leaves in winter just when you want the extra protection. The ivy is evergreen, keeping you cosy when you need it most.

Of course, if you don't want to shut yourself in, it must be admitted that a screen with peepholes, as provided by pre-cast concrete blocks, can stop the wind to a considerable degree, while retaining a sense of lightness in the garden decor. I am assuming, of course, that that very best of anti-wind screens, a most decorative garden feature and the one which provides the most horticultural opportunities, a brick wall with occasional piers to buttress it, is just too expensive nowadays. However, you can make a wall of breeze blocks much more cheaply. But you must render it over with cement, preferably with some colouring in it, for it to be aesthetically acceptable. One technical point here you must be sure to put up piers of brick or concrete blocks to support a breeze block wall.

Now I know they say that what happens with walls is that the wind is thrust up into the air and comes down again some way off. Well, that may be so, but you can still find a comfortable spot behind them to work in on blustery days. They also say that you can trap the frost with a wall or hedge if you're on a slope. That may be so also. Again, I'd rather have frost than wind around the place. Besides really hard frost doesn't do all that much harm unless you are experimenting with tender plants. Most of the things we grow in our gardens are custom-built to withstand it.

A belt of trees can provide a superb windbreak and can usually be left to reach their own maturity. But you need space for a belt. A line is a different matter altogether. And this is all that most of us have room to plant. But what happens when it's no longer a hedge, having grown and grown past clipping height? Are you to allow it to go on and on heavenwards? Gets pretty depressing in time, and weak too, because trees planted close in a line don't get the chance to toughen. They are always drawing one another up. One answer is to remove alternate trees while they are still small enough to be removed without having to call in a heavy gang. Perhaps the real answer, though, where space is limited is to settle for enough shelter to keep you comfortable in one part of the garden and start clipping at 2 m (6 ft). I find one can just reach up to this height with the shears, without having to use steps and keep moving them along.

What to plant? Well, conifers head the list and I will give you my choice later on (see page 36). However, one should not stop at the conifers. (You will notice that I omit recommending the pines which are so often suggested for screening. They just take too long to do their job.) Another method of providing yourself with shelter against the wind is with a belt of tallish shrubs, which can actually be part of the garden scene itself. If deciduous and evergreen shrubs are mixed together it will look after the winter months for you as well as other times. Superficially, this may seem somewhat expensive, but I have now come to the conclusion that a densely planted shrub border, with some standard trees planted at intervals along the front is just about the best garden windbreak you could plant. Such a screen will not only blot out wind, either: it makes your garden a much quieter as well as calmer place in these days of motor mowers and chain saws.

Hedges as boundaries

As well as acting as a windbreak and marking the boundaries of a garden a hedge has other virtues which would make me decide on one in preference to a fence or even a wall. A hedge can actually blur the boundary while defining it. It can be a beautiful thing in itself and it can make a background for other plants that will flatter them, especially if it is evergreen. And of course, evergreens planted in a garden also serve to annihilate winter. There is no close gardening season where there are plenty of evergreens around and they throw into relief every springing bud that shows impatience in February, or even before that.

But don't hedges take a long time to do their job for you, when a fence will do it from the start? Certainly it's never wise to put in tall hedging plants. They take several seasons to get going, and afterwards they never seem as dense as the young plant that has had to get used to the site from the start, being clipped all the while. But there are stratagems that can be employed to overcome the disadvantages and help you to leap the years. In the first place, the site should be prepared as though it was being got ready for some rare plant put in to commemorate some special occasion (see page 58).

However, hedges have another role to play, low hedges that will divide up the garden and give it architectural form, perhaps a touch of mystery too. These are the hedges that help make the garden seem bigger than it really is by emphasising the lines that will set up perspective. Artfully placed they can do so much to make a garden an interesting place. Hedges can entail a lot of clipping though. Some kinds do but by no means all. The best kinds of formal screening hedging plants need clipping only once a year, and there are many types of plants suitable for low hedges that can be kept in order with long-handled loppers with which you chop out the odd sideways-reaching branch right to the ground. In fact, you can do this without bending or reaching up. As for that clipping, with a lightweight pair of modern shears it's not nearly the tedious job it's too often made out to be, while

The romantic Sissinghurst garden illustrates how to combine plants in contrived
profusion: roses, joined by hardy geraniums, violas and alchemilla.

The garden in winter: *Garrya elliptica* and *Pseudotsuga menziesii* (Douglas Fir) take on an icy charm.

battery-powered hedge trimmers are inexpensive and when using one you have only to stroke the hedge with it.

What kind of hedge? For some people beech never loses its appeal as a boundary hedge. They enjoy the freshness of the young foliage in spring and the russet colouring in autumn, though I wonder if they think quite so much of it when they have to start sweeping up leaves again in late winter. However, now it has been shown by many examples that one of the best ways of using beech is to plant the green and purple kinds together in the same hedge to make a so-called 'tapestry' effect. Whenever one comes across a hedge planted in this way it is certainly striking. And so are privet hedges made of either the golden form or the multi-coloured kind. They are much slower in growth than the ordinary green privet which can become such a hard taskmaster!

When it comes to making low hedges as dividers that you can see over, the choice embraces almost every shrub you could ever grow, provided you accept the fact that every so often you have to chop back the growth to keep the hedge thin. The deciding factor can be price, and what you can get a number of plants for. For years we had a fine hedge, of the flowering shrub, *Hebe salicifolia*. Later I made one round a newly acquired statue using the perfumed evergreen *Osmarea* 'Burk-woodii', a lusty grower with multitudes of white flowers in late spring. Another fine hedger of which you can usually get largish plants in garden centres is *Elaeagnus* × *ebbingei*. Even when you have to cut out quite large bits you get plenty of the scented flowers which on a mild day in December can fill the air. This has pewter-coloured evergreen foliage and I am sure that it is as good for cutting down noise from beyond the garden as a holly hedge is supposed to be. Of the latter, it would be well to put a variegated one here and there in a green-leaved holly hedge to relieve any sombreness, though of course on bright days holly responds by reflecting the light with its glossy leaves.

Unwelcome dogs can be kept out, without harming them, with one of the berberis used as hedges. The arching *Berberis* × *stenophylla* is usually available cheaply for hedging, but personally I think I would rather have the stiffer growing *B. darwinii*, for a more formal hedge which can be clipped tight. However, for quite low hedges, up to 1 m (3 ft), *Berberis thunbergii*, which is so fine in autumn, is peerless, and always cheap enough to buy in the quantity needed. Where the soil is very poor one could use the Japanese Briar, *Rosa rugosa*, as a fine hedge that would flower on and on – much better anywhere, in my view, than the lanky 'Queen Elizabeth' rose, with all its flowers on top and none down below. The briar comes with white, pink or deep red flowers and has the added merit of turning its leaves golden before they fall in the autumn.

Also for poor soil the Sea Buckthorn, *Hippophae rhamnoides*, makes a

Hippophae rhamnoides

fine silvery hedge. Here you can be sure of getting a crop of berries, for it is one of those plants that need to have the sexes planted in partnership. The berries are translucent orange, and the birds are slow to take them in autumn, finishing off the red berries of other bushes first. For orange berries one could also plant the almost evergreen *Pyracantha rogersiana* 'Flava'. All firethorns do make good hedges, but this one has the best deportment as a bush.

Recent seasons have seen the promotion and large scale production of young stock of the old *Prunus cerasifera* 'Pissardii' as a hedge plant and because the young leaves are so vivid – and you get so many of them when it is clipped – it has been given the common name of 'Blaze'. This, of course, is an ornamental-leaved plum. Others of its family have been used similarly and given descriptive names also. One is called 'Green Glow' and another 'Purple Flash'. Also in recent years the variegated form of the Portugal Laurel, *Prunus lusitanica* 'Variegata', has come to be offered frequently in garden centres. Each leaf has a silver rim. We have also had put on the market forms of the old Spotted Laurel, *Aucuba japonica* 'Variegata', some with leaves so heavily spotted they appear to be marbled.

Now that so many fuchsias have been found to be hardy when it was once thought that they had to have the winter comfort of a greenhouse, *Fuchsia magellanica* may not be used for hedging as often as it used to be. The others are so much more spectacular when they are in flower. But you do have to be prepared for them to be cut to the ground in a bad winter, though they grow up readily afterwards.

Conifers for privacy

If you want privacy you want it now. You don't want to have to wait years to achieve it. Many times I've been asked where conifers already grown to 2 m (6 ft) tall can be bought. Well, let's deal with that one first. If you could buy them at all they would be wildly expensive, both to obtain in the first place, to transport and to get planted. And then it would be a chancy business. Old plants take a time to settle down once they're moved, if they ever do. In Britain we do not sell many big evergreen trees, but in Europe you can buy a cypress tree 6 m (20 ft) tall quite easily. The nurseries guarantee them for a year, but of course the cost of the insurance is quietly added to the price. I have known yews planted at 1.2 m (4 ft) tall beside some only 76 cm (2½ ft) high. In two seasons the latter had caught up the others, in spite of both having had exactly same treatment and indeed, every attention that a yew hedge could want.

One way of getting privacy quickly if you're prepared for the outlay, and I would have said it was worth it, is to put a cheap wattle fencing and cheaply bought hedging plants in front of this. The fencing would help to draw up the plants and make them do their job sooner. And by the time they had caught up, the wattle would be falling apart and decaying. Conifers would make the neatest, closest hedge which can be clipped. The secret of easy maintenance is not to let the hedge get so high that the top is out of reach. And you want to make sure of keeping a 'soft top', as professional gardeners say, which you can clip with the tips of the shears.

What, then, is the best hedging conifer? A tricky question that needs some pondering. The fastest is undeniably the celebrated × *Cupressocyparis leylandii*. This will grow up to the top of the wattle fence in a couple of seasons, and thicken up in a third. But the trouble with these plants is that they just won't stop when you want them to. Though *leylandii* will slow down later on, you must be prepared to snip its tops several times in the season if you don't want it to be all ragged for much of the growing year. Aren't conifers rather sombre in their dark green? Not necessarily, *leylandii* has a golden counterpart in the cultivar 'Castlewellan' – more expensive to buy but almost as fast in growth.

At the cheap end of the market are the ordinary Lawson Cypress, *Chamaecyparis lawsoniana*, usually called a cypress and the Arborvitae, the tree from which the so-called Western Red Cedar derives, botanically *Thuja plicata*. Both are cheap because they can be raised from seed. Other conifers have to be reproduced from cuttings, either because they are bigeneric hybrids, like *leylandii*, or because they are themselves seedlings or sports which either do not seed or if they did would not 'breed true'.

Now Lawson Cypress is admittedly a deep sombre green but dense, especially if you make sure to clip it right from the start. In this case it should always be kept in mind that cypresses do not break from old wood. You cannot refurbish them by cutting back hard. You would just be left with bare branches. On the other hand, the equally cheap thuja will break afresh if the old wood is cut into, especially if you spray it regularly during the growing season. Is this the paragon, then? No, for it has the weakness of turning a rusty colour during the winter when the weather is cold, though personally I would not hold this against it, especially as it is a particularly fast grower. Accordingly, this must be clipped from the start in order to get it really dense.

Now fortunately, most of the forms of the Lawson Cypress are naturally dense. These are the trees which are sold for so-called specimen planting. They really make wonderful hedges and require the minimum of clipping since most of them are naturally upright growers. However, keep off the most resolutely upright one, appropriately named 'Erecta Viridis' or 'Erecta' even though you may specially like the fresh green colouring it retains all the year. It goes bare at the bottom, always. If you like this tint go for one called 'Pottenii', a much better tree. The golden kinds of Lawson – the name, by the way, comes from the nursery in Edinburgh which introduced it back in the last century – are rather more shaggy, but wonderfully fresh looking, especially in spring and early summer. I doubt if there is anything to choose between 'Stewartii', 'Lanei' and 'Lutea' if you are getting them for a hedge. I would go for the cheapest that can be bought.

Of the grey kinds 'Fraseri' and 'Allumii' look almost the same, while 'Triomphe de Boskoop' is more bluish but again rather shaggy and therefore needs a bit more clipping. When it can be found one called 'Columnaris Glauca' is very neat by nature. The silvery 'Fletcheri' – which was indeed found wild in a hedge in Surrey – is cheap to buy and by no means so slow to develop as it is often said to be. It makes a superb hedge, silvery the whole year and dense.

I have tried to set forth the relevant considerations. What would I choose myself if I were beginning again? None of them. It would be yew every time. One of the sorrows of my gardening life is that I allowed myself to be talked into planting thuja when I was making our garden. Though costly, yew is vastly superior to anything else. A little slow perhaps, but not so slow as it is often thought to be. Now I would beggar myself to provide the garden with walls of yew.

The significance of statuary

The day I found a pair of stone figures in a junk yard among the rusty mangles, the bedsteads of the departed and the silent fire dogs, transformed our garden. We set them up on the plinths that already stood there waiting, and at once it changed the whole prospect, both the perspective and the character of the place. Silent though these were, too, a girl proud of her basket of summer fruit, a boy wrapped against the winter cold, by a paradox somehow they brought with them a new living touch. I suppose really it was the contrast of the stone with the leafiness all around. They may have lost their companions symbolising Spring and Autumn, but they seemed capable of working some special spell in the garden in the way they stood out in relief no matter what season it was. Anyway, the extremes they represent have become a perennial reminder to me of our first vows: that it was to be an all-the-year garden where through the 12 months there should be something out there to enjoy.

This little incident is perhaps in the great tradition of placing statues in gardens. It began in the Renaissance, when the princes and prelates of Italy were plundering the buried Roman remains for stone for their palaces. With the ready-cut building materials they also unearthed many pieces of Graeco-Roman sculpture. Inevitably they wanted to display them and their gardens became something of outdoor galleries, some of the conceits specially fashioned to display their treasure trove. Perhaps the most notable example is the great pine cone, symbol of fertility, which Pope Julius II, patron of Michelangelo, caused to be set up in the Vatican gardens.

The most obvious garden position for a fine piece of sculpture is at the end of a vista. And by vista one shouldn't necessarily imagine anything lengthy. I have known tiny town gardens with a figure at the end of the only path which could have been no more than 4.5 m (15 ft) long. At the purely practical level this gets rid of the small garden problem of where the main path ends. It must lead somewhere and if there's nowhere beyond for it to direct the eye to, why not to some handsome stone object?

Statuary does not necessarily belong to formal gardening either. The occasional figure or urn in a sylvan environment can help relate a wooded bit of the garden, however small, to the more deliberately created areas immediately close to the house. From one of our windows three paths lead into thickly planted shrubby areas in the traditional *patte d'oie* fashion. The scheme became much more significant when I set an urn in the distance in each, using the trailing euonymus.

Some pieces of sculpture go best in pairs and help to make false perspectives, thus extending the size of the garden by illusion. When it happened that I had completed my quarter century on the staff of *Popular Gardening*, to mark the occasion the directors presented me with a fine pair of stone finials from a demolished building. These now look well flanking a short flight of steps in our garden. It was not disrespectful to the donors that I should have painted them over with cowdung after they had been put in position. This was to return to them the patina of age which the antique dealer had carefully cleaned off! The method I used was a favourite recipe with garden makers. It discolours the stone temporarily, and soon lichen grows in the crevices, absorbing the stonework into the leafiness of the garden – and, as it were into time. Another device is to allow ivy to swag a figure to take away the raw newness from it, but you must be very handy with the secateurs and prevent the ivy from engulfing it.

In our own garden I have placed along a path a series of three pairs of terra-cotta pedestal urns which I acquired in a wildly prodigal moment. They are planted with the ever-blooming, ever-silver *Leucanthemum hosmarinifolium*, a name which simply denotes a white daisy, but this is irrelevant to the effect made, which is to lengthen the path and to give the area significance during the winter, while again giving a contrast with the surrounding foliage for the rest of the year.

Terra-cotta is a particularly sympathetic material for garden ornaments but it can be vulnerable to frost, which causes it to become first crazed, then to crumble. There are two ways you can prevent this, however. One is to treat the objects with the same silicon substance used for waterproofing walls, after which you would not think anything had been done to them, for it is invisible. The other method is to mix up a solution of Unibond adhesive in water and paint the terra-cotta with this, but it does put a slight glaze on the surface. Either way prevents the water from getting into the substance, freezing during hard weather and by expanding causing the damage.

The cardinal point about choosing pieces of sculpture for the garden, however, is always to select something bigger than you think the site will take. Best way is to keep a rule handy in the glove box of your car, take rough measurements and before buying make a mock-up from cardboard boxes, site it and then judge what would be to scale with the site.

Paths as decorative features

Paths will play an important part in the design of your garden – how important you will have to decide at an early stage of garden planning. Garden paths can lead you in so many different directions! But you could say they come to the same point in the end.

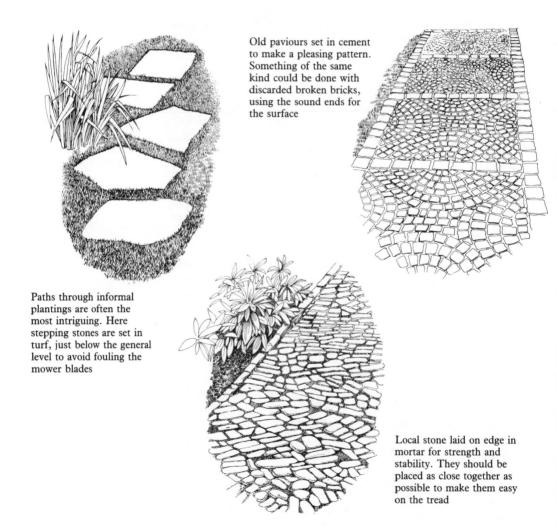

Old paviours set in cement to make a pleasing pattern. Something of the same kind could be done with discarded broken bricks, using the sound ends for the surface

Paths through informal plantings are often the most intriguing. Here stepping stones are set in turf, just below the general level to avoid fouling the mower blades

Local stone laid on edge in mortar for strength and stability. They should be placed as close together as possible to make them easy on the tread

Successful gardens are often built up on their paths. If they are composed of several areas, these can be brought together by using materials of the same colouring and texture throughout. Paths can form the structure of a design that remains constant throughout the four seasons, perhaps taking on its greatest visual importance during the winter when, all else having retreated, you are left with nothing but the pattern on the ground and the third dimension of bare trees and lumpy evergreen bushes.

A sound principle in making paths is that just as they need good foundations for safe walking they should either go straight to their objective or at least take a bold sweep towards it, curling perhaps only to form part of a bold design or to avoid some cherished and perhaps immovable feature such as an old tree or a dominant urn or piece of statuary. Ideally they should be broad enough for two to walk abreast, but at least wide enough to enable one to wheel a barrow without damaging or having to duck nearby plants.

A well-tried strategem in small gardens is to use the path to give an illusion of enlarging the place by curling in such a slight way that it turns just out of sight and leads you to wonder what is beyond. It may actually lead to a concealed shed or compost heap but it will have done its job of making the garden seem a little bigger than it really is. A bold, uncompromisingly straight path can, by perspective, help increase a sense of spaciousness as much as a clean sweep of turf can. Even this can also offer a chance of artistic expression in the interplay of more than one type of material. Random paving, using squared paving slabs in three or four sizes, gives a soft effect within strong outlines.

Paths through informal plantings are often the most intriguing – and least costly to lay – if they are made with stepping stones set in turf, just below the general level to avoid fouling the mower blades. Such a path can take one into a hidden area in a small garden, so adding to its size by illusion when seen from the windows of the house.

3
More about Trees

The deeply loved British landscape depends on its trees. Even those in the wild seem to have greater variety than the trees in other lands. But in our parks and gardens the variety is probably the greatest you will find in the world. Due to the richness of our grass, our fields and hills, and no less from the character of our prevailing light, together they do not make a hotchpotch of vegetation. All these trees of many different species, from many parts of the world, blend miraculously. Many of our wild trees came here by way of seed on Roman chariot wheels, and our arboriflora is almost as diverse as that of our gardens.

We are lucky in being the inheritors of the wealth of trees brought here through the centuries of plant exploring. Not only that, but also from the way they were taken up by garden enthusiasts. France sent its plant explorers to the Far East, though in fact they were amateurs, usually Jesuit missionaries, while ours were professionals, botanists and plantsmen in the pay of botanic gardens and wealthy owners of splendid parks. But in France instead of making their way into new plantings as they did here, the specimens often remained in herbaria dried and stuck to sheets of paper, or at best were confined to botanic gardens.

Here, by contrast, there has always been widespread commercial exploitation of new varieties of plants because we have always had a thriving nursery industry. We have had a spirited camaraderie among our gardeners too, who have been anxious to share their new plants with others. Fortunes could have been made from them, but they weren't. Simply because the plants came into the hands of those who loved them.

Inevitably, then, when we want to commemorate some historic event it is to planting yet another tree somewhere that we at once turn rather than setting up some graven image or lifeless monument. No lapidary words can ever have the eloquence of a tree that grows in beauty year by year. However, trees do need tailoring from time to time. Most of them need to be encouraged to build a fine straight leader unrivalled by other contenders. They need to be thinned early in life so that they are not crowded with branches. They need inner branches that rise at an acute angle removed so they will suffer the least possible damage in heavy snowfalls and in tempests.

Then they need to have weed growth round them kept down for their first three years. Without this they are reluctant to develop. When I see those trees that have been planted alongside our motorways neatly enclosed at the butts with anti-rabbit wrapping but nevertheless sunk in the wild vegetation I am horrified by what amounts to neglect. I feel I would like to pull it all out from round them and spray the soil in a 1.2 m (4 ft) circle with simazine weedkiller. Without such treatment the century will have passed and we shall have entered the new millenium before these trees and bushes make any effect. After all, the highway authorities must have spent, very wisely, great sums of money on these plantings. To leave it at that is certainly not putting it to the best use. But perhaps that's part of our island story today and another matter.

Trees for the front garden

One comfort is that developers are no longer the vandals that got them such a bad name at one time. Today they employ landscape designers who lead them into leaving some of the trees when they break new ground for building. They realise that trees can be as important a part of the environment as the houses they put up, the roads they build and the patches of grass they lay. This fortunate fact offers an idea to the householder when he thinks about planting the odd tree in his patch of front garden. Should it be a neat compact grower such as he would wisely choose for his back garden, or is this an occasion when he can make a real contribution to the appearance of the neighbourhood by planting something that will soar?

Some of the most pleasing roads you could ever walk or drive along are made so by their trees – trees growing in gardens as well as planted at the edge of the pavements. When local authorities plant trees they usually do so formally, making avenues of the roads, but garden owners can plant what they like and gradually the environment takes on something of our wild landscape restored, due to the multiplicity of species of plants that grow in this country. Take the magnolias planted in gardens in the thirties and which have now become mature. They have also become popular landmarks that we look for at flowering time. Exotic you could call them, yes, but they seem to merge perfectly with the sycamores that spring up and are allowed to prosper, the horse chestnuts that arise from discarded conkers, the birches that arrive from no one knows where and the ash trees whose 'keys' once came on the autumn gales. Together all make our suburbs places with an agreeable environment and where residents rise in wrathful protest when anyone so much as talks of taking down a tree, even if it is in his own garden. Of course, there is the problem of drains. You would be a fool to plant a poplar and run the risk of their getting blocked up.

Light is a more important consideration. It seems that legally we have some right to light, and you would be mad to plant a magnolia close to your own or anyone else's windows. It would be delightful flowering on its leafless branches in spring, but in summer those same branches would be covered with dense heavy foliage. And the tree would go on growing, not suddenly stop when you thought it had got to a suitable size!

However, I am sure that deciduous species are preferable to ever-greens (though there are precious few evergreen trees), and this of course includes conifers. Leaf losers give you constant change and ever-renewed liveliness as against the static appearance of evergreens and the touch of the sombre that conifers bring.

Davidia involucrata, the aptly named Handkerchief Tree

My personal choice If I am right in this theory that the garden owner can enhance his road with what you might call parkland trees, what are the kinds that come within this grouping?

First I would put the Tulip Tree, *Liriodendron tulipifera*, a noble tree of soaring outline that one day bears strange and exotic flowers of coral and green but from the start puts on wonderful autumn tints as the leaves turn orange and gold.

Next I would choose the davidia, or Handkerchief Tree, of plume-like outline and bearing in May those large white bracts that pass for flowers. I would consider also the Red-flowered Horse Chestnut, *Aesculus* × *carnea* 'Briotii', two of which planted on the boundaries enhance my own road, to my great and perennially renewed delight.

Someone has planted a liquidambar here, to the benefit of all, for this is one of the most richly coloured of all autumn leaf trees. It has grown into a beautiful cone shape. We also have near us in a similar position a mature golden catalpa, or Indian Bean Tree, the gold colouring the leaves through their first couple of months each season.

Few people ever plant, or even see, the cercidiphyllum, again a superb autumn colouring tree with heart-shaped leaves like those of the Judas Tree, but it is really splendid after some years. As for our ash tree, while the ordinary wild species can be a nuisance with its falling seeds giving rise to countless youngsters, even between paving stones, the so-called Manna or Flowering Ash, *Fraxinus ornus*, is marvellous in white flower in May and in purple leaf in the autumn.

In several garden centres lately I have noticed tallish trees for sale of the Fern-leaved Beech, *Fagus sylvatica heterophylla*, which differs from an ordinary beech in having narrower but more deeply toothed leaves.

If I were planting a roadside birch it would be one with fern-like leaves too. These are to be found in *Betula pendula* 'Dalecarlica', the Swedish Birch. To be sure of the whitest possible trunk, however, one should try to find *Betula jacquemontii*. However, there are several birches with a pronounced pink colouring to their bark. Two of the easiest to find are *B. ermanii* and *B. albo-sinensis septentrionalis*.

For those worried about ultimate spread – though remember that by the time this stage is reached another generation will have taken over who will doubtless accept the trees as part of the natural landscape! – there are one or two upright-growing trees that need bother no one. *Malus tschonoskii*, a crab grown not for its flowers or fruits but simply for the splendour of its autumn foliage, is one of these. Another is the Pyramid Hornbeam, *Carpinus betulus* 'Fastigiata', while a third is the fastigiate birch.

If you seek a certain lightness of touch, then consider the Japanese-looking *Acer negundo* 'Variegatum', or the golden-leaved False Acacia *Robinia* 'Frisia', or again the Honey Locust sold as *Gleditsia* 'Sunburst'. All three are most elegant.

What to plant

Like too many of our herbaceous plants, so many of the trees sold in nurseries and garden centres for planting in small gardens grow too big for them. They look winning enough in the nursery, and it certainly is hard to believe when you see them in their rows that the slender sapling you choose will one day grow into a mighty tree. But that day may come all too soon. And with it the embarrassment of shade, of wide-spreading roots robbing the soil, of branches (and the leaves in summer) taking light from windows.

By tree, of course, I mean one that you can buy ready grown as it were, with three or four branches radiating from a trunk already 2 m (6 ft) tall, giving 2.4 to 2.7 m (8 to 9 ft) overall. And when you begin to look about for something like this but which will not quickly outgrow the site, you realise just how narrow the field is. There are plenty of small bushes about that will grow into trees in time and can be shaped up, like magnolias (see page 72). Another example is the common but attractive amelanchier, which gives a crop of white flowers in spring and has wonderful autumn colour. A third is the rosy-flowered Judas Tree to be found in plant catalogues and garden centres under the name *Cercis siliquastrum* and has everything one can ask of a tree for a small garden.

In the first place it never grows so lustily that once it has gone past a certain stage you are forever hacking it about in the vain hope of curbing it. If you do have to prune it, then you do not have to cut away the flowering twigs and wait another three years before more arrive, for in fact it flowers on the oldest wood, the buds even seeming to burst

Cercis siliquastrum in flower

45

from the bark. Its foliage is a delight in itself. Each leaf is heart shaped, and well worth cutting here and there for putting with sheaves of other flowers in the house. The head that it makes is dense and twiggy. Such a pity that you can never buy this as a standard, only as a 1 m (3 ft) bush which you have to train up, for it is one of the very finest of small garden trees.

Laburnum tunnels are becoming fashionable things to plant in a garden these days, taking the place of the pergolas that have now become so expensive to construct in timber (see page 131). But one laburnum tree in the garden is a delight in May when it is hung with golden tresses. As a member of the big pea family of plants, it likes best a soil that is light, and it shares with others of its kind the habit of making a deep-striking tap root. This means that although it is possible to obtain it as a standard, it is better to buy a small plant from a nursery and train it up as an eventual standard tree, for tap rooters do like being moved when big. Yet young trees start to flower early in their lives, giving rewards out of proportion to their size and orginal cost. The one called *Laburnum* × *watereri* 'Vossii' has two advantages over the common kind: it has a more erect manner and the flowers are longer. It really is a first rate garden tree.

Flowering cherries

The same cannot always be said of the Japanese cherries, of which there are so many in nurseries and which are some of the most captivating things of spring. Not all, however, are suitable for the small garden.

'Mikuruma-Gaeshi' . . . say it over and over again to yourself and you could find yourself slipping into an hypnotic trance. This Japanese flowering cherry actually gets its name from what it did for some remote Japanese emperor who, after they had gone past a particularly beautiful tree in blossom commanded his party of retainers to go back so that he might enjoy its wonder again. Translated 'Mikuruma-Gaeshi' means 'the royal carriage returns'.

I know now, though, that it was folly to plant flowering cherries at all on our damp, heavy soil. It is just the land on which they produce long surface roots which thicken at points and then erupt with new plants – but of the stock, not the choice variety. You chop them off and then find that the relics still foul the mower blades. I am always, it seems, hacking at unwanted cherry trees with a mattock. No matter, when you see them in bloom you can forgive them everything.

I suppose it was folly, too, in an area where bullfinches abound to plant cherries at all. They are busy in the trees most of the winter, pecking away at the buds and scattering them on the ground, the upshot being no flowers. None at all on the early cultivars, those that come with March winds. Yet you see them looking marvellous at that time on the outskirts of cities. The odd thing is that I find the birds leave alone the autumn cherry, *Prunus subhirtella* 'Autumnalis', which puts on a big flush of white blossom in November and early December and then goes on producing more flowers through mild spells into March. Similarly they eschew the kinds whose turn doesn't come until April is almost finished. Nonetheless, if you have lightish soil and don't live anywhere near fruit-growing areas, I recommend planting a few flowering cherries for the sake of that most endearing of blossom early in the season. There are dozens of them and really the best way to choose is to see them in a garden centre in spring.

Much though we may admire it when it is in bloom early in April, I would certainly give the rich 'Kanzan' cultivar, also known as 'Hisakura', a miss. It has been so frequently planted that every spring you can enjoy it anyway, so why not have something you see much more rarely? One I specially like is the March-flowering white 'Pandora', also quite an upright-growing tree and much less robust. I am also very keen on one called 'Accolade', which has deep pink blossom early in April and makes a round head. Another seldom seen is the pale yellow 'Ukon', also rather upright growing. And so is what some cherry fanciers regard as the finest of all, one named 'Tai Haku', which has single white flowers late in the season, the tree making an inverted cone. Known as the great white cherry, it has a most interesting history. It was raised in Japan certainly, centuries ago, but known there only from records in old manuscripts. An Englishman was inspecting these and recognised it as the tree he knew in the garden of an old lady who had got it originally from a Frenchman a quarter of a century before. He asked for cuttings and was later able to restore 'Tai Haku' to cultivation in Japan.

Some cherries make their branches horizontally, and one I have grown with nothing but the greatest delight and success, for it flowers late and is of no interest to the birds, has the name of 'Shimidsu Zakura'. Its white flowers are double and hang on 15 cm (6 in) stems in thick clusters. Another one with outstretched branches of distinct Japanese outline is named 'Shirotae' or 'Mount Fuji'. Again it has double white flowers in reckless abundance. A Japanese cherry that grows like a small Lombardy Poplar has leapt to fame for small gardens in recent years. It has clusters of double soft pink blossom and bears the name 'Amanogawa', meaning Celestial River, the Japanese equivalent of our Milky Way.

Prunus × *hillieri* 'Spire' has rather similar blossom and forms a slim pyramid, very suitable for a small garden.

You will see that Japan figures strongly in the genealogy of flowering cherries. But we do have a native cherry *Prunus avium*, represented in nurseries by its double, or 'Plena', form. It is certainly lovely but so lusty a grower that one can hardly accommodate it in a garden. Unfortunately the same goes, though to a slightly lesser degree, for the cultivated form of our Wild Bird Cherry, *Prunus padus*, which is most distinctive as its small white flowers are carried in drooping clusters rather like a laburnum's.

The Japanese cherries are inclined to have light-coloured decorative bark, as a winter feature, though none can rival the mahogany colouring and texture of the bark of the Tibetan Cherry, *Prunus serrula*. While this is nothing much in flower, the quality has been married by means of grafting good flowering kinds under the general name of Sheraton cherries by the Suffolk firm of Notcutt. Again, this is a tree whose shape has to be encouraged to develop in a symmetrical fashion rather than let go its own way. You hear of gardeners giving this a polish occasionally, too, and certainly it is one to plant in a sunny position, when the bark gleams on fine winter days.

Maples

Such is the lustre of the 'Brilliantissimum' maple (*Acer pseudoplatanus* 'Brilliantissimum'), that I have almost run off the road at the sound of delighted cries of 'stop' from a driving companion seeing it for the first time. What tree could be making so wonderful a sight with its 'blossom' in April? Of course, it wasn't in flower at all but simply opening its young leaves. A sight as fine as any pink-flowered dogwood. For 'Brilliantissimum', which deserves the superlative name conferred upon it better than any plant so endowed that I know, is simply a cultivar of our native sycamore. Where it came from I have never yet discovered.

Spring, though, is not its only hour. For as the leaves broaden the pink in them gives way to bronze markings and not until the season is nearly at an end do they become a plain green. I wish I could say that this effect is in turn succeeded by brilliant autumn colour, but this is not one of the sycamore virtues as enjoyed by many of the other maples. Another of the sycamores notable for this great moment of opening, 'Prinz Handjery', lacks it too, but if I could not find 'Brilliantissimum' then I would settle for this. Or I would have one called 'Leopoldii'. The last is the great tree you see in photographs of the garden at East Lambrook Manor in Somerset, made by the late Margery Fish of imperishable memory, which is admired by visitors there on open days for the speckling on the leaves that sometimes seem so bright that it must be overtaking the green.

A more vigorous cultivar sometimes unaccountably called the Box-leaved type, *Acer negundo* 'Variegatum', is fast enough for nurseries to sell it as a ready-grown standard and once you have planted one the tree soon looks mature. Nevertheless, it never becomes heavy looking. Always its sparse foliage, each leaf conspicuously marked with cream, helps it keep an airy appearance, and you can safely plant it in, say, an 18 m (60 ft) garden sure that it will not seem to be taking over the place within a few years.

If I could have only one Japanese maple to show autumn colour it would not be the most elegant of them, nor the most compact, nor one of those that is bronze of foliage most of the growing season. It would be green until its supreme moment. It would also be tallish. And it wouldn't be one of those which add the appeal of their coloured stems to their overall allure. It would be *Acer palmatum* 'Heptalobum Osakazuki', whose hour comes in October, when the whole thing appears to have set itself on fire in the manner of some oriental martyr. Then it seems finer than any other autumn leaf plant. I used to think that it must be named after some betwitching Japanese lady, but it seems it bears the name of some obscure little place. Well, it may have come from obscurity, but with the low autumn sun coming through its leaves it's an extrovert of a plant.

In our garden we are lucky enough to have some wild Field Maples, *Acer campestre*, which began life long before we did. Their restraint in the neat way they grow, and their marvellous autumn colouring, leads me to recommend them for general planting. Perhaps one could make a group of three of them together to give an informal touch to an otherwise severe plot. They have corky bark which seems to hide many insects for the tree creepers to seek ceaselessly, and it is always fun to watch these lively little birds at work on them. Field Maples are the least expensive of the whole family to buy and they are fast enough as growers for the nurseries to be able to offer them as standard trees.

Acer palmatum 'Senkaki' is always planted for the sake of its coral-tinted bark on the twigs. But I find it altogether a pretty plant for the refreshing green of its leaves through spring and summer, but most of all in autumn when they turn as gold as a witch hazel's. However, in more seasons than one might wish to recall they remain resolutely bushes, refusing to be hurried in their growth.

In contrast to these delicately fashioned leaves, those of *Acer japoni-cum* 'Aureum' are bold as though proud of the gold coating that overlies them through much of the season. April till September seems enough for them, though, for by the later date they start turning green and just when you might think that they would develop autumn colour they fall green and unremarked.

Beautiful bark

The snake bark maples also have highly coloured leaves in autumn but are more often grown for their green and white striped trunks, a feature which develops when they are still quite small. To my idea there is not much to choose between these, and you find them in garden centres and nurseries under the names of *Acer davidii*, *A. hersii* and *A. pensylvani-cum*. They are quite small growing, but you have to be careful to shape them while they are young, selecting a leading growth and training this up to produce a balanced system of branches. Otherwise the trees are

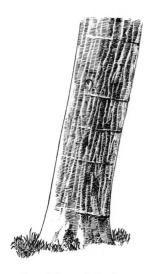

One of the snake bark maples, *Acer pensylvanicum*

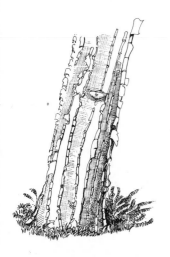

Acer griseum has attractive peeling bark

inclined to throw out odd branches in an ungainly, ugly fashion. Completely different in bark colour, though not in growth, is *A. griseum*, the little tree grown for its flaky brownish-coloured trunk, which people always want to rub their fingers over as they pass, as though, where it has peeled, it was some highly polished piece of furniture. Again it has good autumn leaf colour.

A word on garden training, since you can rarely buy any of these trees as standards. Put a stake to them to make them go straight and upright, but don't take off all the side branches unless they exhibit an anxiety to rival the main leader. They should be left for some years as they will help to thicken the trunk. Take them off in haste to make a tree and it will become whippy and never able to stand on its own.

Birches, the most celebrated of all bark-appeal trees, are always best planted young. Too often they fail when you try to transplant big ones. In addition to our native Silver Birch, *Betula pendula*, there are whiter stemmed exotic kinds that are as hardy. *B. papyrifera*, the Canoe Birch, is one of the best of these, while *B. ermanii* adds the appeal of orange young twigs to the attractiveness of its white trunk. One of the specially good things about birch trees is that they are very airy in appearance and cast little shade, though it must also be said that they are surface rooting and rather greedy for moisture. However, all I can say is that my birches have never done other plants any harm.

Witch hazels

Garden witch hazels are of oriental origin, but the American species, *Hamamelis virginiana*, the one everyone knows by repute from the lotion prepared from it, has a horticultural part to play. For the Chinese one is as reluctant a propagator as its compatriot the panda, and to get a good bush in a reasonable time you have to graft it on to a stock of the much racier American. Undistinguished in flower, the American has, however, another important hand in the whole matter, for it is believed that this was the one from which the common name derives. Early settlers noted the similarity to the hazel at home and some of them would of course try using its twigs for water divining.

The first of its Latin botanical names, *Hamamelis mollis*, comes from the old name given to a Greek tree, supposedly the medlar, the second from the softness of the hairs that clothe the undersides of the leaves. Now though there are other witch hazels grown in gardens, this one is unquestionably the most effective in the landscape for its wispy flowers are the most prominent. They are some of the most curious things in the floral world, consisting of clusters of narrow twisted petals, usually of shining gold, springing from a crimson heart. They spring from the bare stems too, for this is a deciduous tree that casts its leaves in autumn, though only after the foliage has turned from deep, dull green to a gold almost as bright as the flowers themselves.

Like all such winter-flowering plants that lose their leaves, the witch hazel is seen to best advantage when it is set with a background of some flattering evergreen bush. Here, then, is a use for the hardy hybrid rhododendrons which never lose their leaves until a new generation has taken over. The witch hazel will enjoy the same peaty soil, though this is not something it insists on. It does not make a widely searching system of roots and so likes to have plenty of damp peat or rotted leaves round it when it is planted. These are not cheap plants to buy these days, and they are almost always sold as container-grown plants.

Once you have a plant and you want to make more of it there are two courses open – certainly not to try rooting cuttings. One is to layer it by pulling down to soil level a low branch after scratching its bark with your thumbnail and covering the wounded part with peaty, sandy soil and putting a stone on top of this. The other is to 'air layer' it. This means damaging the bark higher up, dusting the wound with hormone rooting powder, wrapping damp moss round it and then enclosing the moss in polythene. Either way it can take two years to make a new plant! In any event it is worth siting a witch hazel within view of your windows. When it comes into bloom the first time you will also want to venture out and sniff its wonderful scent, but you will get the most from it if you can see it from the house. Unlike some winter flowers it is not fleeting but lasts in full bloom for about a month.

Some growers consider that finer than the golden one, since they say it shows up better from the windows, is a canary-coloured variety of this plant called 'Pallida', a seedling whose paternity is in doubt. Though raised at Wisley, the seedling itself came from an old nursery in Belgium, now the Kalmthout Arboretum.

When you see the witch hazels at Kew, not far from the main gate, simply packed with flowers, you might judge that because they are doing so splendidly there in an open site sun is what they need. My own experience is that they do well enough in shade. There are some plants that will have nothing else but sunny, open positions. If you have shady areas, then, why waste the sunny spots on something that doesn't really need it? More important is to provide a position where the bush can open out into an inverted cone standing about 2 m (6 ft) from its point.

Flowering crabs

There are a great many flowering crabs to choose from and truth to tell there is not much between them in merit. The flowers can be white, pink or red. Some have highly coloured fruit in the autumn, which the birds wisely leave alone. Often you can see the crimson fruits of an ornamental crab apple hanging on the trees in January, particularly when the tree is growing on poor soil and the fruits remain hard. They are also bountiful with their blossom. Every year too. They don't take the odd year off as many fruiting apples do. Unlike flowering cherries the birds do not go for the buds during the winter months leaving you only a few on the tips of the branchlets to open.

As trees they are biddable, usually making round heads in time – 7.5 m (25 ft) across after as many years. But in fact you can keep them much smaller than this and more upright in silhouette by cutting out the odd branch from time to time – in good time too, before the process has to be done by an expert in tree surgery.

As for crabbiness of nature, they don't know what it is. They are most contented trees, growing happily where they are put. Of course, like all members of the apple family they are happiest on really good soil, but if you look about in suburban gardens – such valuable indices of what will grow where – you will see many flourishing with abandon in areas where the soil is thin and overlies chalk, just about the least favourable site for all but a few members of the plant kingdom.

Of course, like most flowering trees, they also give their greatest bounty of blossom in places where they get what sun is going for most of the day. You would be unwise to plant one in a position that is shaded by buildings or higher overhanging trees. But some inevitable shade during the day does not mar their performance. Flowering crabs blossom late enough in the spring season to miss the worst of the frosts. Any that they do catch don't seem to harm them. In fact, we owe some of our best varieties to breeding programmes designed to produce both fruiting and flowering varieties that will withstand the harshest of winter conditions. For this one of the parents used was the well-known Siberian Crab, the one that is very familiar from bearing small scarlet apples in gardens during the autumn, and seen along roadsides, since it was planted on an extensive scale between the wars. Another is called 'Dartmouth' and is recognisable from the crimson fruits in the autumn. A third well known for its fruits is the yellow 'Golden Hornet'.

But flowers are our theme. All these have characteristic apple blossom, pale pink fading to white. The most prized crabs as flowerers, however, have deep pink, carmine or even crimson blossom. The richest coloured one I know is named 'Profusion', a tree of Dutch origin. In autumn its fruits are also deep red.

In at least one in general distribution the flowers have quite a strong scent. The deep pink 'Katherine' has this quality, but you have to pay for it by watching the flowers quickly pale to almost white from the fine colouring in which they open. However, in autumn the fruits are a distinct scarlet. Another that is scented, sometimes to be found in garden centres, carries the name of 'Charlottae', relating to the Christian name of the lady who found it growing wild not far from Chicago early in this century. Both pink flowers and foliage, which turns rich colours in autumn, are unusually large for the family. An exceedingly lucky find, appropriate for its place and time.

Flowering crabs, you will see then, actually span the globe in their wild distribution. There is even one to be highly treasured from Japan.

No pet name for this it is simply called *Malus floribunda*. It is actually one of the very best of weeping trees for a small garden. Its nature is to make a tree with a bun-shaped head from which some branches droop, and it never grows very large, keeping a trim little figure. From red buds the flowers open pink and then fade to white, but they are so abundant here.

What I would like to see myself is the quite exceptional autumn foliage quality of one species allied to good flowers and good fruits. This comes from a Japanese species that actually came from the foothills of the sacred Mount Fuji. Its name is *Malus tschonoskii*. In our garden in autumn its colouring rivals that of the liquidambar, and the nyssa, the parrotia and the exotic mountain ash trees. Then in form and colouring it resembles a great tongue of flame. Now wouldn't that be something to have allied to richly coloured blossom and brightly 'painted' fruit.

Mountain ash and thorn trees

Among the mountain ash trees there are several kinds that are missed by the birds because of the pale colouring of their berries. However, one of the red berried kinds is of special concern to home gardeners since its habit is that of a round-headed tree, of rather formal silhouette. This is *Sorbus vilmorinii*, one of the prettiest of the red kinds. The frost rather than the birds brings down the fruits of our tree of *Sorbus hupehensis*. They are like pale pink marble. I have heard that the white-fruited *S. cashmiriana* is on the tender side, but in the south it seems to thrive well enough. To me it is one of the most desirable of all the mountain ash trees. It makes a small dome-shaped head which is covered in May with pink flowers, also distinctive since most mountain ashes' blossom is a dull white. The leaves are rather elegant, being composed of many slender leaflets that give a fern-like appearance. To flower and fruit well *S. cashmiriana* does need a fairly sunny position, and it is better grown in a lightish soil than a heavy one.

Sorbus cashmiriana

Rich colouring is also one of the merits of the mountain ash group. Like the crabs, they do not mind having bits pruned away from them when they tend to get too big. So twiggy are they, indeed that this little amount of surgery is not noticed. Only when they get old however, do they tend to spread. In youth they keep an upright form.

In fact, one can safely plant any of the genus *Sorbus*. This includes the Whitebeam, *Sorbus aria*, which like the Mountain Ash, *Sorbus aucuparia*, has fine leaf colouring as well as bright red berries in autumn.

Also twiggy by nature and therefore easily doctored to keep them to scale with the garden when they are inclined to get out of hand, are the various thorn trees, found in nurseries and garden centres under the name of *Crataegus*. Perhaps the best is *prunifolia*, whose autumn leaves are really splendid, while the crop of berries lasts well into the winter. However, there are double-red, double-white and double-pink forms of the ordinary hawthorn, all first-rate garden trees.

Golden foliage

One of the more agreeable roadside developments of the past few years that you notice from the corner of your eye as you drive along is the rise of the golden tree. Universally admired, the fact is that at least one of them, a False Acacia, is among the fastest growing deciduous trees you could plant. Called *Robinia pseudoacacia* 'Frisia', a tree of Dutch origin, it has the same elegance of foliage that characterised the ordinary False Acacia (*Robinia pseudoacacia*) we know so well. Though it does not grow so fast – few variants with yellow leaves ever do, due to their lack of chlorophyll – the branches are just as brittle and vulnerable to damage in fierce windy spells. But this is no disadvantage, since it usually does no more harm than thinning out the tree, an attention which garden – and street – trees too often lack.

Rather slower and easily mistaken for a 'Frisia' until you get close to it is a remarkable form of the North American Honey Locust tree, *Gleditsia tricanthos* which has been named, quite appropriately, 'Sunburst'. In this the leaflets are much smaller, which gives the whole thing much greater elegance, and I would say that if you are going to notice the tree often in your garden this would be the one to be preferred. Does it flower? Well, yes in theory. But when it does the flowers are insignificant and of no consequence. You could not hold this against the tree as a disability, though. It can amply justify its place, even in a small garden, by the beauty of its foliage, and the grace of its bearing.

Neither of these trees will ever cast much shade in summer, while their effect in blotting out some eyesores beyond the garden may only be minimal. If you want a nice, thick-headed tree under which you can sit and read your book on a hot summer's day, then you want to get the golden-leaved form of the Indian Bean Tree, *Catalpa bignonioides* 'Aurea'. I had always known this as a rather slow grower. When you do see one with a very broad head the thickness of the trunk reveals that it will have been planted many, many years ago. However, a tree I know which was put in only two seasons ago in a garden and is very carefully looked after has doubled the size of its head in this time. So perhaps it is one that pays for generous treatment.

Just as most trees in time produce a sport that has an upright, column-like manner of growth, which is selected and ever after given the extra name of 'Fastigiata', so at some time or other they give rise to golden-leaved forms. These are not always stable and the distinctive colouring does tend to disappear as the season advances, being present only in the early stages. However, in some kinds the yellow colouring is sufficiently strong to make the tree deserving of having the term 'Aureum' added to its other two names to distinguish it. I would not say that in these cases the gold persists all through the leaves' term, but until the end of July, say, it is usually pretty strong.

Fortunately, this quality slows up growth in the forest trees very considerably, making them fit trees to plant in gardens. Even the mighty beech can be so planted, since the variety of the common kind, *Fagus sylvatica*, which also has the pet name of 'Zlatia', remains suitably neat. The Golden Elm, which goes by the botanical name of *Ulmus sarniensis* 'Dicksonii', has both yellow leaves and an upright form of growth, doubly suiting itself to garden planting. I know several gardens where it has been planted in borders where the predominating colours are yellow, bronze and purple and it shows no signs here of outgrowing the general scale of the garden.

Our native alder tree also has its golden sport in *Alnus glutinosa* 'Aurea'. This is one of the few golden-leaved plants that can be safely put in really damp soil without fear that the wetness will get too much for it. Indeed, it would be an ideal tree to add to a bog garden, an area that can be rather sombre once the great spring and early summer flush of flowers is over.

Conifers

As I said earlier the British landscape depends on its trees, so think for one moment what it would look like without our conifers. Vastly different in any region where the hands of gardeners have been at work. To our forbears it was certainly very different indeed in the way that trees influenced it. For until little over a century ago there were hardly any cone-bearing trees growing in it compared with what we have today. Most of the conifers seen at their maturity today came from North America in the great days of plant collecting abroad and of the expansion of the nursery trade here in the last century. Large-scale propagation of them has gone on ever since they were found to prosper here. Hundreds of thousands, if not millions, of conifers have been added to the natural trees of our landscape, remembering that you cannot plant a garden without making some mark upon it.

Proliferation of different forms also goes into big figures. Conifer watchers are constantly on the lookout for new forms arising from existing kinds. They sometimes come as seedlings but more often as curious mutations which just appear as sports on branches, one twig showing marked differences of colour or form from all the rest. A circumstance by no means as uncommon as you might think from the sober look of those tall dark green trees – 'sad cypresses' indeed – that help to compose our landscape.

Britain surely stands in danger today of having too many conifers. Not too many different kinds but too many actual trees that look similar and are already outgrowing their sites. Our nurseries have been to blame in the past. Now it's the garden centres in which we are led astray. Those appealing comfortable looking trees, so beguiling in their pots, show little of their potential in size. As they grow and maturity begins to sit upon them they change character. The winsomeness of childhood is overtaken by the sobriety of middle age too soon, and then appears that depressing solemness that is part of the old age of conifers, a stage that lasts through many, many years too. Just look around you.

Happily, though, the situation is changing. We shall have to fell many of our big conifers – how, it would sometimes be difficult to know – but the seductive conifers in the garden centres now are as often as not dwarfs that remain small all their days rather than trees that become giants.

Range of colour and form In any case the range of trees proper has become much greater. Now there are many tallish conifers in the nursery trade – often the sports from familiar kinds – that have lighter tints in their foliage, either silver or gold. These kinds, due to the reduced amount of chlorophyll in their leaves, do not grow nearly so fast or so large.

An exception, of course, is the golden 'Castlewellan' form of the overplanted × *Cupressocyparis leylandii*, that soaring tree that puts on at least 1 m (3 ft) a year once it has got into its stride. 'Castlewellan' grows almost as fast as its lusty parent. Another to be wary of is the greyish *Cupressus arizonica* 'Conica'. This is a fast grower that becomes shabby in 15 years. I have felled two of them that reached 9 m (30 ft) in 20 seasons, and was glad when another died a natural death. I would be a little careful of the 'Gold Crest' form of *Cupressus macrocarpa*. I daily watch a tree that is 3 m (10 ft) tall after only five seasons with some apprehension, though it is a most beautiful garden feature so far.

However, I do not think one need worry much about the cypress called 'Broomhill Gold', which is in the general nursery trade, outgrowing its site too soon, or one which has been named 'Stardust'. These are superb golden trees, well behaved in all ways since they keep much of their gold colouring through the winter and are elegantly slim. The favourite old *Chamaecyparis lawsoniana* 'Fletcheri' has been around long enough now for us to know that this not only gets too tall for most gardens but fat as well. A much better choice for a small silver conifer is *C. l.* 'Ellwoodii', once sold as a rock garden tree but frankly unsuitable for such a role. It has a sport named 'Ellwood's Gold'.

I wonder greatly what sort of a tree the juniper called *Juniperus virginiana* 'Skyrocket' will make in time. It is one of the thinnest of all, as slim as a Mediterranean cypress, though a bluish grey colour. It was introduced in the 1940s – I believe it was discovered wild in Texas – so no one yet knows. However, the fact that it is so thin may keep it acceptable however tall it gets. Anyway where I have taken out a

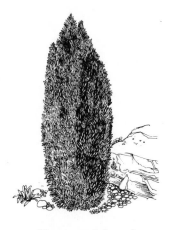

Chamaecyparis lawsoniana 'Ellwoodii'

number of *Chamaecyparis lawsoniana* 'Fletcheri' trees because of their uncomely appearance after 25 seasons I have put this in.

When conifers weep, as many of them do, they are quite slow growing, and here one does not need to look for any new kinds. The old *Chamaecyparis nootkatensis* 'Pendula' is one of the most lovely trees I know, not too dark a green and every branchlet falling to make the whole thing like a cascade of water. It is a superb tree for a key position, perhaps at the end of a vista. So is the unhappily named Coffin Juniper, *Juniperus recurva* 'Coxii', slower growing and always silvery. I have never yet seen a really big one.

Nor I have I seen a grossly large specimen of the elegant *Chamaecyparis pisifera* 'Filifera Aurea', the so-called Golden Whipcord Cypress. Also good for a point of focus somewhere in the garden, this is often a very good choice for a place where a willow sapling is likely to be planted, only to have to be cut down ten years later when it attempts to take over the garden.

Chamaecyparis obtusa, parent of many forms, has one that is in a class completely by itself and in my view one of the most attractive of all golden conifers. This is called simply 'Crippsii'. The leaves arrange themselves like ferns, and no one meeting it for the first time takes it for a cypress.

Modern favourites Today, however, it is the junipers that are really in the ascendant, if one can use the term here, when restraint rather than ascendancy is the desired quality. They have yielded a great many different forms. Some are slender little trees resembling cypresses in miniature. Some make broad cones, others bun-shaped bushes. And then there are many that are just content to spread over the ground, growing almost flat. These are some of the most desirable of all, for they help to keep the garden tidy. These carpeting junipers can be bluish as with *Juniperus horizontalis* 'Glauca'. Or they can be golden, as in *J. communis* 'Depressa Aurea', though this has the added touch of changing to bronze in winter.

The Silver Fir tree, or abies, has several dome-like forms, prickly little trees that can be very appealing at key points in the garden where, say, someone would otherwise cut across a corner of the lawn. One of the nicest of these is merely named 'Globosa'.

And so does the spruce – our Christmas Tree (*Picea abies*) – have beautiful dwarf forms, often coloured yellow or blue. Again, for a dome-like one you can safely look for the name *P. pungens* 'Globosa'. However, when you are dealing with spruces of the blue types, you need not worry about proportions too much, for the blue ones, like *P.p.* 'Hoopsii' and 'Koster', even though they do grow into trees, are very slow about it. In fact you have a problem with them in selecting a leading shoot and have to tie one twig at the top to a cane to make it take over.

Among the pines small enough for a garden I would not be without one that has the strange habit of going gold for the winter and turning green for the summer. It is so slow that you rarely see it as anything but a bush. Again it has a simple name, *Pinus sylvestris* 'Aurea'.

Planting a commemorative tree

What are the qualities one should look for in a well-chosen commemorative tree, whether it celebrates a public or a private family event, happy, sad or by way of thanksgiving? The first requirement is surely that it should be long-lived. Most of the trees we enjoy in our landscape composed of woods, forests, hedgerows and parks began life long before we did. We are their custodians as well as their inheritors. I know a woman who gave away a valuable building plot in the stockbroker belt in exchange for a little bit of land with a great beech on it which she had known and loved from childhood when she heard it was to be felled. She deserves a place among saints, for all who pass that way, and perhaps those for another century to come, can enjoy it.

Personally, I think a commemorative tree should be deciduous. If you go for an evergreen you at once get into the realm of the conifers and conifers can look alien in our landscape where they are over-done. And besides, not all the Cedars of Lebanon (*Cedrus libani*) can endow the delight of the first bright leaf as the spring returns, the weekly comfort of the fashion in which the silhouette grows richer through the summer, the thrill of the autumn leaf colour as the year declines and the dramatic tracery of bare twig and branch against a winter sky. I think, too, that it might as well be small when it is put in, for then it is a symbol of faith, an expression of confidence in a future which it is up to us to make golden. But there's a practical reason too. You don't want to have to wait till the autumn to commemorate this year's occasion. You want to be able to go to some special garden centre and buy the tree at the appropriate time so it can be planted straight away.

You are much more likely to be able to buy some treasure of a tree in a 13 cm (5 in) container and still only about 60 cm (2 ft) tall than a ready grown standard on its 2 m (6 ft) stem. Besides, the range is then likely to be greatest. Then you or those you give it to will be able to watch it as the years pass developing from a sapling to a stripling, perhaps even to its maturity. But you will have the satisfaction of enhancing the landscape for all who follow.

I have compiled a list of trees which I believe are particularly appropriate for commemorating. Some are comparative rarities. By no means all are available in all good garden centres, but it should be possible to get one or other of them, doubtless several, in most such places about the country. All have distinction of some kind. (Though what tree hasn't in some degree?) All are either beautiful in leaf or flowers or in their natural outline.

The ceremony of planting a commemorative tree should not rest with uttering some mayoral incantation over it. (Though I am forced to admit that plants do sometimes appear to overhear what people say in their presence.) It should include thorough preparation of the soil.

Noble trees of handsome bearing

Acer pseudoplatanus 'Brilliantissimum' Bright pink young leaves, turning yellow, then green.

Acer pseudoplatanus 'Leopoldii' Young leaves apricot, yellow and pink variegated later.

Acer pseudoplatanus 'Prinz Handjery' Yellow variegated leaves, purple on undersides.

Aesculus × carnea 'Briotii' Red-flowered horse chestnut.

Aesculus indica Finest of the horse chestnuts, pale pink flowers.

Betula albo-sinensis Birch with pink and red tinted bark.

Betula ermanii Very pale pink bark, orange stems.

Betula papyrifera (Canoe Birch) White bark.

Betula pendula 'Dalecarlica' A silver birch with fern-like leaves.

Carpinus betulus 'Fastigiata' Column-like hornbeam.

Castanea sativa (Sweet Chestnut) Slender foliage and 'sugar-stick' bark in old trees.

Cornus nuttallii Large ivory bracts surrounding boss of small flowers. Gold autumn colour.

Davidia involucrata (Handerchief Tree) White bracts.

Fagus sylvatica heterophylla Beech with fern-like leaves.

Fagus sylvatica 'Dawyck' Column-like beech.

Fraxinus ornus (Manna Ash) White flowers in May.

Juglans regia (Walnut) The 'Laciniata' form has more interesting divided leaves.

Liquidambar styraciflua Magnificent ruby foliage in autumn.

Liriodendron tulipifera (Tulip Tree) Fascinatingly shaped leaves colouring gold in autumn. Old trees bear astonishing greenish flowers in early summer.

Magnolia grandiflora Evergreen species. 'Maryland' is quickest to produce the huge white scented flowers; these appear during summer and autumn. Otherwise get 'Exmouth', or 'Goliath'.

Magnolia kobus Vast crop of early white flowers.

Magnolia × loebneri 'Merrill' White starry flowers.

Morus nigra (Black Mulberry) Do not plant where fruit can fall on path.

Malus tschonoskii One of the finest autumn colouring trees, turning to a torch of flame.

Nothofagus antarctica (South American Beech) Pretty, small leaves turning gold in autumn.

Platanus orientalis (Oriental Plane) Mottled bark and deeply divided leaves.

Arbutus unedo, the
Strawberry Tree

Quercus cerris (Turkey Oak)
Long complexly lobed or
serrated leaves.
Quercus coccinea (Scarlet
Oak) Scarlet glossy foliage,
brilliant red in autumn.

Quercus rubra (Red Oak) Like
coccinea but with matt leaves.
Tilia × euchlora Non-
suckering, non-dripping lime
tree.

Distinctive trees of modest size

**Acer davidii, A. hersii, A.
pensylvanicum** Maples with
green and white striped trunks
and fine autumn leaf colour.
Arbutus unedo (Strawberry
Tree) Evergreen with
mahogany bark. White flowers,
red strawberry-like fruit appear
together in late winter.
Calycanthus occidentalis
(Allspice) Strange reddish
brown flowers in summer.
Catalpa bignonioides 'Aurea'
Golden-leaved Indian Bean
Tree.
Cercis siliquastrum
(Judas Tree) Heart-shaped
leaves turning brilliant red in
autumn.
Clerodendrum trichotomum
Gardenia-scented white flowers
in late summer quickly
followed by violet berries with
red calyces.
Cornus kousa chinensis
White-flowered Dogwood.

Crataegus prunifolia Best
form, with striking red fruits
and fine autumn leaf colour.
Ilex (Holly) Plant any
variegated one, but only the
plain leaved *aquifolium*
'Pyramidalis' is reliable in
setting a crop of berries
without a mate.
Koelreuteria paniculata Stag-
horn like leaves. Good autumn
colour.
Magnolia stellata Small-
growing species with starry
white flowers, pink in 'Rosea'
and 'Rubra' forms.
Sorbus Any species. *S. scalaris*
distinctive with frondy leaves
that turn fiery in autumn.
Massed scarlet fruits in
autumn.
Stewartia Any species. Rare
trees with white flowers in
summer and splendid autumn
colour, also attractive bark
markings.

Weeping trees with drooping silhouette

Betula pendula 'Youngii'
(Young's Weeping Birch)
**Fagus sylvatica 'Purpurea
Pendula'** (Weeping Copper
Beech)
Fraxinus excelsior 'Pendula'
(Weeping Ash)

Malus prunifolia 'Pendula'
(Weeping Ornamental Crab)
Pyrus salicifolia 'Pendula'
(Silver-leaved Pear)
Tila petiolaris (Weeping Silver
Lime)

4
Shrubs through the Seasons

I'm a shrub man myself. Unchanging and unrepentant about it.
During a long-enduring affair with the craft of gardening I've
changed not a little and shifted my ground from time to time. But
never, I think, have I gone back on my shrubs. Others may find
their greatest delight in their prickly roses, their fragments of
alpines, their herbaceous plants that are fodder for slugs, the
house plants that bore everyone else through repetition . . . But I
find the world of shrubs endlessly fascinating.

So vast is the field that one is always discovering new kinds.
The new edition of the standard reference work on the subject,
W. J. Bean's *Trees and Shrubs Hardy in the British Isles*, now runs
to four fat volumes of going on for a thousand pages apiece. Of
course, one could not grow many more than a handful oneself,
but I like to know about as many as I can and to be able to identify
them on sight through seeing them in others' gardens, in parks
and botanic gardens, nurseries too, as well as flower shows at
which there is invariably a shrub competition, no matter what
month of the year it is.

If I ask myself why I should have this horticultural preoccupation, I
suppose the answer would be that next to the soil shrubs are the primary
material of all good gardens, the main architectural element on which
they are built up. And it is the building aspect of gardening that I
particularly enjoy. It is with shrubs that you create your own little
landscape. The success or failure of the project depends on how you
dispose them on the site to create vistas however small the area, to set up
false perspectives, to contrive surprises, to conceal areas of special
pleasure or objects that are eyesores.

You cannot do without shrubs on any count. You need them for
screening your house from the common gaze and from uncomfortable
winds, and no less, if you are a gardener with a universal outlook which
embraces plants of all kinds, to shelter those sorts least able to look after

themselves. A garden whose boundaries are built up with shrub plantings looks bigger than one bounded by hedges – more mysterious, less readily explored.

Shrubs need never have it all to themselves, though. They make the basic framework of the garden but in playing this role they form the best possible background for all other kinds of plants, to flatter and support them. The rhododendrons of spring throw into relief the herbaceous plants of summer. Daffodils will last longer in flower where they are planted among shrubs because the bulbs will have protection from strong sun and untimely frost or snow. The lilies that like drainage so much but a leafy soil just the same will find this among shrubs, for their roots will provide this far more efficiently than could ever be achieved with the spade. Of course, the distinction between tree and shrub is quite arbitrary. Many a shrub grows into a tree in time and many a tree can be kept as a bush all through its life in the hands of an understanding gardener.

Keeping a balance Gardening with shrubs over quite a long time, I have learned not to worry very much about size and scale. Of course, one must arrange them broadly according to their potential. But for how many years must one plan? Five? Ten? Twenty? Certainly not these days for your heirs. The question is impossible to answer. Better to learn about methods of control pruning and which kinds respond to it.

Anything that renews itself from near ground level, like a Mock Orange, will respond, but maples and witch hazels which don't are a different matter. They're in a class to be treated with care. You have to do a cosmetic job on these from time to time, snipping and pinching rather than proper pruning. You also have to learn to steel yourself and jettison a shrub when it has outgrown its site and can no longer suffer pruning.

Then there are always possibilities of moving things around for better effect. This also does something towards controlling growth, for a shrub that is dug up and replanted after four or five years will suffer a check, which is welcome in many cases. The big pea family of plants will not move, but at the opposite extreme all the peat-loving kinds will do so very easily. In between there are hundreds of kinds that will endure being moved if you are wise enough to plant them in plenty of peat in the first place to encourage a tight system of small fibrous roots. I have used it for all the plantings I have ever made.

Evergreen shrubs, quite apart from the importance of their flowers, can be used to provide a background for the deciduous sorts. In the main evergreens are less interesting because they change little and so they are most suited to this background role. Nevertheless, wherever they are sited they help to keep the garden alive during the winter months. It is then that they help to emphasise the curious appeal of the leafless stems of the deciduous kinds which would otherwise be lost. Incidentally, most of the much admired winter flowers actually come on a series of shrubs which, though bereft of their leaves then and apparently at rest, deny this by blossoming during the shortest coldest days.

Deciduous shrubs, though 'always there', unlike herbaceous plants and bulbs, change all through their season, the leaves going through many colour changes, even shapes, as they develop. Thus the garden scene which they make is never static, even though it may be composed, as it can well be, with just half a dozen different kinds. Flowers? Of course – often in great sheaves. One of the most attractive gardens I know is a tiny one so artfully composed entirely of shrubs that few weeks of the year does it lack colour and never does it lack form, or artistic appeal.

Heathers

When I saw the winter heather growing wild in parts of Austria and up in the hills round the Italian lakes I got the idea that a good place for heathers in my own garden at home would be on the sunny edges of the shrub beds, fringing the turf that makes grassy walks round and about. Would it prove labour-saving, in the way that for a whole era of horticultural enterprise it was said it would? In fact, it has done that in more than one way. First of all the heather grows so densely that provided you handweeded for a couple of seasons and mulched well with peat or home-produced leafmould, it kept down all weeds. Indeed, you could fairly say that our heather-edged shrub beds are now self-maintaining.

Next, the heather enabled me to abandon the tedious practice of edging. The margins of shrub beds are always a problem. If you edge the turf sharply and make a gully in the conventional way it looks all wrong in an informal setting. If you don't, the untidiness is a perennial reproach. But the heather grows neatly to the edge of the grass, making an imperceptible join, and the Flymo machine with which I always finish off the mowing round the edges of the beds slips just far enough under the heather to take off any lengthy stems of grass. A cylinder machine, or an ordinary rotary would either shear some of the heather and leave it looking damaged or allow long bits of grass to flourish at the join. Now there are quite a few species of heather and countless cultivars. As ground cover that looks after itself, I would say that the winter-flowering kind generally styled *Erica carnea* but now *E. herbacea* botanically is the best. That little plant which you buy in a 8 cm (3 in) diameter container will spread out in quite a few seasons to make a thick rug over the ground in a circle about a metre across. Of course, it's the same with heathers as with bulbs: you never want to plant one or even three. Better ten of one kind to make a really bold colour effect over a season that can continue for a full three months. Another and perhaps even more important reason for planting many of one kind is the evenness of contour which is set up. No two kinds grow in quite the same way. Among the virtues of a carpet of greenery over the ground between shrubs is that it has a unifying effect on the garden and you want to sponsor this, not weaken it.

Now one of the problems about heather is that most kinds will not suffer lime in the soil, which makes them part of the exclusive province of those who garden on acid ground. The winter-flowering sort does not have any such preferences. Not only will it thrive on poor soil but also on one that has lime in it.

Whereas other kinds of heather are to be found in great numbers of varieties, the winter type is restricted to a mere handful. Rightly, the most celebrated of these is 'Springwood White', a lucky find by two Scottish girls one afternoon on a walk on an Italian hillside in the company of their governess. Its flowers really are the lucky white heather, when the wild *Erica herbacea* is usually a rather dull pink. In cultivation it sported to produce the bright 'Springwood Pink' and has several other richly coloured pink or red cultivars. Two I especially admire whenever I see them are the rosy 'King George', and the deeper coloured 'Pracecox Rubra'. Others worth considering are 'Pink Spangles' and 'Ruby Glow'. The important thing is to see them in flower and choose. They are robust, imperturbable plants. No frost can spoil their flowers, and if it snows they remain as safe beneath it as snowdrops do. Other heathers need clipping over in the spring, when they grow much closer in response, but this kind needs none. It behaves perfectly by nature. I would certainly rate the winter-flowering heather *E. herbacea* in its garden cultivars among the top ten of all garden plants.

Mahonias

Towards the end of the 18th century an Irish immigrant named Bernard M'Mahon set up a seed shop in Philadelphia. Outside the city he established a nursery which he ran while his wife looked after the shop. As those of his persuasion often do, he liked to chat to the other horticulturists who visited his establishment and joined in the arguments. Today he has his memorial not in the specific name of any plant but in that of a whole genus – and one which holds within it some of the noblest of hardy shrubs: the genus mahonia whose members come from the Far East and from the West Coast of North America.

Now mahonias are not merely evergreen shrubs of comfortable size: their leaves are exceedingly handsome. What is technically one leaf composed of many holly-like leaflets is actually a spray of foliage. In some species it can be as much as 46 cm ($1\frac{1}{2}$ ft) long, more than half that in breadth. Those of *Mahonia aquifolium* (and *M. repens*) do not quite measure up to that, but both are admirable plants for allowing to sucker in odd corners, even in the deepest shade, whether the soil is dry there or damp. In fact, I have had this plant growing successfully in near swamp.

However, it is the mahonias which were brought to Britain in a much later era of plant exploration that are now treasured most. These do not sucker but make clumpy bushes about 1.2 m (4 ft) tall and either as much across or only half that width if they are hybrids. They also produce their yellow flowers in the winter. These are also produced in sprays as noble as the leaves. The easiest to obtain in nurseries – and the least expensive – is *Mahonia japonica*. In this case the flowers are pale yellow and formed in lax sprays. They are delectably scented. Like the robust *aquifolium*, this one is very accommodating about where it grows. In fact it is best in the shade because in the sun the leaves are inclined to become coppery instead of their characteristic lush green.

Mahonia 'Charity'

Nearly a century after *Mahonia japonica* had been discovered growing in gardens in Japan there came from Western China a strictly upright-growing species with golden, though unscented, flowers, named *M. lomariifolia*. It did not prove generally hardy, but a very good shrub for planting in a corner where two walls meet at right angles. And it also proved itself excellent breeding material for crossing with *M. japonica*. From this process arose what has become known as the Media group, and you could say that its members have all been endowed with the best characteristics of both parents. Most famous of them so far is named 'Charity', which has the deep yellow flowers of *M. lomariifolia* arranged in the lax sprays of *M. japonica*. They are scented and usually out all through February. But 'Winter Sun', its golden flowers produced in upright spikes, comes in December.

However, mahonia fanciers are now bestowing their greatest praise on one named 'Lionel Fortescue' after the Devon gardener who made one of the crosses in his retirement garden near Yelverton. It certainly has the finest leaves of the group, especially as – in my experience – they are a lighter green than the others, while the arching sprays of flowers can be as much as 50 cm (20 in) long.

Mahonias are a garden ornament at any time and deserve to be planted as individuals. Here they can, as it were, express themselves fully. I find all these as tolerant of where they are put to grow as the suckering kinds. My heavy clay may be wet all the winter, but they don't seem to mind this in the least. On the other hand I know gardens where the soil is light and played out at that, and there they seem equally at home.

Camellias

Naturally enough, when the first camellias were brought here from China through the agency of the old East India Company in the late 18th century they were put straight into glasshouses. And there they spent the next 150 years, collections being greatly added to during this time, but no one ever thought of trying them out of doors. They were too highly prized and the risk seemed too great. During this time, also, they grew and grew. It is recorded that in the last century there were nursery greenhouses where camellias 9 m (30 ft) tall could be seen, laden with blossom in their flowering time. Always tucked up in a cosy atmosphere. In France – and remember a great many camellias have French names – it was the same. And didn't the camellia inspire a novel and an opera? And a film as well in more recent times.

Then the wheel of fashion turned. Then, too, the great days of glasshouses came to an end with the much higher cost of fuel and labour and, you could say, the camellia fell upon hard times. Physically as well as metaphorically, it was left out in the cold. And it prospered just the same. The toughness of the camellia is also shown in an old tale of some plants being left in packing cases after disembarkment at Antwerp. A squadron of cavalry horses came along and trod the lot to pulp. But the camellia among them was rescued and sent to the botanic garden at Louvain where the head gardener at the time, André Donckelaer, propagated from what material there was left, and it became one of the most famous of all time, *Camellia japonica* 'Donckelarii'. Wisley, the Royal Horticultural Society's garden, has played a part in the establishment of the camellia as a garden bush. The man who started the garden there had planted them in his woodlands as early as the turn of the century.

In our own time the camellia has come right to the fore as a garden plant, its hardiness having been proved by winters that one day will be declared the most severe of the century. The bushes don't die of frost. Only their flowers get damaged, and of course this happens to a lot more flowers at times, including crocuses and daffodils. The camellia is one of those plants that makes a lot of buds and opens them successively, so that if one lot goes there is always another relay to take another chance. In any case it's not so much the frost that does the harm as the rapid thawing caused by the early morning sun after a frosty night. Plant them where this cannot reach them and they thaw slowly, and the likelihood is that unless there have been many degrees of frost they will suffer little, no more than a slight browning at the edges of the petals. They may even escape altogether. It is the rapid thawing that reduces the flowers to a brown pulp. A place under trees is very suitable for them for even though they may be bare in winter the branches do keep off some degree of cold and this can be beneficial. If you notice it's always from places under trees that the snow and frost go soonest.

A garden in late spring where a flowering cherry is seen framed by freshly opened foliage and hostas emerge from winter dormancy.

Camellias also like the 'woodsy' soil built up gradually under trees, for they are peat lovers by nature. They do not abhor lime in the soil in quite the same way as rhododendrons. In fact, they seem happy enough in ground that is just neutral. Nevertheless, they will grow successfully in fairly dense soil, as I have proved for myself over many years in the

same garden. Here, though, the best planting technique seems to be to 'plant high', as gardeners say. You add plenty of peat to the site, and just make a shallow depression, piling more peaty soil up over the plant after it is set in this. Of course, you must stake such a plant to keep it upright for the first few seasons.

The bushes make excellent tub plants for terraces and patios, and they lend themselves to being trained against walls – usually a shady one. All through the early winter, and even through the perilous days as spring edges forward, 'Narumi-gata' opens more and more of its flowers – when it is in the right place. For this one none of the woodland in which camellias are familiarly seen planted, but a sunny position against wall or fence. 'Narumi-gata' prefers a place in full sun which it must have as certainly as a cistus or a ceanothus. For this is one of the cultivars – the most easily obtained – of *Camellia sasanqua*, a Japanese species.

Some camellia bushes have a natural inclination to grow upright, others arch their branches, while there are far more of an inbetween outline which just make rounded shrubs. The catalogues issued by the specialist growers indicate this with the descriptions of the plants.

Two main groups Camellias grown in open gardens as distinct from the few that have to be grown against a wall, fall into two main groups. The biggest comprises the forms of *Camellia japonica*, commonly known as the Japonicas. In these there is not only the great range of colouring, from white to deep red, but innumerable shades of pink, many cultivars having mottled and marbled flowers, but there is often considerable difference in their shape. Some are single, others are what gardeners picturesquely call 'very double', the flowers being stuffed with petals in remarkably regular formation. Again in between there are many semi-doubles which still show the great tuft of golden-tipped stamens of the singles. Others have what is styled the anemone form, two rows of petals surrounding an inner disc of small modified petals. Then there is the paeony form and the rose form, the one having a complex domed centre, the other a tufted centre surrounded by several rows of petals pinked at the edges.

A double-flowered camellia hybrid

The other type is styled the *Camellia × williamsii* hybrids, most of which are single or semi-double and pink. In the main they are rather more elegant, though this term could hardly be applied to one of the most famous of them, called 'Donation', which produces a big blowsy flower of sugar-icing pink. This type, though much more restricted in flower form than the Japonicas, has one great advantage over them: whereas the Japonicas hang on to their withered flowers, which have to be picked off one by one, even while the next crop is opening, the Williamsii type drop theirs and are therefore self-tidying garden plants. They are all rather upright-growing bushes too, another convenience in a garden.

Magnolia stellata fits into the smallest of gardens as it grows but slowly with a myriad star-like blooms in March.

Magnolias

These are surely the finest and most impressive of any flowering tree or shrubs with blossom carried in such quantity too, as soon as the plant is old enough to come into bearing. Some kinds may take, admittedly, 25 years for this to happen, even 40 in some cases, but these are the esoteric magnolias they grow so well in Cornwall, and in the West of Scotland. Most magnolias with flowers of various shades of pink, from what you might call wild rose to cultivated rose pink, do grow into trees, not just bushes. Although they take their time about coming to flowering, their habit is to flower early in the year, during April, when in other parts of the country the blooms are likely to get struck down by frost. Not in Cornwall though. Quite different are the everyday kinds that flourish almost with abandon in the suburban gardens around London. These you can plant one year and get flowers the next, with a heavy crop the very year after that.

Ponderous though the foliage may seem at times, it can be put to advantage. So dense looking a tree will in summer make a screen against the common gaze or some eyesore beyond the garden. Apart from this, a magnolia makes a splendid stage on which to display a summer-flowering clematis. Most species, even though they become trees, fork fairly near to the ground so that, soar though they may in time, you have plenty of branches close to eye level where the clematis flowers can be seen.

It happens that the most common magnolia is actually one of the finest in appearance and is a robust grower. This is the hybrid *M.* × *soulangiana*, the one you see in late April, carrying a huge crop of great flowers of white, usually flushed with light purple. In some places where it was planted long ago – usually magnolias survive for generations – you see it as a tree 6 m (20 ft) high and as much across. More often it is a multi-stemmed rounded bush heavily set with blossom. At one time if you preferred a white-flowered form of this truly great magnolia you had to get one called simply 'Alba'. That named 'Brozzonii' was known and the tree sometimes seen, but only very occasionally. Then it was something to marvel at, an occasion for wonder. Now I see it is listed by several nationally known nursery firms. If you come across it, snap it up. The flowers are even larger than the parent's pure waxen-white, only lightly touched with rose at the base.

Fortunately, there have always been plenty of supplies of the purple one called *M. liliflora* 'Nigra'. The flowers are of the same size and shape, but that deep vinous colour. However, the bushes are comparative dwarfs, growing at only half the rate of *M.* × *soulangiana* itself, a most fortunate thing for small gardens. For long I grew *M.* × *lennei* as a separate hybrid, but now it is reckoned to be simply another form of our old friend *M.* × *soulangiana*. For most of us it is the nearest thing we can grow to those rose-coloured magnolias that flourish as trees in the West Country and take so many years to come into bearing. Mine began the very first season, displaying then its large bowl-shaped flowers of rose-pink outside, ivory satin within.

One thing I specially like about 'Lennei' is that it doesn't give you its flowers all in one burst. They open successively between early April and the middle of June, just missing the frost.

Ideal for small gardens *Magnolia stellata* is the slowest grower of the whole genus, and therefore admirable for the smallest gardens, opening the season in March in some forward years. As the name implies, though, the flowers are very different in form, being star-like instead of tulip-shaped. About the only one you have been able to buy has been the basic white form, though there has always been a pinkish one known and offered in the most esoteric catalogues. Now there is a hybrid, or rather a number of them, seen around often under the collective name of *M. × loebneri*, the most freely available having 'Merrill' tacked on to this name. It grows rather bigger and has flowers of the same star shape but they really are pink. One of the parents of *loebneri* is *M. kobus*, which for me in 20 seasons grew to quite a big tree, perhaps 9 m (30 ft) tall. However, I could not say that this is in anyway a garden embarrassment as the whole thing is so light and airy. The leaves in this case are small and the flowers as starry as *stellata's* own. I recommend it as a most elegant tree.

I wish I could be as enthusiastic about the famous *M. grandiflora*, that large-leaved evergreen you see scaling the walls of old houses. I concede that it pays its rent as an evergreen if you have a wall tall and broad enough, but somehow it does seem so mean with its parchment-coloured flowers, only opening the odd one here and there over several months. Still they have a wonderful scent, and evergreens that will grow against walls and make a strong effect with their leaves alone are not all that easy to come by. In this instance, you want to make sure of getting the 'Exmouth' form because it does start early in life to give what flowers it does produce.

Growing both, I cannot see a lot of difference between those two magnolias of a different branch altogether, *M. wilsonii* and *M. sieboldii*. Both are exquisitely formed silvery white, cup-shaped flowers, each enshrining a large boss of crimson stamens and having a delicious fruity scent. Both grow as inverted cones, with conveniently upright striking branches. Neither is very vigorous – in 15 years mine are still no more than about 2.5 m (8 ft) tall.

Now a word about the sort of soil and place that suits magnolias. They have fleshy roots and therefore like it both ways, well-drained and moisture holding. Which indicates a crying need for peat. As for the place, anywhere in the sun. You do get most flowers then, though they will thrive in some degree of shade. The ideal, of course, is one of those spots where the sun doesn't reach it until late in the morning and then goes on shining on the tree for the rest of the day.

When to plant? Early April. Even though it may be in flower. There is no doubt whatever that this is the best time, immediately before the leaves open. If a plant comes from a container, timing does not matter, but if it comes from the open ground some root damage is inevitable but this is least likely to do harm at that time, as the surge of root growth goes forward.

Rhododendrons for the garden

It must surely be admitted that the foliage of the hardy hybrid rhododendrons can be pretty dull once the flowering season is over. Never mind. It has a most important value of its own. With a substantial background of these bushes you could hardly have a finer setting in your garden for the other plants that flower later in the season, nor one, once the plants have grown up, that will work more effectively as a dense screen – against noise as well as the gaze of passers by. The colour range must be large enough to suit everyone – scarlet, cerise, purple, pink, lavender, blood-red and cream. There is even one, called 'President Roosevelt', with variegated leaves, and another with double flowers, named 'Fastuosum Flore Plenum'. Both these extend the range of users of the hardy hybrids by being very suitable for growing as tub plants. The double one has an especially long flowering season.

An important point to know about hardy hybrids: usually the plants you buy – lush, compact and covered in fat buds just waiting to burst into flower – have been grafted. Grafted, that is, on to a stock of the rampant *Rhododendron ponticum*, the mauve-flowered kind you see running wild in the moist holiday areas of Britain. Let a shoot from the base prosper and you'll probably find it is one of the stock's which in time will engulf the lot, like a rose sucker. You have to be on guard against this happening and wrench off each sucker while it's small.

Most of the rhododendrons available in our garden centres are hybrids but some are distinguished by lacking the adjective hardy. There is also a series known as the woodland hybrids, but these are not everyday plants either and are the playthings of those with woodland gardens, often in specially mild spots of the country. Both these and the hardies are derived from forest species. The other set which are most useful for our gardens since they keep small, come from mountainous areas where the tree line gives way to upland meadows. They are adapted by nature to living there. This is the reason for their compact form. I would say, too, that their liking is for quite open positions, though they will content themselves with being in the shade for part of the day. Due to their nature they are exactly right for planting in the foreground of mixed borders where they grow into dome-like bushes.

One of the nicest of these, in my view, is one called 'Bow Bells', with wide flowers of soft pink and especially attractive rounded rather than elongated leaves which are shot with copper when they first expand. 'Oudjik's Sensation', whose longish leaves are always a particularly fresh shade of green has flowers of a much deeper pink. If you have a sheltered spot for it where night frosts in March are likely to pass over it, then try the delectable 'Tessa', a pink midway between the two and again with fresh green foliage, though neater.

Three strong red cultivars are in the garden centres these days, deepest of them being 'Baden Baden', brightest 'Scarlet Surprise', with 'Scarlet Wonder' in between. Deeper, verging on crimson, is 'Gertrude Schale', while 'Bengal' is certainly crimson. Two cultivars have yellow flowers, 'Cowslip' being a lemon colour and 'Chikor' a greenish yellow. In the area of small growers rhododendrons can be blue, a colour not customarily associated with these shrubs. There are lots of plants around of the indigo 'Blue Diamond' and the lavender 'Blue Tit'. Also, a much smaller plant still, of the violet *R. impeditum*.

This section of rhododendrons even includes a few ground-covering kinds, which lie flat on the ground. You will get this effect best from one called 'Carmen', which has quite big crimson flowers.

Rhododendrons of all kinds have an aversion to lime in the soil, so if your ground is the least bit chalky, forget about them. But if a simple soil test shows that your soil is at worst neutral or you know that rhododendrons grow well round about your home, think about adding some to the garden. They will bloom the first season too, if you pick from the garden centre plants with nice fat flower buds on them. The plants are grown in plastic containers and only need a few handfuls of damp peat round the roots to set them well on their way.

Three more acid soil lovers

Pieris enjoys the same soil and conditions as the rhododendrons. Some people call it Lily-of-the-valley Bush, and this name serves well enough since the flowers, though they appear in bigger bunches, really do look like the Lily-of-the-valley. There the resemblance stops, for though they may not be scented everything else about this plant is very different, especially when you also hear it called 'Flame of the Forest'. The facts are that *Pieris formosa* is technically an evergreen bush but not always green. For in the form customarily sold in garden centres under this latter name, the young growths open scarlet. They are more a feature of the plant than the flowers which open in May. Another good form is called 'Wakehurst', after the famous Sussex garden that serves as an annexe to Kew. Rarely do you see a bush of the pieris much above 1.2 m (4 ft) tall, and it is rather upright in form, so it goes well with the red-flowered rhododendrons but particularly with the orange and flame azaleas, among which it will provide a change of texture with its foliage while its flowers will set off these 'hot' colourings.

The gaunt shape of the *Enkianthus campanulatus* makes it especially valuable for interplanting among rhododendrons. So does the fact that this one is deciduous, losing its leaves in the autumn, though not before they have turned a brilliant rust colour. Thus it can increase the season of effectiveness of a little plantation of rhododendrons, providing a hectic moment in autumn when otherwise there would be an unbroken greenness going on into the winter.

Opening a little before the kalmia flowers, towards the end of May, the enkianthus is like the pieris, good for planting among the brightly coloured rhododendrons and azaleas, since its flowers are a coral red colour. The place to plant it is near a path, as each flower in the cluster is most delicately veined, inviting your close inspection and admiration. Fortunately, this is a bush which flowers quite well under shaded conditions, though like many plants that are so adaptable it flowers even better in places where it gets the sun for part of the day.

Yet another good shrub that associates well with rhododendrons and enjoys the same conditions is *Kalmia latifolia*. 'Just like wedding cake decorations' everyone says on first seeing it in flower in June. Every bell-shaped flower that composes the cluster is neatly crimped and pleated as though it had been fashioned through the nozzle of an icing bag. This bush comes out a little later than most rhododendrons, so that if a few bushes of it are added to a rhodo plantation they will help to give succession. But there is a snag. To flower really well they do need a place where they get a good deal of sun. Strange for peat-loving bushes that abhor lime as much as rhododendrons do. But that's nature. They also like the soil moist, so you might say that they are a bit difficult to satisfy. Still you can always see that they are moist at the root by putting a few logs of wood round them over the peat mulch. These will keep in the moisture as much as stones would, and gradually they will rot down and add to the fibrous, 'woodsy' nature of the soil.

The brooms

Brooms have two little quirks that you have always to provide for. One is that they will not suffer being transplanted once they have taken to one particular spot. Always the plants should be set out from pots, never from the open ground. The other is that the great majority will not endure being pruned hard at all. Only the current season's growth may be trimmed over, never anything older. Cut hard into that and the plant will most likely die. The exception is the gorse, which is certainly a member of the broom family of plants. This can be cut to the ground, whether it is the cultivated forms of the wild *Genista tinctoria* or the dwarf Spanish kind, *Genista hispanica*, often grown on rock gardens where it makes a dome-like little bush.

Brooms actually come under three different botanical names, *Genista*, *Cytisus* and *Spartium*, the difference in the plants being related to their seed vessels and therefore more of academic than practical significance. The biggest genus is *Cytisus* and it is among these that you get the highly coloured forms. These are cultivars of *C. scoparius*, which flower during May and early June. They range from 'Cornish Cream' to the crimson of 'Andreanus', and it is here that you find the near orange shade in one called 'Fulgens'; 'Burkwoodii', a hybrid from it, has deep red flowers edged with yellow, and another named 'Daisy Hill' is rich pink and ivory. 'Lord Lambourne' is cream and deep red.

These all stand about 1.2 m (4 ft) high with annual shearing over after they have flowered. On the other hand the yellow *Cytisus* × *beanii* is never seen much more than 30 cm (1 ft) but spreads out to about 1 m (3 ft) across. It is typical of the prostrate brooms which are so valuable for planting at the top of retaining walls which they drape like a curtain. *C.* × *kewensis* is not dissimilar in habit but has cream flowers. Another fine prostrate one has the simple name of *C. purpureus*. You usually see these about 46 cm (1½ ft) high but with drooping branches. It has rich pink flowers early in June. Of roughly the same appearance is the splendid *Genista lydia* whose branches are covered with yellow flowers in May. All these look especially well planted at the top of a retaining wall which they can tumble over.

As its second botanical name implies, *Cytisus* × *praecox* is usually out early in April. Its flowers are cream paling to white in the spring sunshine, but it has a cultivar named 'Allgold' which is yellow, and a pure white form, 'Albus'. The white-flowered broom most often seen, however, is generally called simply *C. albus*. These usually grow to around the 1 m (3 ft) mark. So is a hybrid 'Zeelandia', which has lilac and cream flowers.

The tree-forming brooms all come later on, in July. One of these can even be made to form a most lovely weeping tree, a garden delight whether it is in flower or not. Another interesting feature of it is that it is supposed to grow wild on the slopes of Mount Etna, presumably in the lava. Indeed its name is *Genista aetnensis*, and it has bright yellow flowers.

Even richer in its golden flowers, though not quite so elegant in form, is *Genista cinerea*. The second name in this case relates not to its origin but to its meaning, 'ash-coloured' which goes some way towards describing the colour of the stems and foliage. Both these trees need a very stout stake or they are inclined to get blown over in a gale, since the roothold is slight in the soil where they find themselves planted in this country. For the same reason the best place for the Moroccan Broom, *Cytisus battandieri*, is against a wall or fence in the sun. Here it is beautiful at all seasons because the foliage is really silvery. The flowers come in tightly packed heads and are a rich gold. More than that, though, they have a distinctive scent. It is certainly one of the most attractive of all south wall plants, especially in June and August when its flowers are out. At the same time comes the bloom of the Spanish

Broom, *Spartium junceum* with its 2 m (6 ft) rush-like stems which are themselves bright green, but have leaves so small that you hardly notice them at all. Individually, as though by way of compensation, the flowers are the biggest of all the brooms.

In a garden scene, these plants go very well with heathers and dwarf azaleas. In fact with these three kinds of plants you can get a long series of flowers on the same site, the broom following the azaleas and in turn followed by the heathers. All are in character together and will get along well with a sunny position and well drained soil, though the brooms do not necessarily like it acid as the others do.

Cistus

Never despair of finding plants to grow in the driest, hottest part of your garden when there are cistus to plant. These wiry shrubs will not only thrive there but grow into shapely bushes that keep their leaves all the winter. Sunshine and dryness are exactly what they like. First, one must know a little about their origins in order to understand why they should like to grow in conditions as harsh as these.

The fact is that the parents of all cistus – and there are something like 50 different kinds which can be grown in gardens – grow wild in the Mediterranean region. Some are seen on the hillsides round the plushy holiday areas in the south of France and the Italian Riviera, but most of them come from dry, rocky places in Spain and Portugal. Try to dig one up on holiday and you will find that it has made a woody root that has insinuated itself deep into the rock in search of what soil and moisture there is.

This leads to the two points which must be accepted about cistus. The first is that you can never transplant them. The second is that you must never prune them hard. Their nature is to make hard wood that refuses to break once it has got old. So you must pinch out the tips of the young shoots while the plants are small in order to make them bush out, if this is not already done for you in the nursery.

When you buy a plant, you really want to get one that is bushing comfortably, though not too big a bush, since cistus, it must also be recognised, do have a limited span of life. You are lucky if they go beyond ten years. They just die of early old age. These are definitely shrubs that are vulnerable to frost, except when they are grown in south-facing borders sheltered by a wall behind. In this case a wall is much better than a fence, since in the summer the plants get the benefit of the radiated heat stored during the day by the bricks and this helps to toughen them up. Some are found to be rather hardier than others but the safest thing is to treat them all alike and provide for their vulnerability.

The flower of a cistus lasts but a day, sometimes shattering by mid-afternoon after opening only that morning. But I see this as part of their appeal rather than a drawback, because a bush will produce so many buds that each morning the crop of flowers is constantly renewed. This goes on for almost the full two months of June and July. A big bush set with so many fully open flowers can be a regular summer morning sight. *C. × purpureus*, the most colourful of the entire family, is also one of the biggest, growing to about 1.2 m (4 ft) tall in time and spreading out to an even greater diameter. Even bigger, reaching up to 1.5 m (5 ft) in quite a few years, but growing rather more lanky, *C. × cyprius* is another especially fine one. It has the distinguishing marks of a whole group: maroon blotches at the centre of pure white petals. Not unlike this but remaining rather smaller is one called *C. × verguinii*.

The most famous cistus of the blotched white group, however, is a species of wide natural distribution, even extending into North Africa. Named *C. ladaniferus*, it has leaves coated with a resin that volatilises in the summer heat and gives off the aroma of the South then. The flowers of all these are around 10 cm (4 in) across and really surprising when you see them for the first time. While this also grows big, as cistus goes, there are many small growers, notably *C. × lusitanicus* 'Decumbens', which makes a sprawling shrub, covering the ground densely and producing many smaller flowers of purest white. Another small grower is named 'Florentinus', also with pure white flowers.

Cistus × purpureus

Some cistus have particularly attractive foliage, their likeness to other plants indicated by their botanical names. Thus there is *C. salviifolius* with crinkled sage-like leaves, *C. laurifolius* with shiny dark green leaves, and *C. populifolius* with biggish matt leaves. Again all these have white flowers. Several which are fortunately in general circulation have coloured flowers. 'Sunset' is curiously named because in truth the flowers are light magenta, the bushes very silvery. 'Silvery Pink' has larger cup-shaped flowers of the very colouring its name suggests. Both these bushes keep to around 60 cm (2 ft).

Cistus × skanbergii is in a class of its own, for it has small light pink flowers on a bush that sprawls. Indeed, all the sprawling cistus are exactly the bushes to plant on a lapsed rock garden, looked upon as a menace because it takes too much work to look after. In quite a short time the bushes will help to cover it both decoratively and effectively as labour savers, since by the process of pinching I mentioned earlier they can be induced to grow dense enough to stop any weeds coming up.

They can be grown successfully with all the heathers, though cistus are in fact lime lovers, and with a few brooms to precede them in flower. The heathers will look after themselves in a little community that will make an effect the full twelve months of the year without any close attention. They require no weeding and only a little light trimming, the brooms after flowering, the heathers in the spring and the cistus not at all.

Hydrangeas

The best hydrangeas I have ever seen were in the little cottage gardens of Brittany, where the light was so powerfully bright that you could hardly get a reading on the camera exposure meter. There were no hydrangea leaves to be seen, only flowers. Anyway, they had to put up with what they got for there were hardly any trees to shade them. And they liked it.

As for the colour of the plants you can never be certain where you are with hydrangeas. The blue one you buy in a garden centre or see in a public garden as likely as not will turn out pink or red for you. That's a matter of the amount of iron in the soil and whether it is available to the plants or not, due to the present or absence of lime. But the colours of the flowers are changing all the time.

Again, some make their buds the previous season (in embryo) and no more for another year, so that if they get frosted that's the end of the prospect of any flowers that season. Others, though, have it in them to make buds in the current season and therefore compensate for any winter losses. And then the different groups flower on old wood or new, so that unless you know them fairly intimately you're bothered about just how to prune them.

However, they are just the right plant for the disinclined or those with too much ground to manage. Plant plenty of hydrangeas and they will look after much of it for you colonising and suppressing weeds while giving long returns in flower from July into the autumn.

Now these bushes like a lot of water at times. On a hot day the leaves can flag horribly. Usually the dews of night are enough to restore them, but if that doesn't work then a bucket of water flung over a bush does. The return from apparent languishing to wild health can be dramatic. As for soil, well they are said to like the acid soil that rhododendrons do but those roadside plants show well enough how happy they are with either acid or alkaline soil. It's just that you only get the blue colourings where the ground is acid.

On strongly alkaline soils hydrangeas are always pink. You can apply 'blueing powder', which is really alum, to the ground or you can put flowers of sulphur round your plants. Or you can scatter rusty nails and old hinges round them in the hope of increasing the iron. But if they show that they want to stay resolutely pink or red, then it's best to stop gnashing your teeth about the matter and get on and accept them as they are.

It is worth while every autumn piling round your plants the fallen leaves from any trees you may have in order to build up the peaty type of soil that holds the moisture during the hot days of summer.

Five main types Now one should know that there are five main types, even a hydrangea that climbs, *Hydrangea petiolaris*. It will scale a wall, a

Training shrubs as standards

Just as far more plants than anyone would ever think of can be grown trained to walls and fences in the manner of climbers, so a whole lot more can be grown as standard trees. Often they are quite lusty growers which to keep them neat have to be pruned regularly. So the way they are treated is to train them up as short-trunked standards with a length of stem of about 1.2 to 2 m (4 to 6 ft) before the head of branches opens. At its most sophisticated in this facet of horticultural technique is the standard wisteria. I used to have a set of four which I grew from long branches that had layered themselves from an old wisteria in our garden. I just potted these up in 30 cm (12 in) pots, gave each a stout cane to support its trunk and made a little cartwheel of canes at the top to train out the flowering branches. Standard fuchsias are some of the best trees to grow in this way and are well within the compass of the home gardener who has somewhere cosy to protect these little trees during the winter. They do not even need artificial heat if the plants are kept dry during the winter. However, many shrubs can be trained as small standards. Their value is that they are closely in character with a formal scheme of planting, and they put within the scope of the small garden kinds that would otherwise not be possible.

A shrub that looks very well in this guise is *Hydrangea paniculata* 'Grandiflora'. So does lilac and the hardy hibiscus, *H. syriacus*, though in this case you do not want to prune it too often. Whereas you can cut the hydrangea to the knuckle every year in early spring, you merely want to shape the hibiscus. What is always surprising when you come across one in a garden is a honeysuckle trained as a standard. Every season just when it has finished flowering you simply shear it into a round head. Come the early summer again, the shoots grow out and every one carries several bunches of scented flowers.

The main tip to pass on about training standards is to let the formation of the trunk happen slowly. It will only thicken and become sturdy if it has some side shoots. So you must let it remain 'feathered' for some seasons, only shortening the side shoots, not removing them entirely. Later, of course, you can remove them altogether.

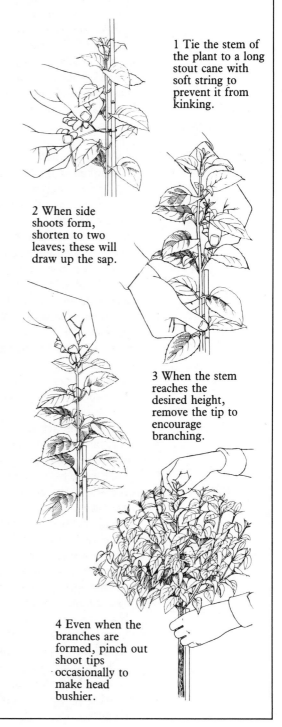

1 Tie the stem of the plant to a long stout cane with soft string to prevent it from kinking.

2 When side shoots form, shorten to two leaves; these will draw up the sap.

3 When the stem reaches the desired height, remove the tip to encourage branching.

4 Even when the branches are formed, pinch out shoot tips occasionally to make head bushier.

fence or a tree, hanging on under its own power. In summer it produces
ivory-coloured lacecap flowers.

Hydrangeas as a race produce two kinds of flowers, insignificant ones
that are fertile, others equally small but surrounded by several bracts,
or modified leaves, that the plant uses for display, to attract the insects
which fertilise the complete flowers. In the lace-caps, a ring of the latter
surrounds a cluster of the former. This is the characteristic of a whole
race that goes by this common title, the kinds that look best in informal
settings, such as the light woodland conditions for which hydrangeas
are commonly recommended. But again, I say, you do seem to get most
flowers in the sun.

Included in this group are two grown mainly for their leaves which
have been coming into the garden centres in increasing numbers in
recent seasons. These are *Hydrangea villosa* and *H. sargentii*. The
former has the better flowers, the latter the finer leaves. The foliage
appeal rests on the texture. It is like velvet and you always want to
stroke a leaf whenever you see either of these plants.

Next we come to the mop-headed type, the everyday hydrangea
available in so many varieties and in which the colour range is greatest,
ranging from white to deep red (on alkaline soil) up to purple and clear
blue on acid ground. Those called 'Parsifal', 'Westfalen', 'Souvenir de
President Doumer', 'Ami Pasquier' and 'Miss Belgium' are all varying
degrees of red but assume violet tinges on acid soil. The best of the
pinks and one that is clear blue on acid ground has the cumbersome
name of 'Generale Vicomtesse de Vibraye', a superlative hydrangea. So
is another named in honour of another French lady, 'Mme Emile
Mouilliere', which always has white flowers no matter what the
condition of the soil. You will also find the deep pink (or mauve)
'Hamburg' and lighter pink (or blue) 'Europa', but again you have to
make sure of the right place for them, for these do get rather lanky. This
is not to be held against them, for certainly in small gardens upright
growing plants can allow you to get more different kinds in than shrubs
that have to be allowed to spread sideways to be seen at their best –
provided you trim out the side growth from time to time.

A fourth type of hydrangea is *H. paniculata*. This is characterised by
pointed heads of flowers that open cream and age to pale pink. Once
there was only the large-headed 'Grandiflora'. Now you can buy an
early-flowering form, 'Praecox', and a late one 'Tardiva', as well.
'Grandiflora' you certainly cut back hard in spring for it undeniably
flowers on wood made in the current season. I am not so sure about the
others. Mine seem to flower on last season's wood like the mop-heads
and the lace-caps. I have not dared to prune them.

The fifth group have rounded instead of pointed leaves and rounded
heads of flower too, always ivory. One is called *Hydrangea arborescens*,
the other *H. cinerea* 'Sterilis'. In the latter the flowers are rather smaller
and neater.

Hibiscus

It hardly seems possible that something so exotic looking could come from the open air in a British garden. Yet the hibiscus is robustly hardy – again in more than one way. I have never known one killed by winter cold, not even in a savage winter. Nor have I known a hibiscus suffer because of any sort of soil. The one thing they seem to insist on is a sunny place. You never see them doing well in the shade. Another thing about them that I particularly like is the shape of the bush. The branches form in a sort of inverted cone standing on a small trunk, and this means that you can grow other plants quite close to them. These can be evergreens and early flowerers because the hibiscus does not break into leaf often until June.

Hibiscus syriacus

Now the hardy hibiscus is distinguished by botanists from the tender kinds which they grow in greenhouses by styling it *H. syriacus*. Poor old Linnaeus who gave it its name got a bit mixed up on this occasion, for the native home of the plant is China, not the Middle East. Apparently it was introduced to cultivation in Europe from there, having been brought west centuries before.

In fact, some years ago a hibiscus appeared that had actually come from China which had been named *H. sinosyriacus*. Its key characteristic was that the flowers were bigger than those of the ordinary kind. They were white stained with deep pink of different shades at the base. I was lucky enough to get hold of a couple of plants then and find they have grown into bigger bushes than the others.

I don't think I have ever found a cultivar to admire more than one called 'Woodbridge'. Its flowers in August are the largest of those of the *H. syriacus* cultivars, and this is an occasion when size does not mean grossness. Nor is the degree of flamboyance which it has out of place in a border of mixed plants. In our garden we grow some of our hibiscus in twin borders in which their only partners are evergreen azaleas planted between them for spring effect, with odd plants of the so-called Gladwyn, *Iris foetidissima* (see page 148). Lately, having some plants on hand I have underplanted the beds with the silver-variegated periwinkle (*Vinca minor* 'Variegata') in the hope that it will flower just after the azaleas and add to the winter effect.

Next to 'Woodbridge' I think the cultivar I admire most is the single white one, called 'Totus Albus' in nurseries, though its correct name could be the much more appealing 'Snowdrift'. 'Hamabo' is one of the two-tone cultivars, its pale blush pink being contrasted with red at the heart, though there is also another actually called 'Red Heart', which is similar.

This is a shrub which will also give you blue flowers. You find plants named 'Coelestis' in nurseries and sometimes 'Blue Bird', which is a clearer shade. A very curious cultivar called 'Meehanii' has lavender flowers and silver-variegated foliage.

Of course, hibiscus can have double flowers as well as single, which all the foregoing cultivars are. But somehow I cannot take the doubles to heart. The flowers seem muddly and in a bad summer they get turned to mush. However, in seaside gardens they can look very well indeed, and when a bush is full of double hibiscus flowers it can be most intriguing, since no one seems to recognise it. Here again there is a good range. 'Duc de Brabant' is dusky red and 'Violet Clair Double' as violet as it says, while 'Lady Stanley' is white with maroon blotches inside the flowers.

Hypericums

When you come to think about it, there are few shrubs yet to flower once the summer is on the wane. The fact that hypericums are golden when others around are blue or pink makes them especially valuable as garden plants, taking us into the golden colours of autumn. Hypericums will do well, even flowering abundantly, in shade of some degree and they thrive in any soil from stiff clay to the thin soil overlying chalk. Most of them are hardy in the face of winter cold and in a wet season they do not sulk and refuse to open their flower buds, as, say, the hibiscus, with which they are contemporaneous, do.

By common consent today the best of the hypericums for everyday gardens is 'Hidcote'. A pity there cannot be the same unanimity about its classification, for it has a somewhat tangled history and its place of origin is unknown. It was once held to be a form of *H. patulum*, the Chinese species. Now the view has been put forward that it must be a hybrid from *H. forrestii*. It is pretty well evergreen. Only in a really bad winter does it lose its foliage. If it grows too big, you can just chop bits off and it will come to no harm. In fact, you can cut it right to the ground and it will spring up again like gorse on a burnt heath.

Even better known and in a way as valuable as a garden plant, though for different purposes, is the old St John's Wort, *Hypericum calycinum*. While 'Hidcote' is a shrub to grow in a border or even as a specimen on its own, this one is a low-growing creeper. 'Hidcote' will stand 1.2 m (4 ft), *H. calycinum* a mere 46 cm (1½ ft). But it suckers and suckers until it has covered the ground with a dense thicket of growth, each shoot surmounted through the late summer with a large yellow flower, its petals enclosing a shaving brush of golden stamens. This is exactly the plant for covering a bank that you don't want to mow or weed. Shear the whole thing over in February and this will make it grow even more dense. It will also allow the daffodils which you can plant in it to take the stage.

Now *Hypericum calycinum* has a hybrid from it called *H. × moserianum*, a useful plant for ground covering if you want something that does this without suckering, but in turn, it has a variegated-leaved form known as 'Tricolor'. It is a small grower, lying almost flat on the ground and pretty enough to plant on this score alone, when it is set with its leaves, which include pink as well as pale yellow and green in their colouring. But as a flowerer, with the characteristic blossom of the family, it is considerable too.

My other favourite is 'Rowallane', a hybrid that occurred naturally in the Northern Ireland garden of that name. It is on the tender side and sometimes gets cut back in a hard winter but it always springs again from the base and flowers just as well on new wood. Its characteristic is that the flowers are more cup-shaped and an even richer gold. I grow it in a yellow and orange patch myself, in front of day lilies, which it succeeds in flower. Some may say 'Rowallane' should grow on light soil in view of its reputed tenderness, but my plants seem to do well enough on some of the worst clay in my garden.

One hypericum is grown not for its flowers, which are pretty but no more, but for its berries. These are bright red and so highly polished that they appear translucent. The name it goes by is *H.* × *inodorum* 'Elstead'. Reaching less than 60 cm (2 ft) tall at most, like growing skimmias it helps put berried shrubs within the scope of the small garden owner.

Berberis

Shade, heavy clay, gravel, scorching sun, wet land, dry land – all are one to berberis, which are determined to live wherever they are put, and ready to defy with a prickly response whoever wants to attack them. If you have little bits of garden where visitors or recalcitrant members of the family insist on cutting corners rather than going round by the path, plant a berberis just there and they will for ever after go right round the proper way. As autumn plants berberis have both berries and leaf colouring. The berries can be brightly coloured or subtle, for many of the fruits are like pieces of translucent coral, very beautiful indeed. Some are blue and some are black. The range, indeed, is greater than any other plant's.

It's difficult to know just how many different kinds of berberis there are. The Royal Horticultural Society's *Dictionary of Gardening* declares that there are around 450 different species. But the new edition of W. J. Bean's *Trees and Shrubs* which ought to get it right since it is the standard reference work on the subject puts the number at nearly 200. Happily, the indispensible Hillier's *Manual of Trees and Shrubs* narrows down the number of garden value, but still includes over 100. The trouble with berberis is that they hybridise readily, whereupon a great many of the resulting seedlings prove better plants than their parents.

Your everyday garden centre has wisely limited the number available very considerably, preferring on the whole garden varieites or hybrids to species.

Autumn Glory and evergreens *Berberis thunbergii* which we all know in its 'Atropurpurea' form, that purplish leaved one with an upright habit which is frequently used for low hedges, has a form called 'Rose Glow', since the purple has paled to pink, adding a bit of silver mottling for embellishment. It also has a dwarf cultivar called 'Little Favourite'. *B. thunbergii* itself, with green leaves, turns the most wonderful orange-scarlet in the autumn. The flowers are pale yellow in spring, the berries bright scarlet in autumn. Most gardeners know *B. × stenophylla* equally well. This is the kind with long arching branches amply covered with orange-yellow flowers in May. This too has a little cousin, called 'Corallina Compacta', whose flowers are paler. *B. × stenophylla* is a hybrid from two South American species. It appeared as a self-sown seedling in, of all places, a Yorkshire nursery. It is wonderful for covering the ground since it suckers so freely, and if you make a hedge of it, it becomes so dense that no intruder, whether animal or human, is likely to try and breach it.

One of *Berberis × stenophylla's* parents is the holly-like *B. darwinii*, tiny in leaf, orange in flower, blackish blue in berry. It clips almost as neatly as yew, and is, therefore, one of the most easily controlled. Darwin himself is reputed to have found this when he was down there on the *Beagle*.

The important thing about *B. darwinii* is that it is evergreen, a quality shared by quite a few of the family, though it has to be recognised that when you plant these you don't get the wonderful autumn leaf colouring of which many other berberis are capable. However you will enjoy a blaze of orange blossom in the spring. Another especially fine evergreen is *B. linearifolia* 'Orange King', upright in form and therefore a fine low hedger. This upright habit is shared by *B. gagnepainii*, also evergreen though turning some of its leaves deep red in autumn. The fashionable form of this one today is 'Wallich's Purple', the colour description referring to the sheen on the stems, which in this case is readily visible, since these leaves are long and elegant.

Some berberis fanciers hold that the most beautiful of all is a hybrid which appeared at the Royal Horticultural Society's Gardens called *B. × rubrostilla*. It is another of those with arching branches and covers these with coral berries in the autumn, and these are particularly large and therefore doubly prominent from a distance. Other berberis buffs favour 'Buccaneer', 'Barbarossa' and 'Pirate King'. They really are marvellous barriers; also Wisley hybrids and members of a group for which the surprising name of 'Carminea' has been coined. The word of course connotes a pigment derived from cochineal, but the berries of this trio are much stronger than carmine, for they are nothing but scarlet and the plants are simply loaded with hundreds of them in some autumn seasons.

Shades of autumn colour displayed brilliantly by *Acer palmatum* 'Heptalobum
Osakazuki' (scarlet) and *Fothergilla monticola*.

This inventive pergola composed of pink and white-flowered Judas Trees, *Cercis siliquastrum*, needs careful pruning each year but is well worth it.

One of the yellow-flowered clematis, *C. orientalis* flowers through late summer into
autumn. The silky seedheads and autumn foliage colour are a valuable asset later.

'Baron Girod de l'Ain' is a vigorous hybrid perpetual rose that can be pruned hard back. Its flowers are strongly perfumed and freely produced.

Pyracantha

Consider this specification. It must be evergreen. It must have flowers that would make it worth planting alone – and at a time when you can enjoy them, not if you shiver from cold when you stand and look. It must be prickly so that it can act as a bulwark against intruders. It must have berries that last from autumn into part of the winter at least. It must withstand pruning, even hacking back. It mustn't mind shade. And it must grow in whatever soil you put it, good soil or bad. Impossible to fulfil? In truth the pyracantha measures up to every point.

True, birds are inclined to feast on the fruits but their attentions are usually reserved for the berries of the oldest pyracantha known, *P. coccinea*, usually seen in gardens in the 'Lalandei' variety, a seedling bred or found in a French nursery at Angers in the last century. Like some cotoneasters and ceanothus, it is easy to keep to a slender profile, fitting it for embellishing or concealing walls and fences, while in this position the berries are less likely to be attacked by birds.

The pyracantha does make quite a good specimen shrub with turf all round it, when it assumes an inverted pyramid-like growth. It can also be used to make a fine hedge. Its wood is stiff and hard, and it also has terrifying thorns, an important matter on some occasions when hedges are planted. It is only necessary to put up a few posts to support the plants in the first place, then, as the branches extend they can be tied on to one another to make the hedge itself. Pruning rather than clipping is practised on this plant, using secateurs, not shears. This allows the job to be done carefully enough to remove only the youngest, unflowered, shoots as far as possible. But it is often necessary to remove bits that have borne flowers and will therefore carry berries later on. This pruning is done most advisedly just after flowering when you can tell young from older wood quite clearly. But it is always advisable to tie in as much growth as possible when the plant is used as a hedge or against walls.

The species most suitable for growing as an open ground plant is *Pyracantha rogersiana*, which has flame-coloured berries in great abundance. Occasionally you can find a yellow-berried form of this called 'Flava'. Recent seasons have seen the appearance in the garden centres of one called 'Orange Glow'. Distinctly orange in the colouring of its berries and therefore more resistant to bird plunder than the red ones, it combines this quality with especially great vigour, which means that you can put in a 60 cm (2 ft) high plant straight from the nursery and expect to have a fine bush in four or five seasons.

Another orange-fruited cultivar is called 'Waterer's Orange', while a third has been named 'Mojave'. The last has been found not only resistant to birds but unaffected by the scab and fire blight diseases which in some areas have caused weakness, even death, to many pyracantha bushes. Fortunately however, these troubles do seem to be on the wane naturally, in the way that plant disorders do ebb and flow.

The fact that pyracanthas are styled evergreen does need a word of qualification. In the worst winters the leaves do get discoloured by the cold. In some seasons one has to scratch the bark to see if it is green beneath to assure oneself that the bush is alive. But this does not happen very often!

Scented shrubs

By common consent among gardeners who know shrubs well, the most richly scented of all – and there are many that are highly perfumed – is one of the smallest, the daphne that goes by the name, appropriately, of *D. odora*. In gardens, incidentally, it is always represented by a form that has a 'wire-edge' of gold to its leaves, *D.o.* Aureomarginata. It does much towards refuting the charge brought against shrubs that they make a dull garden – compared, that is, with the effect made by roses, by annual flowers and by herbaceous plants. What garden can be dull where in summer the air is heavy with the perfume of mock orange – or even of privet in flower? Or in the winter, when you get a whiff of the Lily-of-the-valley scent of the mahonia, or of the true and rich perfume of honeysuckle coming from one of those lonicera bushes that are out then?

The Mock Orange or philadelphus are richly scented in the long days of June. Not only can you prune them hard to keep them small, but this is a group that will endure shade, so that you really can put in a bush wherever you have room for one. Especially when you remember there are at least two cultivars, namely 'Manteau d'Hermine' and 'Sybille', that grow no more than 1 m (3 ft) tall, provided the oldest wood is cut out regularly. Whereas the *odora* daphne, which I don't think I have seen taller than 60 cm (2 ft), though of much greater spread, likes the warmest, sunniest position you can give it, other daphnes do not mind the shade for part of the day. Certainly the early spring-flowering *D. mezereum* does not, and this is richly scented too, nor does the wild *D. laureola*, worth planting in the garden and with green flowers; a tantalising plant, being perfumed at times, scentless at others.

I make this point about shade and sun rather strongly because one always thinks of scent as something belonging to gardens in sunny places. Certainly the herbs are always most aromatic where they are baked.

Shade tolerant shrubs However, the deliciously perfumed *Osmanthus delavayi* will flourish and flower in some shade, producing its small white flowers in great abundance in spring there. So will its more lustily growing hybrid, *Osmarea* 'Burkwoodii', which is also perfumed. Both are evergreen. Others that will do well in these positions are the winter-flowering skimmias, which are generally grown for their scarlet berries but actually have spicily scented flowers, and the winter-flowering sarcococcas which have a privet scent. I can only give a string of names for the best perfumed kinds of viburnum since I cannot judge between them for scent: *V. bitchiuense, carlesii, carlcephalum* 'Anne Russell' and 'Park Farm Hybrid', all producing their white flowers sometime in the spring.

Choisya ternata, Mexican Orange Blossom

Call it Mexican Orange Blossom though you may, *Choisya ternata* is another that does not crave the sun, as you might expect. Indeed, I have seen many fine specimens flowering away with abandon in shady town gardens. While the white flowers of this evergreen with apple-green leaves are sweetly scented, the foliage too has its perfume, but a refreshing aromatic one. On the other hand, the only plants of the Bush Jasmine, *Jasminum revolutum*, that I have seen have been in sunny places. This is a charming rounded bush of 1 m (3 ft) with the same airy grace as the climbing summer jasmine, and its yellow flowers are well scented. I find it a good contrast bush, too, in addition to its other qualities.

A pity that lilac (syringa) itself is not a better looking shrub. The flowers are so abundant and splendid, the scent so rich on a late spring day. Morever, the varieties of colouring are so many. But there it is, a dull thing once it has flowered. Yet its heaviness is something that can be turned to good account later on. With its dense foliage I think it's a jolly good shrub to put close to your boundaries.

I must tell you of a plant I would not be without in my garden, where it has grown flat against a north-west wall for many years. This is the South American *Azara microphylla*. It is very pretty in leaf and an evergreen, but you would not grow it for the sight made by its flowers. Mustard yellow, and a strong shade too, they may be, but you hardly see them, for they are minute, no more than tiny tufts of stamens, and snuggle up under the leaves. But pass it on a February or early March day and the scent is unmistakably of vanilla. My bush is the plain-leaved one, but now I heartily wish it had been of the variegated form which is even prettier to look at and seems to flower as well. And if we are talking of scents to which you can put a label, we must put in a very strong word for the pineapple-scented broom, *Cytisus × battandieri* (see page 75).

Lastly, let us put lavender at the top of all the scented shrubs provided the soil is light and the position for it open. Under these circumstances it is superb. You just can't have too much, remembering that it is evergreen, or rather 'ever-grey', that goes well with almost anything, including roses, which it will complement so well. No wonder people like to plant it in the masses of edgings or – low hedges. And there are kinds to suit every site, from the compact little *Lavandula spica* 'Hidcote' to the massive growing Dutch kind, *L.s.* 'Vera' which makes a bush 1 m (3 ft) all round.

Weed-resisting carpets

Some people will tell you they like bare earth and that they actually enjoy the weekly hoeing that necessarily goes with it. But what happens when you go away on holiday? Or if you've just got other things to do when the hoeing has to be done? It's gardens like those, where the plants and shrubs have bare earth round them, that get unkempt looking quickest. Anyway, it's against nature. The natural process is always for the ground to be covered with vegetation of some kind. To adapt and exploit this principle is to garden really successfully, because then you're working with nature instead of being perennially at war with it. Perhaps it's in the winter that the plants that cover the ground for you make their most important visual effect. At other times their role is partly utilitarian. In winter, they keep the whole place alive – even glowing with colour if you allow that green and grey and gold are valuable garden colours.

Take the junipers. Among these are several kinds that spread almost flat over the ground, making leaves of just these colours that stay that way all the year. Some have appealing names too. There is, for instance 'Grey Owl' which will cover 2 m (6 ft) all round, if you let it. Though I must point out here that all these shrubs are quite easy to curb without making them look mutilated. So intricate is the branch system that you can lop bits off where you like without it ever noticing. In particular, I think one should be especially careful to remove any stray branches that strike upwards.

Then there are the prostrate cotoneasters. One of the best for our purpose is the evergreen *C. dammeri*, which spreads out over an area 2.5 m (8 ft) in circumferance, producing white flowers in late spring, red berries in the autumn. Much more restrained is the little *C. congestus*, though this picks up speed as the branches that lie on the ground root and by forming new plantlets add to the main plant's vigour.

Clump-forming kinds Not only shrubs that creep about in this way are to be accounted as weed resisters. Certain kinds that make clumps are to be thought of in the same context. For instance, the cotton lavender, or santolina, will grow very densely, especially when its branches have flopped around it and no weed is going to get through here.

I have even seen lavender planted to form a carpet and to bind the soil on a bank. Of course, this is a light soil plant, and if you plant it deep, as gardeners say, burying the lowest part of the stems, these will root and help the close spread. The shrubby potentillas will behave in much the same way, only here you have to make sure to get the prostrate types, not the upright growers. The bright yellow flowered 'Elizabeth' is particularly good for this purpose. So is the white *P. fruticosa mandshurica*, which I have seen planted particularly effectively with widely spaced shrub roses. Both can be kept within 46 cm (18 in) even where they may tend to grow up a bit higher.

Everyone knows that heathers are shrubs which spread out over the ground and make valuable carpets of foliage which stay all the winter. Some are bronze then when during the rest of the year they may be gold. The varieties of the winter-flowering *Erica herbacea* are generally considered the best spreaders, since they become very dense too. However, I personally have a great admiration for the cultivars of *E. vagans*, the Cornish Heath. What I like about this is the rich green of the foliage and the appearance of being dense, even though it may grow 30 cm (1 ft) deep. When it tries to go beyond this you want to make sure of clipping it over with shears every season early in March. Then it will perform its job well and truly without taking the place over.

That curious creeper, *Pachysandra terminalis*, is a slow starter but resolute in whatever soil you put it. Lately I have put in more of its variegated form, which is even slower to start, but makes a wonderful winter sight when you have a whole patch of it. Come to that so do the variegated forms of the Lesser Periwinkle, *Vinca minor*. So well does this grow that lately I have planted clumps of it in the dark of conifer trees and it is bringing life to an otherwise dull area in winter.

Autumn colour

Some people will tell you that to get fine autumn colour you need the right soil. Going round gardens hardly confirms this. Another misleading point. Certainly it is an unstable quality, rather like the colouring of hydrangeas. In one garden a known autumn leaf colourer will look marvellous, in another indifferent. But in the following year the indifferent will be aglow with autumn tints. Nor could you ever say that one autumn is better than another for vivid hues. Some years this spectacle may come just a little more quickly than in others, due to the dates when the early frosts arrive. But it is never enough to make a lot of difference.

All the Japanese flowering cherries have bronze autumn leaf colour and the Japanese evergreen azaleas also colour up well, their leaves turning to varying tones of crimson. Of course, the *mollis* azaleas, which are deciduous and thrive in light shade, would be worth planting just for the effect made by their leaves alone at this time, even though the show for which one really plants them falls in the late spring. There is even a type of rose which makes a fine autumn show. This is the Japanese Briar, *Rosa rugosa*, pink, red or white in flower in summer, but with golden leaves in autumn.

Even one of the hydrangeas deserves honourable mention. This is the compact-growing hybrid 'Preziosa', which has mop heads of coral flowers and quite vivid reddish leaves when the blooms are past their best. The ordinary snowball trees, the garden form of the wild

Viburnum opulus, have good colouring in their leaves in autumn. Then it is quite a crimson shade, as are those of *V. tomentosum* 'Mariesii', that spreading bush with white lacecap flowers poised on the horizontal branches in May.

We grow the mountain ash trees largely for their upright form and red berries, but these are soon gone once the birds catch sight of them. Then it is the leaves that continue to make the trees' mark, turning copper, fiery red or crimson according to the species you have in your garden. Quite a few berberis colour their leaves before they fall (see page 84), none better than the ordinary *B. thunbergii*, something of a 'bonfire' in autumn. For some years now the birch has been regarded as a valuable small garden tree since it is so slight, if tall, and admired for the liveliness of its bark. But as its leaves turn gold before they fall it gives a specially good account of itself in the autumn.

Amelanchier canadensis is an inexpensive shrub you can always buy and it proves one of the finest of the autumn colourers as well as being exquisite in spring when the white flowers, pink in bud, come out just as the leaves are unfolding. One shrub which ought to be grown wherever rhododendrons are is the lanky *Enkianthus campanulatus* which comes into its own when the small leaves change from deep green to bright copper before falling.

Everyone who has any interest in gardens knows the sumachs, perhaps because the plants sucker freely and get passed from gardening friend to friend. It is one of the finest of the autumn colourers, and one very easy to accommodate in a small garden since it has that convenient upright manner which allows other plants to be tucked in quite close to it. The one we all know so well is *Rhus typhina*, but if it can be found in nurseries in its 'Laciniata' form – this has more leaflets to each of the compound leaves – it is rather prettier, since the foliage looks like the fronds of some great fern.

Parrotia persica is usually seen as a spreading tree-like shrub with outstretched arms, far too big for a garden, yet its weeping form stays small enough for us to enjoy its crimson and gold autumn leaves. On the other hand, both *Photinia villosa* and *Nyssa sylvatica*, each a small tree, can be grown like a hazel. Then odd branches are cut out every season so that it is always renewing itself from close to ground level.

One could not say that *Liquidambar styraciflua*, the Sweet Gum and one of the most splendid of autumn colouring trees, with leaves like huge rubies then, is anything but a tall tree. But it grows very slowly and takes more than a lifetime to develop its full stature. I have had one in the ground for more than ten seasons now but it is still no taller than I am. I have had a bush of the strange *Euonymus alatus*, characterised by the wing-like formation of its bark, for much longer, and this still stands no more than 1.5 m (5 ft) tall and the same across.

Fothergilla major will make a charming little bush, developing quite a thicket of its own no more than 1 m (3 ft) high. Like the Sweet Gum its leaves turn to gold at first, then red and then to deeper scarlet before they fall. It takes up little room and you hardly notice it except at that time and in late spring when you are one day struck by the peppery scent of its flowers on the air. *F. monticola* also provides a spectacular autumn display.

Shrubs for winter

Brave? Foolhardy? Precocious? Versatile? What would be just the right word for those shrubs that curiously and confusingly decide to put forth their flowers at a time when they must know – and plants do know things – that the weather is likely to do its worst to them and that there will be few insects about to fertilise them anyway?

Garrya elliptica What persuades a garrya bush far away from its native California and Oregon, down there on the sunny Pacific coast, to produce its elegant tassels in winter? It is in autumn that you realise this winter-flowering bush is eager to get on with its job. Gradually the embryonic catkins elongate until one day you notice that they are now several centimetres long and that it's winter. Their evergreen foliage, not particularly distinguished in this case, sets them off very well.

At one time, basing the beliefs on gardeners' talk and published accounts, I assumed that the garrya had to have light soil. Personal experience, however, has shown me that this is false, for our plants grow very well in the most awful clay and in a good deal of damp too. I also thought, again because you didn't see the plants grown anywhere else, that it had to have the shelter of a wall, even though this might be facing north or east. False again. There are open ground plants that again do very well, growing to 3 m (10 ft), though this is a bush you can easily keep much smaller by cutting out some of the oldest wood from time to time, once the flowers are finally done towards the end of March.

Stachyurus praecox My other favourite winter shrub, one which starts to fashion its buds in the autumn like the garrya, has the strange name of *Stachyurus praecox*. I have been glad to find in recent seasons that this bush is making its way into local garden centres – at a price, again because it's slow to increase. No one who sees this plant for the first time can ever put a name to it, even gardeners of great experience.

The flowers of stachyurus seem little more than pale yellow buds, yet they hang on the bush most elegantly weeks before the leaves ever come, and share with other flowers that come out in winter a long life. Two months' flowering season is not unusual, the buds expanding in January and continuing till March. They are seen at their most abundant in sunny positions, though half shade suits this 2 m (6 ft) shrub well enough. In autumn it gives a fine bonus, when the leaves turn to rich gold and red before they fall, which is not until December in many seasons. It seems content with what is customarily and inexactly known as ordinary soil. I have seen it on light soil and have grown it on clay.

Viburnum × bodnantense

Winter flowers Flowers that come out in the winter have to make their presence felt somehow in order to attract the insects to them to perform their private processes of reproduction. Usually it's by way of scent. Wasted on the winter air? Not if you plant them close to some path you use often, preferably close to the house where your visitors can enjoy the perfume too. The winter weather may be doing its worst in fogs and rain, frost too perhaps, but *Viburnum × bodnantense* will be doing its best to shame it all – with big clusters of palest pink flowers that open from rose-coloured buds from November onwards. They fill the air around the bush with the most seductive perfume – scent would be too tame a term in this case – that no sunless day can diminish. Usually the bushes are seen standing about 2 m (6 ft) tall, the branches arching halfway up. They don't seem to mind what sort of soil or spot they are planted in, whether it's damp or dry, shady or sunny. It's the best tempered of shrubs, and one that suckers a bit so that you often have a rooted piece you can pull off and give to someone who admires it – always one of the pleasures of having a garden.

Another winter-flowering viburnum is the old Laurustinus bush. The strange thing about *Viburnum tinus* is that though it is one of the toughest evergreen shrubs you can have in a garden, it actually originated in the Mediterranean region. The rough texture of its leaves is actually its way of protecting itself against long periods of drought. However, it grows well enough in soil that sometimes gets waterlogged. It is not surprising, though, given its origins, that it should flower during the winter, usually starting in January. Usually the flowers are white, produced in quite big heads from clusters of pink buds. The best form for home gardeners to plant is one called 'Eve Price', a more compact form, slowly growing into a close dome of a bush about 1.2 m (4 ft) high, while the buds are a deeper shade of pink. Another pale pink-flowered form sometimes found in garden centres is 'Gwenllian'.

Long before the leaves come the flowers of *Cornus mas*, the so-called Cornelian Cherry, are out. Tiny individually, they are produced in rounded bunches all over the bare branches, and in full bloom on a cold February day when the sun is making a welcome appearance a bush appears as a golden cloud. It would have to be a pretty old bush that would stand more than about 2.4 m (8 ft) high and as much through. Usually it is seen much smaller. Even so it makes a splendid host for one of the smaller flowered clematis of the type that are out in the late summer. Though a wild bush in southern Europe, it is nevertheless robustly hardy in all parts of Britain and well worth growing, whatever soil can be offered it.

I don't think you would ever see a Winter Sweet, *Chimonanthus praecox*, flower in an open ground site. It's hard enough to get this wonderful thing to flower in the highly favoured position of a south-facing wall. This it must have, not because it is tender, but so that during the summer it gets the ripening influence of the radiated heat, which must be one of the factors in persuading it to bloom. Make it think it's only hanging on to life by a thread, for I also believe that in places where it grows successfully but never flowers this is because the ground is too rich in nitrogen and lacking in potash. The perfumed flowers appear in February and are most intriguing to peer into, a crown of molten gold surrounding a maroon centre. Real cold will turn the flowers glassy looking, but they are equipped by nature to with-stand quite a few degrees of cold without showing distress.

Daphne mezereum In theory this is a wild plant in Britain but it is now so rare that few people have ever seen it growing in the damp woods it once inhabited. The rosy purple flowers hugging the bare stems open in February and fill the air round them with sweet perfume. However, it is the pure white form, 'Alba', of this daphne that is the great prize among plantsmen. The ordinary kind has red berries but this one's are yellow. Both are liable to die suddenly after a few years but these freely produced berries drop seeds and provide replacement bushes. However, remember, whatever the colour, these berries are deadly poisonous. Most flowers are found on plants that grow in a sunny place in 'woodsy' soil with plenty of humus. Scent is one of the qualities of the majority of winter-flowering plants, though one must admit that the Winter Jasmine has none. Of course, the Winter Honeysuckle is perfumed, though. There are several of these, the most easily obtained being *Lonicera fragrantissima*. Others carry the names *L. standishii* and *L. × purpusii*. To me they all look the same, so it doesn't seem to matter which one you get. The flowers are small and ivory coloured, with a perfume out of all proportion to their size. Whereas the Witch Hazel makes outstretched branches so distinctive that you would know it from these when it had neither flowers nor foliage, the lonicera makes a bush like a small Mock Orange. It doesn't twine like its summer cousins. As for its position, well it will tolerate shade, the same as the Witch Hazel, but it also gives most flowers in a sunny spot, preferably near the house where you can enjoy it on a winter's day.

Winter stems The two shrubs that make the strongest effect are also two of the most easily grown. They will thrive anywhere. These are *Cornus alba* 'Westonbirt' with light scarlet stems and *C. stolonifera* 'Flaviramea' with egg-yolk yellow ones. But here it is the young wood that is coloured, not the old. So you want to encourage plenty of this. The technique is to chop the bushes almost to the ground at the end of February.

The result will in time be a thicket of young stems radiating from what gardeners call a stool, and standing about 1.2 m (4 ft) high. This can be a most striking midwinter garden feature. I would not say that it is worth a prominent position, since both plants are undistinguished for the rest of the year, but one advantage they have is that they are among the few shrubs that will flourish in boggy soil and do well in shade.

Several brambles that you would hardly give a second glance in summer are most remarkable in midwinter, for then their young growths have pure white bark. They are found in plant catalogues under the names of *Rubus cockburnianus*, *R. biflorus* and *R. thibetanus*. All are very pleasing. Again it is best to cut out the old wood and leave the new to take up the relay every season.

Two very common shrubs which have highly pleasing winter bark are hardly ever recommended for this quality. The double-flowered *Kerria japonica* ('Pleniflora') which produces those rich yellow flowers for so long through the spring and early summer, growing conveniently upright, makes a marvellous winter plant since its stems remain bright green. So do those of the Old Elisha's Tears, *Leycesteria formosa*, which produces dangling and, it must be admitted rather dreary flowers in the late summer. Still, both of these are also plants that will endure shade and damp soil. You would not cut these down in February like the dogwoods, however.

For long I have grown a little bush called *Stephanandra tanakae* down in the boggy part of our garden. It has never minded the constant wet and repays the hospitality by revealing very attractive golden-brown stems when the leaves are off. The leaves are maple-like and deeply ribbed with veins.

One of the Mock Oranges has mahogany stems speckled with white. This is the fabulous *Philadelphus delavayi*. You also find winter appeal in the summer-flowering deutzias. Their bark is either ashen grey or reddish, and this is a bonus from these so easily grown shrubs that give such a great bounty of flowers in June and July.

Some of the willows have very pretty bark, and if you hesitate ever to introduce a willow to your garden, let me say at once that these are more shrubs than trees, since they are also of the kind that you chop back really hard in late winter in order to encourage as many young shoots to grow as will. *Salix daphnoides* has purplish stems dusted with white, *S. alba* 'Chermesina' is orange and *S.a.* 'Vitellina' is deep yellow.

Berries for birds

Birds and berries – the two go together always, if not for long. They make an uneasy pair. However, it must be said – hesitatingly, because you can never be certain about birds – that they do have preferences and can sometimes be selective. Red and orange berries are to their taste, yellow less so. But I have noticed that they leave the white and the pink ones till last, only going for these when there are no more red ones to gobble up.

For all this, you can't do without a holly with red berries in your garden, one of the few kinds the birds considerately leave until after Christmas. You generally need two kinds, a male and female, to produce a crop of berries. Happily, there is one kind which to my certain knowledge reliably gives a good crop of berries in isolation. It would have to be a bad holly year for *Ilex aquifolium* 'Pyramidalis' not to bear. It lives up to its name also in its manner of growth.

Though the birds may sit there all day long and gorge the berries, I still would not be without a red-fruited cotoneaster. If I could have only one it would still be *C. horizontalis*. To my mind this is a shrub with everything. Even in winter you can admire the herringbone formation of the branchlets. In late spring it is covered with white flowers that the bees simply throng. In autumn, with the big crop of scarlet berries, its leaves become crimson. You can grow it against a wall or to lie flat on the ground, in the sun or in the shade with equal effect.

Nevertheless, there is at least one cotoneaster that makes a good evergreen hedge, 'Cornubia'. It does not work out too expensive, as you need to plant it only 2 m (6 ft) apart or even 2.5 m (8 ft). Then you tie the branches sideways. Easily kept to 1.5 m (5 ft) high, or you can let it go on and on up, when it will turn into a weeping tree eventually. The deep red berries last into December, sometimes longer. Among the Snowball Tree family there are some good berriers that also have the merit of turning their leaves to rich colours while the fruits are still on. One I have much admired season by season is *Viburnum opulus* 'Notcutt's Variety'. But it does make a good big bush, large enough for screening. So those with little space might like to know of a dwarf kind, making a rounded bush 1 m (3 ft) high. It simply has the Latin word 'Nana' after it. Pure turquoise are the berries of *Viburnum davidii*, a low evergreen bush useful for ground cover, especially as it thrives in the shade. In this case you must put the sexes together, but not in pairs. One gentleman will look after half a dozen ladies very well indeed.

Callicarpa was once a rare shrub and is now in almost every good garden centre in its cultivar called 'Profusion'. In this case the berries are violet. But there is more to it still, for in autumn the leaves go a nice pink sometimes mauve, before they fall. They say that to be sure of callicarpa berries you need to plant three or four bushes all together. But my one bush berried so well and I liked it so much that I pegged down some branches to make more of it.

If you live on acid soil and can grow rhododendrons you should also find room in close company with them for a few bushes of the evergreen pernettya. This has big berries that can be pink, white or soft red. The rhodo foliage shows them up well, and the pernettya foliage itself, which is small, contrasts well with that of the rhodos. Together they make a good little plant community.

5
Roses are Shrubs

What is it that endows roses with universal fascination? Is it that they represent better than any other the ideal of beauty in a flower? Is it their scent, their colourings, their shapes? Is it that their ancestry, reaching back into the earliest days of gardens, has become an inescapable part of our own inheritance?

Why has more breeding been done on roses than any other flower in the search for perfection, different shades of colour, resistance to the troubles that in the natural world lie in wait for every plant? Why should the genealogy of roses be more carefully documented and more widely published than any other flower's, even orchids? It all underlines the fact that roses are supreme among garden flowers in popularity, in esteem and in affection. Even people who may not like them all that much, or have some fault to find with nature over them only confess to it shame-facedly, if they have the courage to at all.

People say to one another as though it were one of the great universal truths of gardening that 'roses like clay' the real fact is that roses will grow anywhere on any soil, or at least there's a rose that will thrive on the most unfavourable site. 'You have to know how to prune them', they say too. But when I attempted what I thought was a definitive analysis of wise pruning, no less a rose personage than Harry Wheatcroft wrote to the newspaper saying that it didn't matter how they were pruned or who did the job. They grew well just the same.

You used to know where you were among the main garden roses. There were four groups: climbers, shrubs, the hybrid teas (or large-flowered roses) that usually produced one flower to a stem, and the floribundas (or cluster-flowered group) whose flattish flowers were carried in clusters. Then the cluster ones were produced with stylish pointed flowers, blurring the main divisions. So the great and wise ones decided it was time for simplicity. Height was all that mattered.

Fortunately, the old names – hybrid teas and floribundas – for these two groups do persist in nurseries, in the conversation even of rose fanciers and in some rose catalogues, giving some indication of the way in which the bushes – and we are talking of what most of us know as garden roses – choose to display their flowers. Then we know whether they are to be chosen for cutting for vases or to be planted in the garden for display.

All such roses are termed perpetual, a misleading term since what it really indicates is that they will put on a show, usually broken only by short intervals, between mid-June and the end of October, with the biggest flush early in July. You could fairly say that their maximum height is 1.2 m (4 ft), though the average, with annual pruning to encourage the bush to renew itself frequently from near the base, is around 75 cm (2½ ft).

A new race in the ascendant is the miniatures. These make bushes about 45 cm (18 in) tall with flowers of a size in proportion. Today they are being bred on a large scale in the United States and the bushes are being produced every season in tens of thousands. They bring rose growing within the scope of those with the smallest gardens. The next thing we are promised is dense, flat-growing ground-covering roses.

In choosing roses it is important to decide at the outset how they are to fit into the garden scheme and what purpose they have. Equally, it is wise to consider their position carefully. For instance, today there is a reaction among gardeners against making rose beds in view of the house windows on the grounds that for much of the year the plants are not very decorative, and the site could be made much more pleasing throughout the twelve months by using other plants there.

Indeed many gardeners now prefer to have large-flowered roses (hybrid teas) those which produce their blooms singly on longish stems, in rows alongside vegetable plot paths just to provide cut roses for the house. Again, it is widely recognised that it is the cluster-flowered rose, the floribunda type, that is best for display.

If roses are not particular about the actual soil in which they are put, whether it is acid or alkaline, light or heavy, they do like a bit of feeding up, like all plants whose natural tendency is to renew themselves frequently. And they like a nice place prepared for them. What they abhor is enclosure. They like space and air.

This is why, apart from the use of the miniatures, rose growing is difficult in very small gardens, unless you make use of the 'perpetual' climbers. These adapt themselves readily to a position against walls and fences, though they need to be tied to some sort of trellis. They also prove a worthwhile proposition on poor soil that just lacks enough humus for most others. The other main exception is the Japanese Briar, *Rosa rugosa*, which in its pink, red or white forms will actually grow happily on sand dunes.

In their present day form, the climbers – which are totally different

Rosa rugosa 'Frau Dagmar Hartopp' has pale pink flowers

from the outdated ramblers which begin life afresh every year from the bottom and become a prickly mess unless pruned rigorously – are decorous roses. They can flower for as long and as often as the best of floribundas. They do not make an uncontrollable amount of growth and their life is to be counted in decades not years, like hybrid teas and floribundas which as a general rule have lived out their lives in about 12 seasons, though there are many exceptions of longevity.

Climbing roses can be used to advantage trained to wires to make screens round, say, the composting area or perhaps round an ugly oil storage tank. If they are fed as well as all roses deserve to be the foliage will be ample and the plants will be made to provide dense cover by having their shoots tied in repeatedly.

In recent seasons the hedge of roses has come into its own. For this climbers which flower repeatedly can be used with the branches trained sideways to wires, or some of the shrub roses, or where height is not important, the cluster-flowered types. This is one of the more practical aspects of rose growing.

The shrub roses, those growing over 1.2 m (4 ft) and up to 2.5 m (8 ft) and which have many subdivisions, including all the old-fashioned types with romantic names, are very long lived, however. Partly this is because they are either natural species or do not have a complex parentage. They are naturally vigorous growers, and are the best kinds for planting in close companionship with other shrubs, hardy border flowers and bulbs in mixed groups, but if they are fed well the smaller growing cluster-flowered cultivars can also be used successfully in this way.

What constitutes that magic of old-fashioned roses? Roses bred by an earlier race of fanciers, largely in the last century, before the subject became complicated and there were so many different kinds for them to work with. But some old-fashioned roses actually date back to the time of the Crusades. Back through all those centuries the rose has had plenty of time to insinuate itself into the consciousness of mankind, to weave a spell from which there is no escape, nor the wish for it. What would life be like without roses? An unlikely proposition. It is unthinkable. In the whole genus there are more than 2,000 wild species encircling the earth. And their progeny is without number.

Planting and aftercare

The modern roses flower continuously whatever the weather and wherever they are planted, even though they may sometimes get affected with disease. From late June through to the end of October they give you flowers to cut and to embellish the garden in a succession that hardly ceases.

Rose planting time is in November when it is the moment to prepare the soil for them. Not only do such splendid plants deserve it but they grow and flower all the better from being given extra preparations. In practical terms this means plenty of bulky manure added deeply to the soil for texture improvement and some coarse bonemeal to nourish the roots over several seasons. If roses have been grown on the site already it is folly to replant in the same soil. You must dig out a fairly big patch and replace it with soil from elsewhere in the garden. Somehow or other roses poison the soil for their own kind.

While so many shrubby plants these days are sold not direct from the open ground but in containers, and some roses are indeed containerised as the nurserymen put it, many more are in fact sold as bare-root plants, which makes planting that little bit more trouble. The main thing to watch, something which confuses amateurs too often, is to lay the plant against the side of the hole, not put it in the middle. Then you can shovel soil up to it and tread it really firm, making sure that the graft, the point from which the branches emerge, lies just below the surface. This is the point at which the growth of the selected cultivar has been grafted on to a stock of a vigorous wild rose. Grafting is done for wholesale production of rose bushes and uniformity of growth.

The other thing amateur growers find difficult to bring themselves to do is to prune hard after planting – at least the hybrid teas and the floribundas. The other two kinds have usually been pruned enough when you get them from the nursery. Cutting back hard really does prompt roses to make a vigorous response.

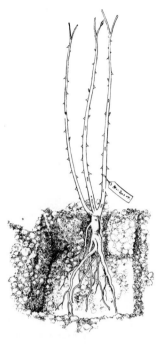

Planting a bare-rooted rose

So immediately after planting your new large-flowered and cluster-flowered bushes in autumn, prune them fairly hard to about six buds, even if this means removing shoots that have already started into growth. This is one of the factors which makes for healthy, stocky bushes that will produce plenty of main branches for plenty of flowers in succeeding years. Fortunately, bush roses produce their flowers on the new wood and this can be easily produced between spring and midsummer so that the plants bear in their first season. Shrub roses and the true climbers, however, flower on twigs made from the main branches which take longer to develop. Accordingly, these types of roses are not pruned after planting in the same ruthless way.

Ensuring vigour While roses have to be fed with a special potash-high rose fertiliser during the spring this treatment to encourage health and vigour is wisely supplemented by removing the spent dead heads soon after the flowers have withered. It not only makes for tidiness but prods the plants into making more and more flowers.

Vigour is also aided by regularly spraying with an insecticide against greenfly, which can have a crippling effect on the bushes by sucking the sap and sometimes damaging the buds so much that they either fail to open or are distorted. The plants should also be sprayed regularly with a fungicide against mildew and black spot disease, which can have a similarly debilitating effect on the plants.

103

Taking rose cuttings

Roses do not always grow readily from cuttings, but amateurs often find it worth while producing new climbers and shrub roses in this way. During the late summer unflowered shoots are pulled off the parent (1), the tag of tissue at the base trimmed up to leave a rounded end (2), and these are then pushed into a patch of sandy soil in a lightly shaded place (3). If possible cover with a cloche. Such cuttings take a year to grow into a new plant

Modern garden roses

More books have surely been written about roses than any other flower. And still they come. Yet these days roses of the most popular kinds have their detractors as well as their admirers. Those agin them declare that hybrid teas and floribundas, the collective terms by which they continue to be known in spite of a new classification for them having been instituted calling them large-flowered or cluster-flowered, will not tolerate other plants grown in close company with them: they want the place to themselves. Broadly true, I suppose, if you reckon that their character is so strong that they just don't assort well with other plants. However, what other plants give so much for so little attention, when you recall seeing in roadside gardens huge billowing bushes full of flowers, that no one ever seems to do anything to or for!

Cluster-flowered (floribunda) roses are the best kinds to plant for making a good show. Often they flower continuously throughout the summer and into the autumn, and their tendency is to become stocky bushes, though heights vary from less than 60 cm to 1.2 m (2 ft to 4 ft). The colours vary from hard reds and near oranges to soft pinks. When they are planted in mixed borders the best results are achieved with the soft colours, since these blend more happily with the flowers of other plants. So let us give a word of commendation to that incontestably superb floribunda the white 'Iceberg', to the red 'Evelyn Fison', to the

Bays of bearded iris in a border. By planting warm colours in the foreground and misty blue further from the house the impression of distance is given, thus increasing the apparent size of the garden.

Nerine bowdenii, an exotic bulbous plant from South Africa, will flourish in a well drained spot at the base of a sunny wall.

pearl-like 'Margaret Merril' (so free with its scent), to the yellow 'Allgold', to the near violet 'Escapade' and to the apricot-cream 'Chanelle', all roses I never cease to admire and that usually appear in the Royal National Rose Society's audit of the most favoured cultivars.

The best way of pruning this group is to cut out at least one old branch every season in order to encourage them to make new wood from close to the ground. Then the whole bush is renewed over several seasons.

As for large-flowered roses (hybrid teas) in their newer classification, we must pay due awesome respect for the perfumed, deep rose-red 'Wendy Cussons', for pink and cream 'Silver Jubilee', for 'Alec's Red', for 'Piccadilly' (red on one side of the petal, yellow on the other), even for old, old 'Peace' itself, and hardly much younger, the rose and silver 'Rose Gaujard'. Princes among roses, all of them. These large-flowered roses are the kinds which produce the flowers most suitable for cutting, but the bushes themselves are the least attractive. They are therefore best grown in rows to provide blooms for this purpose alone. There they can be planted closely so that they draw one another up, lengthening the stems. Blooms of exhibition quality are only produced on them by disbudding, removing any surplus buds on a stem in order that all the plant's energies go into making one flower to a stem. Hybrid teas are also the most greedy feeding roses, requiring a special rose fertiliser in the spring and a mulch of nourishing organic refuse laid over the rooting area. Spraying against greenfly is also essential for getting perfect blooms.

Shrub roses

Of course, all roses that are not climbers are shrubs. And if truth be told a few of the climbers will behave a bit like shrubs given the chance. So it's all pretty confusing. In truth, the term is made to embrace three or four distinct types of roses, which they loosely term the hybrid musks, the rugosas, the Chinas and the moderns. This is to distinguish them, most inexactly, from those romantic old-fashioned roses which have such intriguing names and equally intriguing flowers. The shrubs are roses for display rather than to inspect individually with a fancier's eye. They are plants to make hedges of, to plant in mixed borders, to grow in banks in otherwise unoccupied areas of garden, which they will fill with such richness.

For a shrub rose proper will grow 1.2 m (4 ft) across or more and as much high. In summer you would soon get tired of trying to count how many flowers it carries. Some of them have exceptionally fine foliage to complement the flowers, and the Chinas actually keep their leaves through most of the winter. Thus besides the actual size of a bush of one of them, which can make such a substantial contribution to the garden in itself, they give particularly good all-round garden value.

The one thing against them that I can see is those wretched thorns. Such big bushes tend to claw at you whenever you go near them. So be warned, and approach them as little as possible. In practical terms this means cleaning the ground thoroughly of perennial weeds before they are planted and growing some effective ground-covering plant underneath them, so you don't need to weed or hoe as you go round the roses.

Never think shrub roses necessarily grow too big for what you might reasonably call everyday gardens. Roses have it in them always to renew themselves from near the base, just like hazel bushes and blackcurrants do. Exploit this characteristic by cutting out one or two of the oldest branches from time to time. This prods them into making some of the latent buds down below grow when they would otherwise remain asleep so you have new and shorter growth coming along all the time. For home gardeners the great thing about the roses that are termed shrubs is the huge bounty of flowers they produce. Usually it does come all at once, in June and July like the old-fashioned types but in quite a few cases cultivars exist in this group that in sunny spots and where the soil is well fortified with enough goodness to keep them properly nourished will go on flowering past the summer days into the autumn as the large-flowered (hybrid teas) and cluster-flowered (floribunda) roses do. But not everyone wants every plant in his garden to flower ceaselessly for weeks on end. The more seasoned and perhaps discriminating garden-lovers of my acquaintance like the effects their gardens produce to ebb and flow.

Now an important thing about shrub roses is that whereas large-flowered, and cluster-flowered roses to a lesser extent, want beds to themselves in order to flourish really well, the true shrubs have such lusty vigour as one of their qualities that you can satisfactorily put other plants with them. The best of summer gardens these days have herbaceous plants set between their shrub roses. In fact, it can be an advantage to have other plants close to them in that they can drain off some of the nitrogen in the soil, as it were, and slow them down.

The first roses of summer are produced on large growing shrubs, and usually they have yellow flowers; 'Canary Bird' is one of these, often flowering in May. It can be trained into very pleasing little standard trees with arching branches where there is not room to allow it to grow in the form of an inverted cone, to reach up to 2 m (6 ft). Paler in colour and always seen as a large bush is one called *Rosa × cantabrigiensis*. This is very suitable for planting at the back of a mixed border. Also here one might plant the series with names always beginning with *Frühling*, which have big single flowers of pale yellow or soft pink in profusion in early summer. Afterwards they leave the stage to other plants set in front.

Hybrid musks I think I would put the hybrid musk roses as supreme among the shrubs – as a race, that is. These actually have almost nothing to do with the real musk rose, though they do have a wonderful scent. This type of rose is a distinctive group making rather dense rounded bushes set with bright green foliage that is very healthy. They grow 1.2 to 1.5 m (4 to 5 ft) tall and in late June and early July are covered with flowers of pale pink, bright pink or apricot according to cultivar. When this burst is over the twigs are snipped back to encourage them to produce more flowers later in the season. This group make very good hedges as the main branches last for many seasons without having to be cut away for renewal. They are also particularly good in mixed borders, giving a good show of flowers for comparatively little trouble and in relation to the amount of space they occupy. They respond to being cut back, but if you want you can leave them to go their own sweet way.

Best known among this type is dear old 'Penelope', palest blush in colour, again as gardeners like to put it. I think my next favourite in this group is 'Buff Beauty'. Again, it is a little mistakenly named, for you would reasonably say that a blend of apricot and yellow would be a closer description. It really is a superb rose of unusual colouring.

'Vanity', whose flowers are single when most of the other hybrid musks are double, is a brighter colour altogether, bright pink, and therefore better named. 'Prosperity' is white, while 'Cornelia' is an apricot colour. The little pink 'Ballerina', whose flowers are just like apple blossom, is often classed as a hybrid musk, though it looks very different. Its story is worth outlining, if only as an example of the value of maintaining breeding stocks.

It has been going for more than 50 years. But the rose growing firm of Fryers rescued it from ill-deserved obscurity in the 1960s and have used it as one of the most valued of rose parents for a new race of roses. Mystery surrounds its birth. 'Ballerina' turned up at the little nursery in the village of Havering-atte-Bower, Essex run by one J. A. Bentall, who took over the stock from the vicar, the Rev. Joseph Pemberton, who had been busy hybridising roses in the early part of this century. It was put on the market but there was no record at all of its parentage. Perhaps it was a foundling. Certainly at the time there were no other roses like it. Nor were there in our own time until Jack Harkness, the rose breeder of Hitchin, took it up. He saw its possibilities.

Meanwhile it got pushed around in the rose lists and encyclopaedias. Some called it just a shrub, others a floribunda, and others dared to label it a hybrid musk. Today 'Ballerina' does have two direct descendants that are in the currency of roses: 'Red Ballerina', crimson, with flowers rather double, and 'Marjorie Fair', rich carmine, each flower with a white eye. But this is only the beginning of a new phase in 'Ballerina's' history. 'Ballerina' and those who have come after it are continuous flowerers. They produce massive heads of bloom that are quickly succeeded by more when the first are spent and snipped off. This shows the importance of keeping stocks going somewhere of garden plants of all kinds, even if only for breeding with them. Work which the National Council for the Conservation of Plants and Gardens is doing.

Rugosa roses Next in importance as shrubs is the fine group of Japanese briers, cultivars of *Rosa rugosa*. These are of special value to those who try to garden on poor soil. They really don't mind how light and sandy it is. They flourish and flower freely just the same. In fact, all that you could find to say against them is that their stems are most horribly prickly. Not set with the odd hook-like thorn but covered all the way up with multitudes of little prickles that get into your hands whenever and wherever you touch them.

Exactly right, then, you might well say, for using to plant as a hedge. I do know some jolly good hedges of them that look efficiently intruder-proof. They are abundant with flowers at the height of the rose season, and if the spent heads are regularly snipped off they will flower repeatedly into the autumn. At that time the dead heads can be left for the hips to mature, and they will turn scarlet and reach the size of small tomatoes. In the late autumn the leaves turn to golden and rich copper shades before they fall.

The two favourites here are the white 'Blanc Double de Coubert', and the deep red 'Roseraie de l'Hay', both excellent roses that anyone would be well advised to plant. Especially when you know that they do sucker a bit so that you always have new plants to offer to a friend or to plant elsewhere in your own garden.

However, there is one that to my idea is supreme in this section. It is called 'Sarah Van Fleet'. Its flowers are bright pink, and all through the summer and autumn it never seems to be without them. I also like one called 'Schneezwerg', a white rose, and the pale pink 'Frau Dagmar Hartopp'.

China roses Small gardens have special need of the compact so-called China roses. My own special favourite among these, which I have grown ever since I have had a garden, and repeated in a new planting only a few seasons back, is the soft pink 'Natalie Nypels'. Never a day goes by between early June and the end of November when it is without a flower. Its acquaintance is one of the many things for which I am grateful to a former *Popular Gardening* editor, H. H. Thomas.

A great favourite among the Chinas is the well named 'Little White Pet'. Another is the charming 'Cécile Brunner', with miniature pink flowers of perfect buttonhole formation. Also in this section is to be found the strange *Rosa mutabilis*, which produces orange buds, opening to yellow flowers which change then to pink and later copper.

Modern shrub roses The group known as modern shrub roses is very hardy. They tend to flower repeatedly all through the summer. Best known of them is the ivory 'Nevada' but others which lend themselves to mixed border planting or for hedges are the crimson 'Fountain', pale yellow 'Golden Wings', shell-pink 'Sparrieshoop' and cherry-pink 'Elmshorn'. Brightly coloured cultivars for hedges are orange-scarlet 'Bonn' and 'Kassel'.

Some of these I grow myself in shrub borders rising from among the evergreen azaleas, which seem to make a good groundwork for them. Cultivars I have tried and would not part with now are the well-named 'Lavender Lassie' and the splendid 'Aloha', with buds opening to rich pink flowers. 'Cerise Bouquet', another one well named, is distinctive among roses in having a scent like a dish of raspberries. In this case the bright cerise flowers are set off by greyish foliage. Another in my most admired group is 'Golden Wings', mentioned above, which has perfectly formed single flowers. I could wish that 'Raubritter' was a bit more generous with later flowers, but for a long time in summer its arching branches are set with rounded flowers of a strong pink often tinged with silver.

Encouraged to grow bushy by having the older wood cut out frequently, these shrubs can be made to grow into thickets in beds that will in time look after themselves, especially if, say, three plants of the same variety are planted in close company and allowed to grow into one another.

China rose 'Elmshorn'

Old-fashioned roses

Come June, with its warm days, long evenings and sunny hours when the air is filled with a pot pourri of scents, the old-fashioned roses once again get their rightful share of admiration. Tousled and heavily stuffed with petals, their flowers have an enduring charm that lasts in the imagination long after the blooms themselves have withered and dropped their petals. Then it is time to muse over their names and wonder how they came to get them. Who were those elusive figures they enshrine? Are they only remembered by the roses named after them? Were they distinguished, famous and fashionable? Or were they village Hampdens who bred or found a rose, or perhaps had some endearing quality that someone wished to acknowledge in this most felicitous of ways?

Alas, perhaps we shall never know now, but at least we still have the roses to delight us every year when June with all its flowery delights and summer perfumes comes again.

Though the characteristic old-fashioned rose is a blowsy flower, they are divided into groups and to understand this class of rose you must know something about these, for then you can get to know at once something of the nature of the bushes on which they grow.

In nurseries and garden centres they are found under the group names of centifolia, damask, gallica and Bourbon. In general they flower only once, towards the end of June and early in July. Moreover they tend to be rather lax plants that are best tied to three or four stakes, the stems being wound in serpentine fashion. This both keeps them in control and encourages the plentiful production of flowering twigs. In fact, it is better to tie in as much wood as possible rather than prune them every year.

Most of the old-fashioned roses are pink of one shade or another. A few are white, but none are yellow. But to compensate for this you get a violet colouring in some of them which no modern rose can offer. Again, some of them are striped and mottled with a richer pink or with white, again a charming effect that cannot be found in modern roses. As for the scent for which old-fashioned roses are famed, I could not put my hand on my heart and say there is nothing like it in the roses of today. Scent is subjective and some may be able to declare this. But for my part I believe that there are scents just as strong, just as delicious to be found in the roses of the present. Not all old-fashioned roses are scented anyway. Let us run through the different classes of them.

Gallicas These are single or semi-double and 60 cm (2 ft) high. They naturally make thickets because they sucker freely. Best known is the crimson 'Tuscany' and the striped 'Rosa Mundi' (*Rosa gallica* 'Versicolor'). But also worth growing is *R.g.* 'Officinalis', the so-called Rose of Provins, once grown widely around the French town of that name for the perfume industry that flourished there. A deep crimson cultivar of this group I cherish is 'Charles de Mills'.

Alba and damasks These roses make stiff bushes whose leaves are a light green colour. Here the most adored cultivar is 'Céleste', a soft light pink flower of flattened form, but another of great appeal is the paler 'Maiden's Blush'. They make rather tall lax bushes that are best trained to stakes or to tripods about 1.2 m (4 ft) high. Then the branches can be tied round them in serpentine fashion. The same goes for the damask roses, whose flowers are rather ball-shaped. 'Ispahan' is typical, a lovely clear pink, another is 'Blue Damask', a cultivar in which the pink is tinged with purple to give a mauve tint.

Centifolias The centifolias or cabbage roses have a similar form, but here the flowers are still more sumptuous, for the first name means 'rose of a hundred leaves'. Often the blooms are quartered, the petals disposing themselves in four segments in the flowers. Indeed, you would want to look no further than *R.* × *centifolia* itself, though there are also several cultivars around. Most notable of them is 'Chapeau de Napoléon', a cultivar so heavily encrusted with 'moss' as to resemble a cocked hat. Moss roses are a separate kind and get their name from the frilly green growth covering the sepals from which the buds break.

112

Here there are many pink but also white cultivars, all with the characteristic mossy appendages.

Hybrid perpetuals By comparison with the centifolias all of them ancient roses, the hybrid perpetuals of the last century are new. In appearance they resemble the centifolias, but the bushes are rather stiffer, and you can certainly prune them almost as hard as you would a cluster-flowered rose of today, whereas with the other classes you get most flowers by tying in all the growth you can and pruning only surplus wood. The famous white 'Frau Karl Druschki' is a hybrid perpetual rose that characterises the whole race. Others are the crimson with white edges, 'Baron Giron de l'Ain' and the similar 'Roger Lamblin'. 'Reine des Violettes', well named for its colour, is another and a famous deep pink one is 'Ulrich Brunner'.

Bourbons Last come the Bourbon roses, in which the beginning of our perpetual flowering roses is seen, for these flower recurrently through the summer. 'Zéphirine Drouhin', that bright pink thornless rose, often classified with the climbers, is one of these. Others are the cream-pink 'Souvenir de la Malmaison', silvery pink 'Mme Lauriol de Barny', palest pink 'Mme Pierre Oger', and deep pink 'Mme Isaac Pereire'. All these are roses rich in scent and full petalled. They are buxom roses with that sense of abundance that gives the old-fashioneds their perennial and enduring appeal. Look for them in gardens opened to the public during early summer.

Rosa 'Zéphirine Drouhin'

Climbing roses

It's one of the absurd paradoxes of gardening that the smaller your garden the more you need the tallest growing of roses, the climbers. As a group, that is, not the biggest growing of climbing roses. I feel the possibilities of vertical gardening have yet to be exploited on a scale appropriate to the limitations of our late 20th century gardens.

The larger proportion of bush roses will need fully 1.25 m² (4 sq ft) of ground apiece for a start. Then in a small area they tend to grow up as well as outwards and look out of scale after a few years, no matter how you try to curb them with the secateurs. Miniatures? Yes, but they too seem to look out of scale with the rest of the plants in the garden. Now climbing roses need simply length and depth without breadth, a single plane. Not if you let them have their own way, you may well say, and certainly many climbers will reach out and claw at you if you give them a chance. But the possibilities are there for keeping them neat and tidy even if it does mean climbing a ladder pretty often. This is of little account, however, once you get used to it.

It is important always to distinguish between rambler and climbing roses. The former begin life afresh from the base every season rather like loganberry and raspberry canes do. The old branches will flower again, but it is best to cut them out and leave the new ones to take their place. On the other hand the climbers build up a framework of branches which go on for many years, and these are the best for the average garden, whether planted against walls, fences or against posts, which they are tied round in spiral fashion.

Here's another point about climbing roses. Other kinds need feeding to make them grow well and flower abundantly. Climbers seem to have it in them to produce cascades of flowers. In general climbing roses will tolerate poorer ground than bushes and often live to a great age, provided they are occasionally allowed to reproduce themselves by having the oldest wood cut out when there is young growth for replacement.

For 'wall' read 'fence' too, for climbing roses go just as well on fences. Better sometimes, one might think, for it's easier to knock a galvanised nail into a fence than it is into a wall when you want to tie in the odd straying branch. And here we get on to this intricate matter of training. The conventional thing for training climbers on is trellis of some kind, whether it's made of wood or wire, so that you always have handy some secure support at any point to tie in any bit of growth. In fact, though, you don't need to go to so much trouble or expense at all.

Watch the professional. What he does is to keep tying the rose branches back and forth to the plant's own strong growths, using the older branches as supports for the younger ones. Of course, you have got to make sure that the old ones are firmly attached to the wall or fence, but you can do this by knocking or screwing in here and there the odd vine eye, as they call them in garden shops – those big eyelets they sell for holding wires to fences.

Now the effect of this actually benefits flowering. It is one of the facts of gardening life that if you train a branch of a climbing plant sideways or even downwards to restrict the upward surge you encourage buds to break that would otherwise remain dormant and you get many more flowers as a result. This is why if you grow climbing roses against the posts or pillars of a pergola you want to train the branches round them in serpentine fashion instead of just lashing them to the support with string. In this case, however, it would seem to be well worthwhile encircling the post or pillar with rings of stout galvanised wire every 38 cm (15 in) or so to provide a foothold for those main branches, remembering that it is a much more artificial process than training on a wall or fence. But you may well say your climbers are always making lanky new growth low down that you can scarcely cope with. Well, there are climbers and climbers. The most biddable kinds just don't do this. They make a framework of tough wood and from this produce twigs of varying lengths on which the flowers are borne.

The famous 'Albertine' one of the very best of roses for a wall, occupies a place midway between ramblers and climbers. It makes new wood every year from part way up the old. Therefore the wood above the point of origin of this can be cut away or the new tied in to supplement it. By the latter process high walls can be covered in roses, but the plants will only flower really well and justify this lavish treatment if the tied in wood is always trained sideways as described above.

True climbers don't only flower in one glorious burst through the longest days of the year, but produce a goodly quantity of further flowers for as long as the floribundas do. That superb climbing rose 'Handel', now reckoned by the pundits of the Royal National Rose Society to be about the best repeat-flowering climber, appeared almost unnoticed. Perhaps that was because its ivory flowers rimmed with cerise look so much like those of a large-flowered rose that they didn't stand out. But that's just what makes this such a valuable rose. Among this type of rose 'Compassion', so named because it was first sold to help raise funds for heart disease sufferers has many admirers. If you were to call it salmon you would be doing it an injustice, for besides this there are many other tints depending on the stage of development of the flower; it is delectably scented too.

I have unbounded admiration for the brownish-apricot 'Schoolgirl' which is the successor to the old 'Phyllis Bide' our parents grew for so long. The latter was always reckoned a fawn colour, and it flowers and flowers. I long thought it had gone right out, but now I notice that Harkness, the rose specialists, are cataloguing it, which means that it cannot have lost its vigour or become a martyr to disease.

Yellow roses are always thought of as being a bit on the difficult side and certainly they come and go. One of the most splendid is called 'Royal Gold', but this only seems to do well in favoured spots. However, 'Golden Showers', which has now seen more than 20 summers in gardens, holds its position, though it could be challenged by one called 'Dreaming Spires'. The best white of the day is 'Swan Lake' and the pale pink 'New Dawn' shows no sign of giving up. Everyone I know is delighted with 'Aloha', having the copper-pink colour of 'Albertine' but without its rampant ways.

Climbing rose 'Golden Showers'

Indeed, the restraint shown by these roses also fits them for growing in mixed borders on tripods of stout stakes, or, better still, obelisks, when four are used and brought together at the top. You wind the branches round and keep tying in just as you would on a wall, and though you may have only a little border you can still have roses in it by the hundred.

The miniatures

Try to find out something about the genealogy of what are known as miniature roses, in the way that rose lovers eventually come round to studying the history of their favourite flower, and you are in for a confusing time. Their pedigrees are not at all reliably documented like those of other roses. Some accounts tell you that they came from a little rose noticed in a chalet windowbox by a Swiss army doctor and taken up by a celebrated rock plant specialist. But this is only one strand of the story.

What we can be sure of is no more than that they were grown as pot plants on quite a wide scale early in the last century, though few of those early cultivars have survived. One I grow myself, called 'Pompon de Paris', is reported to have appeared about 1839.

A friend gave it to me and I daresay it has been passed around from friend to friend for the last century. It is a most charming little rose, making a neat bush with semi-doubled flowers of light carmine striped along each petal with a lighter bar. When I was given it I wondered if it would prove the climbing form, which is seen now and again in old gardens, but so far it renews itself from the base, I notice, and has made stems no more than about 45 cm (18 in) tall. As such it is perfect for tiny gardens, proclaiming across a century and a half a type of rose that is only today in the ascendant as a garden bush.

Every year now, along with the shrubs, the hybrid teas and the floribundas, the lists of new roses always include a few miniatures, though some are styled dwarfs and others patio roses. It does not amount to quite the same thing, as some grow as little as 30 cm (1 ft) tall, while others will go up, if you let them, to as much as 1 m (3 ft).

What characterises them all is the size of their flowers. They are just perfect little replicas of their everyday brethren, some keeping a pointed hybrid tea shape, others opening flat and being produced in quite large clusters.

Among those to be found in the rose catalogues and whose flowers have the admired pointed form are 'Little White Pet', another quite old cultivar, growing about 45 cm (18 in), dating from the latter part of the last century, the pink 'Cécil Brunner', of the same size and a contemporary, and the execrably named 'Peek a Boo', a spreading grower with apricot flowers that belong to our own time.

A miniature of the 1930s that has only lately won recognition is 'The Fairy', a most charming pink cultivar with plentiful sprays of flowers but an appalling flopperty habit of growth. Yet so charming is it that you could not damn it on this account. I grow a line of it as a low hedge and have it propped up with stakes and wire, like the support for a row of broad beans. Angela Rippon and Anna Ford each have a miniature rose named after them, both 45 cm (18 in) growers. Angela's is coral, Anna's bright red, and both have flowers that open out into a rosette form. In the same height range Jack Harkness has named a yellow one 'Kim', and Cockers of Aberdeen an orange one 'Little Prince', and they have followed this up this year with 'Boys' Brigade' in which the red colouring is set off with a white eye.

Showing just how many there are and how intense is the breeding programme to produce more and more, a current specialist catalogue, lists over 50 cultivars, more than half of them of recent raising. Not only are all the British rose raisers working on them but in New Zealand Sam McGredy is busy too, and so is Alain Meilland in the South of France at the home of the 'Peace' rose. They are very selective in what they introduce, however, all of them producing little roses hardy enough to grow out of doors here. In the United States, however, new cultivars are tumbling from the rose breeding stations. They are produced mostly for the indoor pot plant trade, or for standing out in their 'yards' or on their balconies for the summer.

What role have the miniatures to play here, then? In the smallest gardens, of course, they are of special value where other types of roses would be ungainly, but elsewhere as tub plants they excel as their confused ancestry has made sure that they will flower continuously from early June till the end of October, perhaps for even longer.

It is when they are raised up in containers that you find them so intriguing individually, as well as making such a fine 'bedding' show. The only pity is that some of them are being given such embarrassing names, like 'Darling Flame' and 'Little Bucharoo', 'Little Flirt' and 'Yellow Doll'. They deserve better!

Roses for ground cover

Since it came out nearly 20 years ago now, the ground-covering 'Nozomi' rose of Japanese origin (its name meaning hope) has stood by itself. It forms a mat 15 to 20 cm (6 to 8 in) deep and which produces apple-blossom-like flowers in early summer. It was thought to be the forerunner of many more of its kind, but only recently has a series been introduced. These come from Denmark and are named 'Pink Bells', 'Red Bells' and 'White Bells' and they have been put on the market together with 'Snow Carpet' from New Zealand.

The newcomers are much denser in growth than 'Nozomi', and whereas this had silver leaves, they are a rich green. The plants lie flat on the ground, each covering a circle 1 to 1.2 m (3 to 4 ft) across and rising more than 30 cm (1 ft) at the centre. Thus they are exactly the right plants for using to cover banks and odd pieces of sunny ground where you want them to look after themselves. It would be wise to destroy all perennial weed growth with glyphosate and handweed afterwards for the first couple of seasons until the plants have become dense enough to do their own garden housekeeping for you.

6

Climbers and Wall Plants

Surely enclosure is essential to a garden? Essential, too, once you get to know the many plants that climb or can be trained up fences and walls just waiting to be given a home where they will be cherished. A porch entwined with honeysuckle, roses swagging the walls, a wisteria reaching up to the eaves ... they add up to a persistent idea of a home embowered by climbing plants. But it's not so easy to achieve and live with as to conjure the image. Broad picture windows leave little wall space on modern houses to plants. And once climbers have got over their first years of establishing themselves they tend to go on the rampage, hopelessly outgrowing the space allotted to them, especially if they are encouraged with the unwise feeding that is liable to be given too often to anything living close to the house.

If there is one elementary piece of advice to offer universally on wall plants, whether they are natural climbers or have to be trained to keep them upright, it is to leave them alone at the root but never to let them have their head or even let them go their own way for long. All wall plants need frequent curbing, by pinching and trimming. Then they will have the romantic, cascading touch without the wild abandon.

Year-round interest

One of the most challenging of gardening ideals, it seems to me, is to try and create a garden when there is no week, perhaps day, in the year when you need to be ashamed of it, not even in the winter. Always, if this is the aim you set yourself, as I do, it should have something interesting to offer, I confess to being a very long way from achieving this even after working the same plot of ground for a good many seasons. But it does remain the ideal to which I am committed. In the garden of my dreams every square metre of ground will have some pleasing feature that stops you in your tracks throughout the four seasons. One plant will follow another there either with its flowers or making some appeal with its leaves.

Of course, this is only one part of the year-round effect. The other is an architectural one. The outlines drawn in green should survive the ebb and flow of other plant life. After all, many of the most admired gardens in the world don't have a flower in them. They depend solely on their design which is more often worked in hedges and topiary than it is in masonry.

But it is the way that plants and their flowers are disposed that makes the greatest contribution to the idea of year-round effect. This is achieved by interplanting, almost like catch-crop vegetables. Climbing plants and those wall-trained shrubs are of the first importance in this technique. It's one of the elements of successful gardening that when you cannot garden outwards, either because your garden is tiny or because you've taken up all the available space, you want to examine the possibilities of going upwards. Not, though, with one climber at a time but always with partnerships.

First, though, one should always appreciate that anything growing against a wall is likely to come into flower earlier than its twin set in the open ground. At once, then, this is a point that aids succession. Exploit the shelter of your walls and fences to give plants a chance they would not have in the open ground, thus extending the range of plants you can grow and therefore the interest of your garden and the length of the season when it yields flowers.

Companion planting Take the climbing roses that have one main season of flowering. Plant a clematis to make use of the framework the rose provides and you will get either flowers before the roses – if you use one of the spring kinds – or later on in the year, if you grow one of the large-flowered kinds that are pruned hard in spring and therefore flower late in the summer. Here too the annual climbers come in so useful. You just push the seed into the ground close to the rose, or other wall plant, cover it with a glass jar to act as a miniature cloche and wait – first for the seeds to germinate, then for the plant to grow encouraged by the scope offered it by the host plant.

I find that the spring-flowering ceanothus also act as accommodating and encouraging hosts to clematis, annuals – and vines. It is not realised often enough that vines are plants that can be cut back really hard in the spring, provided you are careful not to cut back the one-season wood to a stump every year. The new stems grow out 2 m (6 ft) in a short time and carry a crop on this new wood.

Similarly, there are many plants that can be cut to the ground every season to grow out over more permanent kinds that make an enduring framework. The fuchsias are some of the best examples, while another is the Lemon Verbena (*Lippia citriodora*) which if the frost does not destroy it to ground level and do it for me I hard prune every year training in the new growth to the arms of a ceanothus.

Wisteria is a somewhat difficult case, but once you realise that it flowers on stubby spurs like a cordon apple you can exploit its basic framework for other plants – clematis and annual climbers again. You simply have to prevent them getting swamped by the wisteria's exuberance by nipping it whenever it gets a bit unruly, which is something that promotes flowering abundantly in the following season.

Of course, you do not need to confine such intercropping to wall plants. Any tall tree, any flowering cherry or crab, can have its rose growing over it to follow up the spring show. Or smaller trees make good hosts for clematis of the small-flowered late summer kinds. On the other hand any tree that happens to flower in the summer can have an early clematis. Not the wild *montana* type but one of the *alpina* or *macropetala* forms which are much more restrained in growth. Each of our eucryphia trees, covered in white flowers in August, in late spring look as though it is growing pink or blue flowers – from one of these clematis. For tree, however, one should also read shrub. Most kinds will suffer slender climbers using them as hosts. However, to make full use of climbers it is always wise to interplant next to each other spring and later flowering types. For instance if you set a honeysuckle beside the yellow-flowered Winter Jasmine the latter will fall into insignificance while the first is performing, and vice versa.

Jasminum nudiflorum, the Winter Jasmine, enlivens the winter days with its yellow flowers. However, it was treasured in greenhouses when it first reached this country from China. How mistaken this solicitude was is shown by the fact that today it can be planted to face the north or the chilly east with a confidence that it will thrive there as well as it will on a more favoured site. Though it looks as though it ought to be scented, perfume is the one quality it lacks. Having to tie its lax branches to a trellis is a small price to pay for such treasure in the dead of the year, when the rest of the garden is at rest.

Two words of warning about the practical aspects of growing climbers in close partnership with other plants. Don't make the mistake of using a twiner to grow up something else. The two main twiners are wisteria and honeysuckle. They will throttle anything within their grasp – unless it's a mighty tree, and you do sometimes see wisteria in this role. Twiners should be the privileged hosts with first claim on the trellis.

Low wall shrubs

What about those low walls under windows? How can they be exploited and embellished to extend the scope of one's gardening? What will grow there without always having to be trimmed back so that you can see out? For convenience' sake you can divide what will grow there into two groups of plants; those which enjoy or must have a south- or west-facing aspect, and the others that will put up with facing north or east. None are climbers: they are shrubs that have to be trained to some sort of trellis, however simple.

One of the finest for the latter aspect is the old 'Japonica', a plant that has gone through several changes of botanical name having finally come to rest as *Chaenomeles*. The flowers can be blood-red as in the favourite 'Rowallane', rose in 'Pink Lady', deep red with conspicuous golden anthers in 'Crimson and Gold' and even white in 'Nivalis'. All give you golden fruits in the autumn that can be used to make a perfumed jelly.

Next in merit comes *Cotoneaster horizontalis*, the one that forms its branchlets in herringbone fashion flat against a wall, covering them with white flowers in late spring, with scarlet berries in autumn, lasting into the winter. In this situation the birds go for them last! Since in an open-ground position *Osmanthus delavayi*, which has scented white flowers in great abundance in the late spring, makes a flattish bush, this is something to put to good use against a wall. There this neat foliaged evergreen will also grow flat, but the 'right way' up.

In certain garden centres lately I have seen the once rare *Mitraria coccinea*, another South American that has flowers like elongated foxgloves of rich crimson in late spring and summer. It actually likes the shade and damp, but also plenty of peat in the ground. Lastly, for the shade, that gold-splashed evergreen, *Euonymus fortunei* in one of its choicer forms like 'Emerald 'n' Gold' (see page 130).

Let us now come round to the sunny spots, whether they face south or west or something veering to either side of this aspect. Never would I be without a Lemon Verbena plant, *Lippia citriodora*, grown just for the sharp lemon scent of its leaves. Nor without that most remarkable of all hebes, *Hebe hulkeana*, whose plumes of lavender-coloured flowers are often 30 cm (1 ft) long and a third of that across. By now the plants I would recommend for such a site are queueing up. I could never have a garden without a bush of *Daphne odora* 'Aureomarginata' under the sunny window (see page 90).

Myrtles flower about midsummer and then they are aromatic rather than scented, always white in blossom but for the rest of the year the dark green foliage is also found to be aromatic when a leaf is crushed in the hand. A related plant in its Mediterranean origin is the greyish-leaved, yellow-flowered *Coronilla glauca*. It would be hard to say just when it is time for this to flower. In fact it is hardly ever without a few clusters of its circlets of bloom, each like a crown.

There is ambiguity, too, about the bright salmon blossom of the *Penstemon isophyllus*, so long is its season, running from rose time until the autumn colour is at its most dramatic. Again, indispensable. As, in my judgement, is an abelia, preferably the fuchsia-like semi-evergreen *A. floribunda*, the most splendid species when in deep red flower in June. However, if I could not find this species I would always like to

Coronilla glauca

121

have one of the others, any of them, for they are much the same with their cloud of small pink bells in the autumn.

Slightly tender Over the seasons I have never been without a grey-leaved blue-flowered *Teucrium fruticans* under the low windows in a sunny, well-drained spot. Frost has carried them off from time to time, but since they flower for so long through summer and are so elegant, always I come back to planting another. The same goes for the Dwarf Pomegranate, *Punica granatum* 'Nana'. If I gardened near the sea or high up, where the air was clearer and the light stronger and there were no nearby hills to pull down the clouds, as happens near us, I know it would flower superbly in its vermillion livery in summer. As it is, it and I live on hopes.

No problem, though, about getting the woody red-flowered salvias, of which there are many, to flower against a low wall. They too go the way of teucrium in some years but they come so easily from cuttings that it's no trouble to have a stock with which to replace a lost bush or to offer to friends who admire them. Also I must put in a good word, a very good one, for the New Zealand leptospermums, also plants that once grew only in the gardens of those who would have styled themselves connoisseurs but are now to be found in many a garden centre. The flowers are like pink or red dolls' house roses, the leaves matching them in neatness.

Now in a position against a low wall, all these plants do need some sort of training. They need the support of a trellis to keep them fairly flat and they need to have surplus growth pruned out pretty often and unwanted shoots pinched before they have spread too far. This job can be done when you think of it, all through the year.

Clematis

First of all what is it that these plants really enjoy? They like soil where the wet doesn't hang about for long, but they insist on having in the ground plenty of the compost that holds moisture. Just the same sort of demands, in fact, that lilies make on you. Magnolias too. Indeed, if you were ever to dig up a clematis you would find that it does have the rather fleshy roots characteristic of plants with these basic requirements.

When you see a well-trained clematis romping away as though it really enjoyed being there you can be pretty sure that the plant has got its roots comfortably under some area of paving or other. Either that, or planted in front of it is a dense low-growing evergreen bush that will shade its low parts. Couldn't this be taken as a sign that clematis will succeed on shady walls or fences? They will grow there but not necessarily flower well. The summer-flowering kinds that is. Curiously, the spring types are happy enough in shady situations. Like lilies again, what clematis really delight in is to be able to clamber out of the shade into the clear light. This at once indicates one of the best ways of growing them – up trees and over bushes.

Where they are grown in one vertical plane they do need some kind of trellis to cling to. They hang on by elongating their leaf stalks and turning these into coils like tight springs. Right from its earliest days in the garden a young clematis must have something to cling to to be stimulated to reach further and further. Wire netting will do, even plastic netting. They will climb canes, and I have found you can make highly pleasing features to inset in mixed borders of shrubs and herbaceous plants by putting in four 2.2 m (7 ft) canes in a 60 cm (2 ft) square and tying them to form an obelisk. I grow two plants on these, one for spring, the other for summer, the two intertwining and sharing the same support.

Two groups But what kind of clematis do you want to plant? There are in fact two main groups of clematis, one succeeding the other in flower. The much used term 'spring flowering' is a little misleading for in most places the daffodils are over and gone before these clematis open. Most celebrated of them is the one universally known simply by its second name of *montana*, a sure sign of general admiration and affection. This is white but it has several pink forms, notably 'Elizabeth' which is also distinguished by having a scent. In a way it's a pity that C. *montana*, which in time becomes rampant, has rather overshadowed the other spring kinds whose flowers, *macropetala* in particular, resemble colum-bines. They are bluish mauve and white, but pink and white in the very lovely 'Markham's Pink'. This is quite a slender grower and the one I have used up some of my obelisks. However, you should know that C. *alpina* is very similar, though a slighter grower still. Of its cultivars 'Columbine' is blue, while 'Ruby' and 'White Moth' describe themselves.

A third type of spring clematis is *Clematis armandii*, which is technically evergreen, though in a cold winter the leaves get turned to brown paper. Its small white flowers are perfumed. Only against a sunny south- or west-facing wall will it thrive.

At this point we come on to the summer-flowering kinds, but here again they divide themselves into two. One embraces all those large-flowered kinds that everyone knows, in purple-blue, red, pink and white which includes the archetypal *Clematis × jackmanii*. However, few home gardeners ever see a double clematis. Yet they do exist and are well worth looking out for.

Few also ever see the small-flowered late kinds, the plants which are best suited for planting to clamber over arches and for allowing to scramble over trees and shrubs. They are generally not so vigorous as the large-flowered ones. You find them in nurseries and garden centres under collective names of *viticella* and *texensis* hybrids. Of the former there are purple, white, crimson and pink. 'Minuet' is raspberry pink

Getting the best out of clematis

It is commonly held among skilled gardeners that you can kill a plant by putting it in too deeply. But not clematis. In fact, it is advisable to bury a few centimetres of the bottom of the woody stem. New roots will develop there in the way that heathers can root from the old wood.

(1) Take out a hole 45 cm (18 in) deep and wide at least 30 cm (1 ft) from the wall or fence and fill in with 15 cm (6 in) of old manure and a couple of handfuls of bonemeal or hoof and horn.

Top up with peat and garden soil and plant your clematis 5 to 8 cm (2 or 3 in) deeper than it was in its pot to induce vigorous shoot growth.
(2) Prune back stems to just above a pair of buds some

23 cm (9 in) from the base. This will encourage a bushy plant and plenty of flowers.
(3) Lay some pieces of paving stone over the soil to keep the roots cool and active. Remember – heads in the sun, roots in the shade.

but white at the heart. 'Elegans Plena' is dusty purple and double. 'Alba Luxurians' has green tips to its white flowers. The *texensis* hybrids are much more scarce and have flowers that look like tulips. There are only rose-coloured forms. 'Etoile Rose' is the most celebrated.

Did you know too, that there are yellow clematis? Both *C. orientalis* and *C. tangutica* have small yellow flowers in great profusion and they keep them into the autumn, when all the leaves are turning to red and gold.

Pruning Once they are happily sited and comfortably suited at the root clematis grow so well that you just can't let them have all their own way. You have to prune them – at the right time and in theory in the right way according to variety. No trouble with the spring ones. As soon as flowering is over you cut out any offending bits. Once in a while you can refurbish them entirely by cutting away whole branches and allowing slender shoots low down to provide an entirely new plant.

But the summer kinds – with characteristic cussedness some flower on old as well as new wood. Others only on new growth. In theory, again, you can get two displays from a plant of the ambivalent first class, by preserving some of last season's wood but cutting some back to encourage young growth to give a second crop. Personally, I can't be bothered. The rough but very ready way in which I deal with them and which I find works well is to prune them all hard, almost to the ground every year in early spring. They soon grow up again.

Come to that, you can be too soft with clematis after all. Why, when you plant one in spring from a garden centre you want to crop it back hard straight away – by at least half. It's the root you want to start with, not the rudimentary top growth.

Ceanothus

Although no one here ever uses the common name of the ceanothus, Californian Lilac, the very title says quite a lot about these bushes. Sunshine, first, of course. After all, many of our annual flowers are of Californian origin, and everyone knows how much they crave sunny garden spots. They languish without the sun. Light soil too. Almost all sun-loving plants grow best in soil that drains sharply, as you would expect of ground that has been baked throughout time. But the birthplace also indicates an indifference to whether the soil is limy or not. They thrive where the soil is acid or alkaline. And they will grow at a considerable rate, reaching their potential in three or four seasons. Their one weakness is a certain vulnerability to hard winter weather. Yet even this can be counteracted by growing most of them in the shelter of a sunny wall, where they will be protected from the cold winds and where they will benefit from the radiated heat in summer that ripens and toughens their wood.

Most ceanothus have blue flowers, produced in plume-like clusters, though a few kinds have pink ones. This prevailing feature is a valuable one, since blue-flowered shrubs are scarce. Most ceanothus bloom in the late spring, but a few, mostly hybrids, are late-summer flowerers. For general purposes, however, they are divided into ever-green and deciduous kinds, though technically this is arbitrary, for those that do drop their leaves in the winter are derived from evergreen species. All these we call the evergreens respond to the close pruning needed to keep them trim against walls, while those termed deciduous will all endure really hard pruning every year.

Easy to propagate – which is why they are seen so often in the garden centres – ceanothus are also easy to cross one species with another, and this facility has resulted in many different kinds.

Evergreens The hardiest of the late spring kinds are to be found under the names 'Delight', 'Southmead' and *C. thyrsiflorus*. Others flowering more or less at the same season, generally available in garden centres, and to be strongly recommended as making, when in bloom and properly pruned, those surprising walls of bright blue are 'Dignity', 'Italian Skies', 'Cascade', 'Edinburgh' and 'A. T. Johnson'. The individual characteristics of these are botanical rather than horticultural. Any garden lover would be delighted to have any of them on his wall.

Cut back hard all the side shoots as soon as they have borne the flowers, leaving some of the strongest growths to enlongate and make a framework of branches. What must be understood about this group is that pruning should be fiddly rather than summary: no ceanothus will put up with the old wood being cut into. This becomes hard quickly and won't break afresh. So never cut into any growth more than a few months old. And never cut a shoot right off, but rather leave several leaves at the base. From each cut branch or twig several new ones will spring and give even more flowers in the following season.

To this group belong the two prostrate ceanothus which make dome-shaped bushes or can be trained to tumble from the top of a retaining wall. Correctly they are named *C. prostratus* and *C. thyrsiflorus repens*. Both bear the same plume-like blue flower heads in massive quantities.

'Burkwoodii' and 'Autumnal Blue' seem ready to flower from spring till late autumn, in spite of the name of the second. In practice, though, it is best to trim back their sideshoots in the spring rather than let them go their own way. Otherwise they get top heavy.

Deciduous forms Experience over generations has shown that the deciduous hybrids are tough enough to be grown in open beds provided they get the sun in summer to ripen the wood. Pruning these is quite a different process. You treat them harshly, cutting all the branches back every spring, right to a few centimetres above their point of origin. This keeps them as sturdy compact bushes. If left to grow as they will, they could well be blown out of the ground.

The collective botanical name for the whole group is *Ceanothus × delinianus*, but nobody ever uses it. They are always known by their cultivar names. Most famous of them is the celebrated 'Gloire de Versailles', which has light blue flowers. Those of 'Henri Desfosse' are rather deeper. The cultivar 'Indigo' describes itself, while 'Topaz' is rather paler. The two pale pink ones are 'Marie Simon' and 'Perle Rose'. This group have larger leaves than the evergreen kinds, except for one selection of a spring-flowering species, *C. arboreus* named 'Trewithen Blue' after the garden in Cornwall where it was found. Flowers are rich blue and continue to be produced sporadically for the rest of the summer when its main flush is over.

No ceanothus lives to a really ripe old age; ten years is full maturity for these shrubs. But fortunately, they all grow so easily from cuttings. You only have to pull off shoots of the current season's growth in late July, push them into a pot of sandy soil, cover with a polythene bag and watch for the signs of new growth at the tip that denotes that rooting has been accomplished. Then give each new plant a small pot of sandy soil, keep them sheltered in a frame or under a cloche for the winter and you will be able to put them out in the spring, to begin a new ten year cycle.

Wisteria

The wisteria is content with any soil, acid or alkaline. Garden centres always stock them as container-grown plants so you can plant them in late spring just when they are fresh in the minds. All they ask is for a sunny place and a good start in life by way of some comforting sandy peat being placed round their young roots and more for them to run into. After that, they can fend for themselves. Sun, though, they really must have. After all, though you do see such wonderful wisterias in this country, it is in sunnier places than our own that you find it even more prodigal with its flowers. There too you can discover, if you have not found it out here, that the flowers of wisteria actually have a delicious scent which needs greater heat than we customarily get on an early summer's day to bring out its full essence.

The wisteria we all know best and see most often is of Chinese origin. It was brought from a garden in Canton to Britain in 1816, though it is actually wild in the distant northern provinces of China. While its flowers are usually mauve, hanging in tresses about 23 cm (9 in) long, it also has a white-flowered form, which is very elegant indeed. On rare occasions you may come across one in which the mauve flowers are doubled, though this may seem to you more curious than beautiful.

There is also a Japanese Wisteria, *W. floribunda* 'Macrobotrys', which is quite astonishing. The flower tresses can be as much as 60 cm (2 ft) deep, though usually they are seen around 45 cm ($1\frac{1}{2}$ ft). Its effect is lost on a wall, and it is here that the wisteria's capacity for adapting itself comes in. For this is best grown as a little standard tree, in which form its long flower trails can be properly appreciated.

The truth is that wisteria can be tailored as well as apple and pear trees can, by a system of pruning that is very similar to the summer pruning practised on them. Towards the end of the summer, about the end of August or early in September, you cut back all the new slender shoots to about 15 cm (6 in). This toughens them and in the early winter when all the leaves are off they are easy to see – and easier to prune again then. For it is in winter that they are cut back again, this time to two buds. Now this is a principle that you can apply to every new shoot a wisteria makes in the summer and by this means you can make it into a bush. Of course, it will always try to display its basic nature as a twiner, many of the shoots curling round other parts of the plant. But no harm comes from unravelling them.

Recent seasons have seen the import from Japan of early flowering forms of wisteria. They have the name 'Prematura'. The idea is not that they flower earlier in the season but earlier in their lives, for if truth be told you do sometimes have to wait for the plants to settle down before they begin flowering. Sometimes you can come across the pink form, *W. japonica* 'Rosea', which can be very elegant. I have seen darker coloured wisterias in continental gardens and they have been even more striking. 'Black Dragon' is one sometimes available here.

Plants for a south-facing wall

I really know no better south wall plant than the Blue Potato Vine. It's just such sheer good value. Starts early in June, and is still in flower when the evenings really close in on you. Everyone who sees it marvels at its great bounty of flower, no matter what month or week in between when they come to your garden. Inevitably when I want to give someone who gardens a retirement present or a wedding present, one of the plants they get is *Solanum crispum* 'Glasnevin'. However it is tender and during my gardening lifetime I've lost several plants to the frost, though I've never been sorry to see them go and give me the chance to start again with a new small young one. I have always grown it on a post in a sheltered corner, but those I ask to accept one always get the advice thrown in to plant it on a sunny wall.

Solanum crispum 'Glasnevin'

Here you can grow the most ravishing and tantalising of plants. Some day they go figuratively to the wall under the effect of frost, but our climate being what it is, you can get seven or eight seasons of flower in a row from them, perhaps more, before they are put to the ultimate test.

Another of them is the related potato vine, *Solanum jasminoides*, which in late summer cascades with white blossom as you would expect to get from Summer Jasmine itself but which you never do. My present plant has now been in its position for eight years, so I am wondering if the time hasn't come to take some cuttings for its replacement. Still, even if it dies to the ground it usually springs up again. That's the nice thing about south wall plants: they develop so swiftly.

Take the mimosa, *Acacia dealbata*. The plant you buy in a garden centre in late spring and plant in a sheltered nook will be half as big again by the time the winter comes on, and by the same time next year will be more than twice the size. The following winter it will be flowering in anticipation of spring. The same rate of progress is made by *Abutilon megapotamicum*, that captivating plant with red and yellow flowers for half the year. *A. vitifolium* is not in bloom for so long, but is wonderful when it is, with clusters of pale lilac blossom, delicate in colour and in texture. Nowadays you can sometimes get a hybrid from it called 'Suntense', with flowers that have a purplish touch about them.

Not dissimilar in its golden flowers is fremontodendron, a sunny plant with leaves like those of an ivy-leaved geranium. When it's in full bloom it's a miraculous sight, really suggesting hot sunny places. The scent of the trachelospermum does too, though the white flowers produced in late summer aren't much to look at. Once you've enjoyed it somewhere you would want to grow this Mediterranean plant just for the perfume.

No one ever seems to recognise *Hebe hulkeana* as a shrubby veronica, so huge – without being coarse – are the sprays of its lilac flowers. This is one that you must grow in the shelter of a south wall, trained to some kind of trellis. So you must *H.* × *andersonii* 'Variegata', a plant worth growing for its silver marked leaves alone, but which also produces rich mauve flowers.

The Loquat, *Eriobotrya japonica*, rarely flowers in this country but this again is one I would grow against a south wall just for its foliage. The leaves are big and jagged, dusted with a silver down that makes them look as though they were carved in jade. A comely plant for one of those extra special clematis to clamber through.

Seldom seen in gardens outside the West Country, *Cleyera fortunei* deserves a trial elsewhere in a sheltered position in front of a south-facing wall. For it is one of the most dramatic of variegated leaf bushes. The term 'evergreen' is inadequate as the foliage, thick in texture, is coloured with pink, even cerise, on the green ground which is often the colour of jade, while each leaf has a cream margin. It came from Japan as one of the plant introductions of Robert Fortune, who brought the first forsythia to Britain. Its manner of growth makes it suitable for training flat against a wall, but it will also sprawl over the ground. It is a bush for light soil, and the poorer this is the more pronounced the leaf colouring.

The handsome-leaved drymis produces intricate blooms of ivory with a peppery scent. The leaves themselves smell of bay when crushed. So big has my plant grown that I have to cut it down really savagely in order to get the house painted! For some years I did have a mandevilla growing, a South American plant with massive white trumpets like a morning glory's. They were scented too, and often I think it would be worth replacing this now, especially as it used to twine round a drainpipe for its support. Several of the Australian bottlebrush bushes, callistemon, have come my way and always flourished for years, making red or yellow flowers.

As I look back over this list I notice that in fact most of these plants are of southern hemisphere origin. No wonder they want the most highly-favoured position in the garden.

Self-supporting climbers

The ways of climbing plants are curious and individual. Honeysuckle and wisteria, for instance, hang on to anything within reach by twining round their host in an apparently desperate embrace. Clematis are more decorous, twirling the tips of their leaf stalks round their host support. Others, like the sweet pea and the vine, put out tendrils which do the hanging on. Some don't even climb at all. They have to be fixed for they are more floppers, like the Winter Jasmine and the Blue Potato Vine, which just loll. Roses have their own way: they claw their way up, grabbing what support they can find with their barbarous thorns (see page 113). All must be offered a helping hand of some kind in a garden.

But there is yet another class that need no help from anyone in embellishing a wall or fence, nor support provided for them. They can hang on to timber or masonry either by way of little suckers along the stems or of aerial roots that serve for attachment as well as for gathering food. The climbing hydrangea (see page 78) is one such plant. *H. petiolaris* will in fact thrive on a north-facing wall or fence, flowering abundantly in July, when it produces its ivory-coloured lacecap heads. There is a winter bonus, by the way, in the light brown of the younger stems. The hydrangea family has two other members that are similarly endowed. One, indeed, has similar flower heads too. This has the awful name of *Pileostegia viburnoides*, which is one of the few evergreen self-clinging climbers. In its brother plant *Schizophragma hydrangeoides* it is the bracts which surround the flowers that are ivory, too, and hang like patriarchs' beards.

However, there are much less esoteric climbers that cling under their own power. Every kind of ivy does, for one thing. And some of these are highly decorative indeed. The variegated kinds are especially useful as they will enliven a north or east-facing wall with their silver or gold colouring. Choose one with the largest leaves, for this will make the strongest impact – where you have plenty of room, as is usually found on a sunless wall.

Much more restrained, though clinging firmly, are all the cultivars, new and old, of *Euonymus fortunei*. They are usually variegated with silver or gold, and sometimes you find pink tones in them too. 'Emerald 'n' Gold' is a very nice one of bright colouring for a dull spot. They are particularly useful for covering dustbin containers that can disfigure gardens, but they can also be used to cover ugly plinths or north-facing retaining walls that are getting crumbled by frost and damp. They will bind the brickwork as well as obscure it.

Vines While most vines cling by means of tendrils a few ornamental kinds will cling with suckers. Their names are tangled, but correctly today the best of them should be called parthenocissus, though you may still find them in garden centres under ampelopsis or vitis. Anyway, the one called *P. henryana* is especially decorative, for each vein is heavily outlined with a broad chalk mark. In autumn the foliage goes the fiery colour of the Virginia Creeper, also a self clinger, *P. quinquefolia*.

The Mediterranean heavily scented trachelospermums are self-clingers and very beautiful in a really hot position (see page 128). As for that other most desirable of self-clinging climbers, asteranthera, it defies me, yet, I shall go on trying it until I can make the wretched thing grow, and produce its midsummer flowers of rich red, the bravest of self-clinging climbers. The Scarlet Trumpet Vine often called a bignonia, *Campsis radicans*, grows lustily on a sunny wall. This does cling, but so abundant is its growth that it needs the odd tie here and there for fear that, soaked with rain and dew, the weight of its leafage will become too much for its aerial roots.

Pergolas

The pergola, that familiar feature of the English garden is in fact a foreign import. It belongs to countries hotter than our own, much hotter, where to enjoy a walk in the open air you need to be sheltered from the sun. Nevertheless, in its adapted form it's a convention that has a place in any garden, large or small, to which it will add a romantic touch, or an air of sophistication according to the materials of which it is constructed or its general character.

The pergola can indeed take many forms today. The shaded covered walk is an absurdity in our climate. But the term has come to connote a rather large archway or a simple colonnade of posts joined by cross members of timber or lengths of rope in the manner of those Edwardian rose gardens that persist in public parks.

While it will add a third dimension to a garden from the day of its construction without getting any larger and therefore out of scale as trees do, the pergola is a stage for climbing plants on which roses and clematis, the annual morning glory and canary creeper can be displayed to an advantage not possible when they are grown on fences.

Why should the pergola not be a living thing altogether, composed, in fact, of trees closely spurred to keep them in order? That is just what the pleached alley of old gardens was and still is very occasionally. To pleach, is, of course, an ancient verb meaning to intertwine, and in such an alley the branches are certainly woven into one another.

Another example of this kind of garden feature I have always found thrilling whenever I have seen it in flower in a friend's garden is an arcade composed entirely of Judas Trees (*Cercis siliquastrum*), one tree of the rare white kind planted to every three or four of the ordinary red one. The branches are trained over the path that runs beside them and pruned every season, a job which involves quite a lot of work on steps, but the result is so astonishing that it is worth all the trouble.

Training apples and pears Apples and pears especially lend themselves to being closely pruned and tightly trained. I have been trying this myself for some years, creating what could be called extravagantly a cupola, more modestly a pair of intersecting arches over the point where kitchen garden paths cross. I started with four cordon apples trees which I planted in pillar fashion and when they were more than man high began to train them towards one another.

In such a case the trees are not pleached, or interwoven but all their side shoots are spurred back hard.

As the base of every sideshoot the leaves form themselves into a cluster, whereas for the rest of the way up the shoot they grow one by one at intervals. Be sure to prune not in winter in the conventional way but in summer, at the end of July or early August. Then all you have to do is to cut back every new shoot – to four leaves beyond the basal cluster of leaves if it springs from a main stem, to one leaf beyond this point if it arises on a secondary stem that has already been cut before. When the main branches have reached their optimum length you nip off the ends at the end of May. Any shoot, however, that is needed for extension in some position or other is left until the winter, when it is shortened by about a third.

The principle you have to remember always in training apple and pear trees into shapes – producing an arcade or even just an arbour with them – is that winter pruning promotes growth, summer pruning controls it. Knowing this you are ready to create a living pergola with them, or any other kind of structure. It can be a pleached alley, simply like a strip of wall on stilts, it can be an arch or an arbour to shelter a seat from the wind. Or it might be a circle enclosing an area where one could take meals in a certain amount of shelter.

Of course, apple and pear trees are almost as attractive as any flowering tree when they are in blossom, especially when they are close spurred, for then the flowers are simply abundant in a restricted area. Grow a mixture of varieties to ensure successful pollination; two earlies and the rest lates should ensure a succession of fruit for eating from September to February.

There is no reason why the pergola should not be embellished further with still more plantings, for the late-flowering clematis which are pruned hard in the spring will readily clamber up the trunks with a little support and over the top unbidden. I am not quite so keen on having roses, for they can just get too exuberant, though if you plant the more restrained kinds of climbers that tend to make a permanent framework instead of being always anxious to renew themselves these can be satisfactory and not reach out to claw at you whenever you go a bit too close to them.

7
A Colourful Border

Home horticulture being something affected by fashion as much as anything else, the turn of the wheel of fortune is bringing back the herbaceous plants that once filled almost every garden border but which went into a decline because 'they were too much work'. After shrubs had taken their place the realisation dawned that shrubs just didn't offer the summer colour that the old hardy border plants had. But shrubs had also brought with them so-called woodland garden plants, a selection of herbaceous kinds that would thrive in the shade. These, it was discovered, were exactly the plants needed for small town gardens whose ground was necessarily shaded for much of the day and much of the year. Under these twin influences, plus the rise of the big wholesale nursery that found an opening in the market, herbaceous plants began a new ascent to favour.

And so much favour did they win that many forgotten kinds were sought and restored to cultivation; a process still going on, while a whole new hardy plant breeding industry grew up, resulting in cultivars more suitable to the new era, not of the discredited herbaceous border but of plants that could comfortably coexist with shrubs, among, under and in front of them. Nevertheless, there has always remained a public for the 'fancier's' type of herbaceous plants, like delphiniums and irises, plants of such distinction and variety that they each have a society dedicated to the cultivation and development of the flower.

Herbaceous plants Border plants, herbaceous plants, hardy perennials ... they're all one and the same: plants that grow up from an enduring rootstock in the spring, flower in summer and die down again in autumn, to renew themselves afresh the next spring, and for many more seasons to come. They increase themselves with no encouragement from the gardener. Some so much that they have to be taken up, split into small pieces and these replanted every few years for fear that they will either engulf the less vigorous species or exhaust themselves from too much effort. But most of them can safely be left in for a term of seven years at least, many more in a few cases, and watch them build up into colonies that will maintain themselves or need no more than a little propping up in late spring and cutting down in the autumn.

The colourings are many and varied, and the plants offer scope to the artistic instincts in the gardener. With these you can work out the colour schemes in which plants of all kinds always look their most effective. In planting them, however, it is always wise to set those with rich and bright colours in the foreground of a bed or border as it is seen from the windows of the house, or from a terrace, and the soft colourings in the distance. This is one of the ways by which the garden can be made to seem bigger than it really is. If there is one golden rule it is to plant perennials in groups as bold as the garden will allow, restricting the number of different kinds.

One special advantage of hardy perennials is that a colour effect can be achieved in the first season from planting. Or if the performance falls short a fresh start, without much financial loss or waste of time.

In their form border plants can vary from spire-like growers to bun-shaped hummocks. Some reach up to 1.2 to 1.5 m (4 to 5 ft), though in the main these are the least garden-worthy types, while others hug the ground. The latter class embraces a whole range of ground coverers that in broad patches become utilitarian plants, helping to keep the garden tidy while resisting weed growth.

Ground-covering plants Somehow the idea persists that there are cultivated plants, if you can only find them, that will banish weeds and take over from them. The supposed principle is that you can put one kind of plant over another and the former will win. That's the popular conception of ground covering, anyway. It's false. Covering the ground with plants, of your choice rather than nature's, may be something of a natural method of gardening but the exclusive occupancy of a patch of ground by one kind of plant doesn't happen naturally, does it? You usually get a whole lot of different wild plants coming up together.

Nevertheless, you can garden without labouring with the help of ground-covering plants provided you understand what their capabilities and limitations are. The general idea is certainly that once you have a tight network of vegetation over the earth wild plants – the weeds – just won't get a chance.

Well, this may apply to annual weeds that propagate themselves by way of seeds. Once the ground is densely covered they're not going to get much of a chance to settle. But those kinds like nettles, couch, creeping buttercup and ground elder which spread by way of their own roots, these will continue to come up through the toughest of introduced ground coverers.

So to exploit the system you first have to eliminate these with complete weedkillers. Glyphosate works very well, since it destroys everything. Only then is it wise to plant. Even so you still have to weed for the first couple of seasons – largely by hand, unless you choose to daub any interlopers with glyphosate gel, which is supplied in a bottle with a brush for painting it on the leaves.

Only when your plants have joined hands and interlocked can the area be left to itself. Then it will certainly become a self-maintaining area of ground, the ground coverers keeping the soil moist to the benefit of the roots of the shrubs whose area they carpet. Provided, that is, you have chosen the right kinds.

Ground coverers can be divided into trailers and clump-formers. Some of the trailers that have been used go too far too soon and just won't be kept under control. Some go upwards as well as sideways and provide you with an unholy tangle. Some are not dense enough. Some clump-formers take such a hold on the ground that you find yourself with worse weeds than those you are trying to avoid. Some don't join hands quickly enough. Some seed themselves about and become a nuisance. In my effort to try to maintain quite a large garden single-handed I have had a go, I believe, at all the ground-covering plants on offer, but now I have narrowed down those I continue to use to very few. Some are evergreen, others disappear for the winter. Chief of these are several of the hardy geraniums but one among them is supreme, *G. macrorrhizum*. It makes a dense carpet about 30 cm (12 in) thick, almost evergreen, and has a big flush of pink flowers in early summer. Another is *G. endressii*, not quite so thick or so dense but its pink flowers go on through all the summer and autumn. Again it is nearly evergreen. *G. nodosum* is one to avoid as it is a prolific self-seeder. Wherever I take on a new patch of ground I use *G. macrorrhizum* for a time, even if later I abandon it. It is no trouble to pull up, and one doesn't even need to plant it in the conventional way. You just make a slit with the trowel and push in a bit of stem. I have never known it become a nuisance.

I have turned my back on the silvery *Lamium galeobdolon* 'Variegatum' which runs everywhere, even up into the shrubs it is meant to carpet. *L. maculatum*, even in its superior forms, seeds itself too wildly. I have the greatest respect and regard for London Pride, using this and other evergreen forms of creeping saxifrage. I specially like one called *Saxifraga geum*, whose leaves turn red for the autumn and back again to green later. As for bergenias they are simply superb. Evergreen, flourishing anywhere, never a nuisance, flowering pink, red or even white in the spring – they have everything as plants to grow between shrubs in self-maintaining areas of garden.

The evergreen pachysandra is excellent, making a dense 23 cm (9 in) carpet, though not much in flower, but it is slow to get going. I use it as a contrast to bergenia, but also lots of the Common Male Fern (*Dryopteris felix-mas*) in the same role.

A little known plant of the greatest value is pachyphragma, a cultivated relative of the Wild Milkmaids or Lady's Smock. About 23 cm (9 in) deep and evergreen, it produces masses of white flowers early in spring and looks particularly well carpeting a bed of camellias.

I have found it necessary to get hold of ground coverers to run between hellebores and some of the special-named kinds of hostas, so expensively bought as they increase so slowly. The one I now like best is a relative of the bramble, namely *Rubus calycinoides*. It hardly rises 5 cm (2 in) from the ground.

Where you want such plants as hardy cyclamen to have the place to themselves in winter and early spring but want to see the ground covered over for the summer, a tiny ornamental rhubarb is excellent. This is *Gunnera magellanica*. It is dense, fresh green and only 2.5 cm (1 in) deep.

So much for the kinds that run about. Now for the clump-formers. I have settled for two. You always want ground coverers that will close over decaying daffodils when they are over. Here two lily-like plants are supreme – hemerocallis and hostas, the first giving flowers of yellow, orange or bright pink and mahogany at midsummer, the other flowers of white or lilac just afterwards. Both conveniently die right away, only to renew themselves in the late spring.

I promise you that with the help of these plants and a few shrubs rising above them, but following the preparatory techniques, you really can make patches of garden that will look after themselves for you and always present a well-cared-for appearance.

Planting for succession

Is there a labour-saving way of gardening which will keep up a succession of colour, really colour effects, in our borders? I believe there is by way of contrived interplanting so that one plant rises while another beside it retires below ground or discards its flowers and has nothing left for this season but its leaves, ready to help the neighbouring plant strengthen the effect it makes in its turn.

Take this very simple example. Oriental poppies flower early in the summer, monkshoods or aconitum later on when they reach up taller. If you had half a dozen plants of the poppies and spaced them out well, then interplanted them with as many monkshoods, it would look as though for one month that patch was filled with the one but later on equally well filled with the other.

Again, say you have built up a collection of day lilies or hemerocallis and put them all together in one part of the garden to flower with abandon during July and August, you would save any dullness in spring if that was where you also planted your daffodils. Someone would come to see you one April day and see the area of garden a mass of daffodils and be surprised to find it filled with day lilies on their next visit. The

Ferns and grasses

Wider experience of growing ferns in small gardens and in borders has shown their tolerance of soil and site. While of course they are seen at their most lush in damp, shady spots, they have also revealed themselves to be plants that can be satisfied with 'ordinary' soil and with places where the soil stays pretty dry for longish summer periods. Even the giant Royal Fern, *Osmunda regalis*, of the permanently damp west of Ireland has been found to grow in such ground.

One of the special appeals of ferns is that many of them are evergreen, and once a gardener has begun to take an interest in them he also finds that almost every species has a number of different forms. And most hardy ferns suitable for growing in gardens are actually members of our native British flora; the forms have been discovered in the wild by sharp-eyed collectors. The Hart's Tongue Fern, *Asplenium scolopendrium*, is one of these and has forms that are either fanged at the tip or waved at the margins. Another is the Common Polypody, *Polypodium vulgare*, whose evergreen fonds can be subdivided several times in the varieties. One of the most prolific with its variations is the British Soft Shield Fern, also evergreen, *Polystichum setiferum*. Again they differ in their degree of complexity, one requiring no less than five Latin names to distinguish it. Among the noblest of the evergreens, however, is of

Chilean origin, *Blechnum chilense*. Other ferns mostly keep to clumps that grow larger year by year: this one spreads by way of underground stolons. While the beautiful and well-named Ostrich Feather Fern, *Matteuccia struthiopteris*, is technically herbaceous, the green leafy fronds dying away in autumn, it makes a splendid winter sight with its stiff, blackish fertile fronds which are present all through the months of bad weather.

Once established in the garden ferns often increase themselves by way of their curious means of reproduction, the young sometimes appearing mysteriously some distance from the parent. To build up the close colonies that will help resist weeds the 'seedlings' or rather 'sporelings', are best lifted and replanted where they are required while they are still young, since ferns are inclined to sulk if they are transplanted after they have become established.

In a border planted for permanent effect with minimal maintenance ornamental grasses do have an important place as accent and contrast plants, especially as some, like *Helictotrichon sempervirens*, are silvery, *Milium effusum aureum* golden, and *Hakonechloa macra* 'Aureola' yellow striped. A few can be used as non-invasive ground coverers and these include the grey *Festuca glauca* and *Phalaris arundinacea*, the striped Ribbon Grass; one of the very few to have a common name.

Polystichum setiferum plumosum

idea can actually be used for one type of plant. Daffodils, of course, come in so many varieties that their season lasts from early February till the end of April. Well, by choosing, say, three types that flower successively and carefully interplanting them with the day lilies you could span the whole season.

Nature is doing this sort of thing all the time. If you watch through the growing months a roadside verge or railway embankment where the wild herbage is allowed to grow as it will, you will see that one kind of plant is always taking up the relay from another. One day it might seem filled with primroses, another with cow parsley, another with ragged robin, and yet another with meadowsweet, each taking its place in an orderly sequence, yet dominating only at its appointed time.

With some planning and ingenuity it is not difficult to apply this to garden borders. The sequence is particularly apt for those borders that are enfilade, from one end. Then it doesn't matter if two plants out together are 1.5 m (5 ft) apart. From that viewpoint they will seem close, and so on down the border if the same plant is repeated several times over. It does mean, of course, restricting the number of different kinds of plants you have in your borders.

By what I have, perhaps a bit pompously, called the transformation scheme type of planting, you can have a strong effect through most of the growing season. Over the years, and it does take some seasons to learn your mistakes and gather your ideas, I have worked at this for the whole of our garden. I am a long way from reaching the ideal but I hope one day to stroll round the garden – perhaps when I can't do much more than that! – and find everywhere at my feet is a flowery patch.

Here's one of the schemes which I have evolved for our little blue and white garden. Four white camellia bushes take their chance on March days but blue primroses start the real flowery season in April, though already some of the giant snowdrops have done their turn there. White daffodils follow and soon it is time for four big clumps of white hardy geraniums. While they are still performing, out come four big clumps of single white peonies. And soon it is time for the four small thickets into which the dwarf mock orange, *Philadelphus* 'Manteau d'Hermine' has grown. Then is the turn of the 'White Bonnet' cultivar of perennial chrysanthemum, to be followed by the hardy agapanthus. Meanwhile, scrambling about over all, though harmlessly, is that extraordinary Michaelmas daisy called *Aster divaricatus*, or *A. corymbosus*, which by the time September comes is covering everything with its white stars. Rising from this groundwork, though, are four little obelisks on which the summer-long indigo *Clematis × durandii* has been trained, and on the same posts for late spring are four plants of *C. alpina* 'White Moth'.

And how much room does all this take up you may ask. This little enclosed garden, where the octagonal beds are edged with silver variegated euonymus, occupies no more than 6 m (20 ft) square, though always something is happening there, in a bold outburst.

Making a tiny garden is a challenging enterprise. Paved areas, containers and raised beds, even a miniature pool can be successfully integrated.

Pelargoniums, helichrysum and artemesia fill to overflowing a large terra-cotta container.

Lately I have created a new woodland path where snowdrops – thousands of them transplanted from elsewhere in the garden where they have seeded themselves and spread – begin the season. They are followed by early rhododendrons in March which are accompanied by a few camellias. As they go over, an edging of ivory tiarella appears, helping to set off the May-flowering rhododendrons. Their day over, it is time for a repeated planting of the raspberry-coloured astrantia which I managed to provide us with by acquiring half a dozen plants and breaking them up. By now it really is summer and there are many astilbes here, soon to be followed by hostas. Then it is time for the hydrangeas to take over, and they in fact continue the succession of colour into October.

Is the principle emerging clearly? You do have to work it out on paper first, watching other plantings besides your own for plants that will maintain a sound succession and flower boldly, not wispily. They also have to be compatible in the ground they like and the site where they are most at home, whether it is sunny or shady. They have also to be fighters that can cope when a neighbour tends to get a bit too close.

Two basics you have to be sure of. One is to hand-weed during the first few seasons. The other is to manure the ground well in advance, just as you would for intensive cropping in your vegetable garden, and then you must mulch to give all the ingredients a real chance to shine. It boils down to this: choose a plant for every month and repeat it in your border until everything is full.

My personal selection of hardy border plants

In choosing hardy perennials one should always watch out for the kind that have a compact way of growing and therefore do not need that staking and tying that traditionally goes with growing herbaceous plants. These kinds are capable of standing up under their own power, but if they do flop in windy, wet summers they do so decorously without making the garden look a storm-rent place as many of the taller growers do when they have become lanky.

All the plants mentioned on the next few pages have been chosen with this in mind and also, with just one or two exceptions, because they can stay in their position for many seasons, as distinct from other herbaceous plants that need lifting and dividing every three seasons in order to regenerate them. By choosing judiciously half a dozen or so plants from this selection you should, indeed, manage to provide successive patches of colour and interest throughout the year.

Aconitum (Monkshood) Shade-tolerant plants with helmet-shaped flowers, usually indigo in colour, and handsome jagged foliage. They usually grow up to 1 m (3 ft) tall. They are especially good in damp soil.

A particularly good form is called 'Bressingham Spire', with almost violet flowers. 'Ivorine' is white but grows only 60 cm (2 ft).

Anaphalis One of the few silvery-leaved plants that will flourish in shade. It can be dry or damp too. The plants make a thick tuft of silvery leaves from which in summer rise stems bearing clusters of papery white flowers, each a complex daisy. These can be dried for winter decoration. *A. triplinervis* 45 cm (1½ ft) is the best one to grow, but *A. yedonensis* reaches up to 75 cm (2½ ft) and is more inclined to spread from a creeping rootstock below ground.

Anemone hupehensis (Japanese Anemone) Really excellent plants that actually dislike being disturbed. The foliage is dense over the ground and highly decorative itself, and the flowers are carried on stems around 1 m (3 ft) tall. The most familiar white one is called 'Louise Uhink', but there are many pinks, notably 'September Charm', 'Bressingham Glow' and 'Krimhilde', to be found in nurseries. While the plants flower best when they get some sunshine, they will also do well in some shade. In either position they will spread into large colonies.

Anthemis A daisy-flowered plant that is generally inclined to 'flower itself to death', so prolific is it. But one kind is robustly perennial in light soil and a sunny position. This is *A. cupaniana*, which has silvery leaves in a tight network over the ground and white daisies early in the summer. Its foliage effect continues over the winter.

Artemisia lactiflora (Wormwood) This is a family of herbs with a pungent aromatic quality. Usually the plants have silvery leaves. This singular member has antler-like foliage in a tight mat over the ground and spires of ivory flowers surmounting 1 m (3 ft) stems, growing in a tight bundle. It grows well in any position, but is found at its best on damp soil and is particularly good to contrast in form with rounded shrubs.

Aruncus sylvester (Goats Beard) One of the largest of hardy plants, growing in a single season to a plant 1.2 m (4 ft) all round, carrying sprays of white flowers in July. It is best on damp soil and will put up with considerable shade. For smaller gardens it has a brother plant in a form called *kneiffii*, in which the leaves are more fern-like and make a plant only half the size.

Aster amellus This is the finest of the perennial asters or Michaelmas daisies. Unlike the others it needs no frequent lifting and dividing. Flowering goes on from August to October, the leaves making a dense tuft. Though the flower stems stand 60 cm (2 ft) tall, they are woody enough to remain upright without any staking, again in distinction to the other kinds. The flowers range from pink to purple but are mostly a mauve colour. The most notable of the group is *A.* × *frikartii* which has proved especially robust. It is a candidate for being supreme among hardy border flowers. Just a Michaelmas daisy, certainly, but no ordinary one at all. It suffers from neither mildew nor mite. It never strays, never needs to be lifted and divided. And it flowers for longer than any other of its kind. July sees it opening. In September it is in its full glory, and then in sheltered places it can even stand witness to the fall of the leaf in October. It doesn't need any of your stakes and twine either. 'King George', violet, has particularly large flowers and is almost equally tough.

Astrantia (Hattie's Pincushion) A group of plants that always arouse curiosity and admiration. Each flower seems like a tuft of big stamens (though in reality they are petals) of a greenish pink colour, and they are surrounded by a 'starched' ruff of pointed bracts, also greenish. They grow around 60 cm (2 ft) tall. Astrantias are usually sold as *A. major* or *A. carniolica*, but *A. maxima* has pink flowers, its form *rubra* with strawberry-coloured flowers. The plants are quite happy in the shade but do need rather damp soil in order to flourish.

Aster × *frikartii*

Astilbe × **arendsii** (Spiraea) Excellent plants for damp places. They do not mind some shade, but flower best when they get sunshine for part of the day. The foliage is complex and fern-like, usually a deep red. The flowers, which appear in feathery plumes in July, are borne on stiff stems 60 cm to 1 m (2 or 3 ft) tall. There are a great many cultivars most of them ranging from white, soft pink and salmon to glowing garnet red, but occasionally a white one is found. This is one of the toughest of hardy plants and endures as long as paeonies do.

A series of dwarfs has been raised which grow to a mere 46 cm (18 in), less if the soil does not get all that wet. 'Sprite' is the best known cultivar with dark red leaves and shell-pink flowers. Other small-growing types are *A. chinensis* 'Pumila' with fluffy mauvish flowers and *A. simplicifolia*. *A. taquetii*, a species from China, is a splendid plant. The foliage stands 1.2 m (4 ft) and the fluffy flowers almost purple in colour show what an astilbe can be like in the wild.

Bergenia (Elephant's Ears) The common name in this case comes from the rounded, leathery leaves which the plant produces and which it carries all through the year. The pink or red flowers come quite early in the spring. Some of the cultivars turn their leaves red in the autumn and this coloration persists through the winter. It is most notable in one called 'Sunningdale'. Richest flower colour is found in 'Evening Glow', but in default of this try to get 'Ballawley'. 'Silberlicht' has white flowers. While these plants which originate from Siberia will all grow well on stiff clay, they also thrive on poor soil, even along the bottom of

Bergenia cordifolia (see also page 144)

hedges. Sun and shade are all one to this plant, too. In a garden planted to save labour you cannot have too broad a patch of any of these varieties of bergenia, or even the common ones, *cordifolia*, soft pink, and 'Schmidtii', paler.

As for increase, propagating the bergenia is as easy as making new irises. Just above the ground the plant makes the same sort of woody rhizomes which in turn root into the soil on which they loll. Break a bit off with two or three roots and you have a new plant.

Brunnera macrophylla (Caucasian Forget-me-not) A spreading plant 15 cm (6 in) deep with good weed-resisting foliage and sprays of blue flowers 30 cm (1 ft) tall in spring. It grows well between shrubs and on any soil, even land that remains damp most of the year. It is best in shade, when the leaves give the most effective cover.

Campanula (Bellflower) Of the huge family of plants a mere handful are acceptable as reliable easy-going garden plants. One of the best is *C. glomerata superba*, with rounded heads of purplish flowers early in summer and a dense 30 cm (1 ft) spread. While this is easy to divide and make more of, the other excellent kind, *C. lactiflora* 'Prichard's Variety' 1 m (3 ft), cannot be divided and will endure planting only in spring. Nevertheless, it is a long stayer with deep mauve flowers in summer. *C. latiloba* 'Percy Piper', 75 cm (2½ ft), is a refined form of an otherwise coarse and invasive plant, with deep blue flowers. Another good one of the same type is 'Highcliffe'. Some of the rock garden campanulas can be used as border plants in the foreground of shrub plantings, notably *C. carpatica* and 'Birch Hybrid', both with rich blue flowers.

Centaurea (Perennial Cornflower) While the blue-flowered member of this family, *C. montana*, is a most invasive weed, *C. dealbata*, with bright pink flowers, is a most desirable hardy plant, especially if it can be obtained in the 'John Coutts' form. It has most attractive silvery leaves and large cornflowers throughout the summer. In rich soil this plant is inclined to spread rather invasively, but on light soil and in sunny positions it deserves high marks. The yellow *C. macrocephala*, while liking the sun, is good on all types of soils. Its flowers are like giant thistles and appear in early summer. Take care when it is not in flower, though: it can easily be removed in mistake for a dock.

Coreopsis verticillata This is the sole member of its well-known genus which can be relied on as being truly perennial. Its flowers are like golden stars, its leaves feathery. It spreads well though not invasively and soon builds up into a large clump covered with bloom on 60 cm (2 ft) stems throughout the summer. While it is not particular about soil, it does like a sunny place, as do most daisy-flowered plants. A cultivar called 'Grandiflora' is rather larger in stature.

Dianthus (Pink) There are many cultivars of pinks which are suitable for growing in the forefront of borders, provided they get the full sun and the soil is light. Here they will make year-round tufts of silvery foliage and the flowers come either in a big burst in late June or appear sporadically all through the summer and autumn. Of the latter group the best kinds are the pink 'Doris' and crimson 'Thomas', each with a deeper zone of colour at the centre of the flower.

One tip about keeping them in good health. Plants that have it in them to go on flowering as long as these will, can 'flower themselves to death', as gardeners say, or at least into a decline. So about the end of September it is best to put a stop to their season by pinching out the flower buds. Like the carnations they can also do with a little feeding up from time to time, again with the same fertiliser used for nourishing roses in their beds. I also favour putting bonfire ash round both types of plants from time to time.

Dicentra (Bleeding Heart) Beautiful plants with fern-like leaves and locket-shaped flowers of pink or light red. Growing to 60 cm (2 ft) and the most easily obtained kind is *D. spectabilis*, flowering in June, but a hybrid from it called 'Bountiful' has deeper pink flowers and continues to flower all through the summer. The plants thrive in moist soil and in lightly shaded positions. Take care to mark where they are planted with canes, as they die away completely below ground in the autumn and are not seen again until the following spring, leaving no traces.

Doronicum (Leopard's Bane) One of the earliest herbaceous plants to flower, opening its yellow daises in April or even in March in sheltered places. It is also one of the few daisies to put up with shaded positions. Any soil suits it, and after flowering the plants continue growing outwards to form large weed-free mats. The most familiar kind is *D. plantagineum excelsum* or 'Harpur Crewe' which has single flowers on stems of 45 cm (18 in), but a double form which lasts in flower much longer is called 'Spring Beauty'.

Epimedium (Barrenwort) Excellent ground-covering plants with very pretty heart-shaped leaves of bright green often marked with chocolate. The flowers are small and yellow or pink but are produced in very dainty sprays. However, it is the foliage mat which counts, this lying 30 cm (1 ft) above the ground and becoming absolutely dense and weedproof in time. Patience is needed, though, before they spread into broad clumps. All kinds offered in garden centres are worth growing – and planting in any position and on any soil. They are first-class plants for setting between flowering shrubs to make self-maintaining areas.

Erigeron (Fleabane) Mauve-flowered daisies whose 60 cm (2 ft) stems spring from a tight mat of leafy growth. They like the sun and fairly light soil, where they will grow compactly, but on heavy soil they become too lush, 'Darkest of All' is near-violet, 'Foerster's Liebling' near-pink. When it can be obtained 'Elstead Pink' is a very good dwarf kind, spreading out particularly well over the ground and flowering for many summer weeks.

Euphorbia (Spurge) A group of most valuable ground-covering plants with greenish-yellow flowers all blooming in early summer. For the rest of the year they are evergreen. Best ground coverer is *E. robbiae* 45 cm (18 in), with greenish flowers, but *E. polychroma*, 38 cm (15 in), is more yellow and makes a most imposing weedproof clump. A dramatic, architectural plant, *E. wulfenii* grows to 1 m (3 ft) with an equal spread and looks more like a shrub. Its great plume of yellow flowers lasts for many weeks. While this one is best in sun, the other kinds do not mind the shade and though the leaves have a glaucous hue, which usually indicates a liking for light soil, they all do well on heavy land.

Geranium Not to be confused at all with the scarlet geraniums grown in summer flower beds. The hardy kinds can be left out the whole year, and these are valuable spreaders. In fact, for a labour-saving garden they are some of the most useful of all perennial plants. Most rampant grower, but not difficult to eradicate if it spreads too far, is *G. macrorrhizum*, which has pink, rose or white flowers in early summer rising on stems 45 cm (18 in) from a 30 cm (1 ft) deep mat of dense aromatic foliage. Scarcely less strong growing is *G. endressii*, with pink flowers throughout the summer and autumn, and having still more complex leaves. A good blue one is *G. grandiflorum*, 45 cm (18 in), flowering from June well into August, but 'Johnson's Blue', also 45 cm (18 in), makes a greater burst of colour in late June. Also blue, *G. wallichianum* 'Buxton's Blue' does not flower till late summer, and while the others spread perennially this one dies back every year to a tight rootstock and grows out to form a 1 m (3 ft) circle every year in late spring, standing only about 23 cm (9 in) high.

The 60 cm (2 ft) geranium seen in purplish flower in early June is *G. magnificum* (*ibericum*), and the familiar magenta one seen in bloom all through the summer is *G. sanguineum*. From this has come a hybrid name 'Russell Prichard', which is a much more pleasing plant with carmine flowers which continue through most of the summer.

While all these will grow in shade they flower best in positions where they get sun for part of the day. They are not fussy about soil either, and are especially valuable for planting in places where the soil is very light or of poor quality. Thus they will spread right over the rooting areas of flowering shrubs, steadying up the growth and also preventing weeds.

Gypsophila Though the tall-growing kinds which are traditionally grown for cutting to put with sweet peas in summer are not reliable hardy plants, one member of the group is. This is called 'Rosy Veil', a spreading plant reaching hardly more than 30 cm (1 ft) high, but in a single season growing out in a circle a metre or so across. Through the summer it is covered with light pink flowers. Must have a sunny place and light soil.

Helleborus (Hellebore) The famous Christmas Rose, *H. niger*, can be a somewhat disappointing plant. It rarely flowers at Christmas and can suffer from Chocolate Spot disease which somewhat debilitates it. However, its close relation *H. orientalis*, the Lenten Rose, flowers reliably every year from late February into April, producing its exquisite flowers in clusters. They can be varying shades of dull red, pink, yellowish green or white and have remarkable weather resistance. The leaves stay on the plant much of the year and help to make a weed-defying barrier. The average height of the flower stems is 38 cm (15 in). These are plants that like heavy damp soil and shade, but once they are established it does not matter if tree and shrub roots stray beneath them, for they are natural woodland plants although they will also adapt to a sunny position.

Helleborus orientalis, the Lenten Rose

The Corsican Hellebore, usually named *H. corsicus* but sometimes also called *H. argutifolius*, is a more imposing plant, standing nearly 60 cm (2 ft) high and each year in February producing a huge cluster of greenish yellow flowers above superbly sculptured leaves. These do not die down until there is another set ready to replace them, and thus the plant has all the appearances of being an evergreen shrub. Again it is good on heavy soil and in the shade.

Both these hellebores seed themselves freely once established, so that it is possible to make large colonies of them very easily. The same is true of our native hellebore, *H. foetidus*, an unhappily named plant whose common name of Stinking Hellebore should never be allowed to put you off. In foliage it is most beautiful, being deeply divided into several toothed leaflets. Its pale green flowers, each marked with a deep red rim, appear in late winter.

Hemerocallis (Day Lily) These rank with the hardy geraniums as some of the finest of all no-work border plants. The leaves are rush-like and very tightly packed in the clumps which spread freely. The flower stems rise to about 1 m (3 ft) and are surmounted by trumpet-shaped flowers that last but a day but are followed on the next day by another crop, this succession continuing through late June and July into August. The flowers come in many colourings ranging from pale yellow to mahogany, and there are many copper shades and even some of a pink tone.

The plants are almost indestructible and can be moved or divided at any time of year, just by chopping pieces off them with a spade. They will do in light shade but the best displays of flowers come when they are grown in sunshine. However, they do not mind what soil they are planted in. Traditionally they are grown on damp ground by water, but light soil gardeners find that the plants adapt themselves to this sort of ground quite well, though not growing quite so lush there.

Heucherella 'Bridget Bloom' A dainty plant with sprays of pink flowers on 45 cm (18 in) stems through most of the summer. Likes light soil and light shade. The leaves form a dense mat over the ground.

Hosta (Plantain Lily) Another absolutely indispensable plant for helping to avoid work in keeping the garden tidy. The leaves are magnificent, often deeply etched by their veins and sometimes variegated. Though small, the flowers are of lily form and are mauve, purple or white. The plants range in height from 30 cm to 1 m (1 to 3 ft), and the leaves spread out densely. Every known kind is worth planting. It is a wildly proliferating plant. Many species are being introduced from its native Japan where it is being hybridised on a large scale resulting in newcomers with more strangely variegated leaves than those already in general cultivation. Hostas look best in shade, flower longest here and also grow best. While they are usually considered damp and heavy soil plants, they will flourish on any ground and can be divided at any time of year by chopping off pieces with a spade and replanting them. Although they die right away in the winter, they return every year in late spring.

Iris Selective breeding has produced a wide range of irises in many colours with flared falls (front petals) and an overall sophisticated elegance. There is a movement away from the tall bearded irises towards the intermediate forms which instead of reaching up to 1 m (3 ft) tall stand a mere 45 cm (18 in) or so. A miniature race which doesn't exceed 30 cm (1 ft) provides a pleasing ground cover – I particularly admire 'Green Spot', 'The Bride' and blackish blue 'Chieftain'. All irises increase very rapidly and should be divided in July after flowering. Set them just below the soil surface. They enjoy light soil and ensure a sunny position so the rhizomes get baked every year for health and good flowering. If the tips of the foliage turn brown after flowering, chop off the top half of the leaves at an angle.

Iris pallida 'Dalmatica' is a plant I value highly and looks well in clumps along the forefront of my twin borders. It has light mauve flowers. *I. foetidissima*, the Gladwyn iris, is planted not so much for its flowers but for its scarlet seeds which are revealed as the pods burst in autumn. This is a true evergreen growing to 45 cm (18 in). It tolerates most situations and will seed itself most usefully, too. The Algerian iris, *I. unguicularis* shows its pale mauve flowers in midwinter. In order to do this it must be given a warm, sunny place by a wall so that its rootstock is well baked in summer.

Kniphofia (Red-hot Poker) Dramatic plants for an isolated position. It must also be sunny and preferably on light soil. All kinds generally on offer in garden centres are worth planting where something standing 1 to 1.2 m (3 to 4 ft) high in summer can be accommodated. However, recent seasons have seen the appearance of a race of dwarf red-hot pokers which always seem to win the hearts of those who meet them. Unfortunately, they are not quite so robustly hardy. What they must have is sharply draining soil. This at once puts them among the plants with which those who garden on gravel and sand, and always complain about it, can excel. It also means that these kinds make admirable tub plants.

These are usually seen about half the size of the red-hot pokers we know best. Indeed, they are rather less dramatic than the big ones. However, the colour range has been widened, running from ivory through pale yellow and gold to amber tints. It also includes greenish shades.

Lamium (Dead Nettle) While the cultivated form of the Wild Arch-angel, *L. galeobdolon* 'Variegatum', which has handsome silver-marked leaves, is a plant to be planted only on banks which have to be covered permanently; several of the dead nettles are highly attractive plants, some runners, others clump-forming. However, they are extremely vigorous spreaders, so be warned! Of the latter class *L. maculatum*, purple and a less strongly growing pink form, are worth setting among shrubs to spread over the ground. They flower throughout summer and into autumn. Both have leaves striped with white. *L. garganicum*, pink, and *L. orvala*, rose flowers in early summer, make tufts of foliage and are much more restrained in growth. Some flowers appear in shade but more in sunshine.

Ligularia These are large-leaved plants for moist soil with huge deep yellow daisy flowers, making an imposing sight beside water, where they form clumps 1 m (3 ft) high and as much across. 'Gregynog Gold' has green flowers, while both 'Othello' and 'Desdemona' have leaves in which the green is shot through with purple. *L. przewalskii* 'The Rocket' produces distinctive spires of yellow flowers.

Limonium latifolium (Sea Lavender) Essentially a plant for light soil, where the cabbage-like leaves spread flat over the soil and the stems rise to 60 cm (2 ft) and carry broad heads of tiny lavender flowers. It must have sunshine. The flower heads not only last for many weeks but can be dried for winter decoration.

Liriope muscari Said to be a light soil plant but actually flourishes anywhere except in deep, damp shade. It has grassy leaves like a daffodil's, which grow into thick clumps and remain all the year. In autumn it produces spires of deep blue flowers resembling the Grape Hyacinths of spring. An ideal front-of-the-border plant.

Lupinus (Lupins) These well loved country garden flowers which bloom in early summer, should not be eschewed just because of their bulk and for the fact they are soon over. I suggest you grow them at the back of your borders between spring-flowering shrubs. There, provided the 60 cm (2 ft) high spikes are removed, they will keep weeds at bay and provide a flattering background for later summer flowers. Where do they grow well? Any sort of soil, even where the going's lean. I recommend 'Joy', orange; 'Thundercloud', violet; 'Harvester', peach; 'Fireglow', orange and gold and 'George Russell', pink. New shoots from the base of the plant provide cuttings in spring. These quickly root in sandy compost in a frame. Seeds will germinate readily if sown in a box of peat-based compost in summer.

Lychnis chalcedonica (Jerusalem Cross) One of the very few scarlet-flowered hardy border plants. It grows 1 m (3 ft), the flowers appearing in rounded heads on top of the stems in summer. Likes sunshine and light soil. Does not spread much but is valuable for rising among low shrubs, like evergreen azaleas, on which it can loll if damaged.

Lysimachia punctata (Yellow Loosestrife) A rampant plant but a pretty one that will grow anywhere, though it has a special liking for damp soil. The yellow flowers appear in spires and last through the early summer. Takes hold resolutely, so plant it only where it can be allowed to spread as it likes.

Lythrum salicaria (Purple Loosestrife) Though a natural waterside plant, this will flourish in any soil, provided it has a fairly sunny position. There are several cultivars, all growing around 1 m (3 ft) and standing almost as wide when fully grown. The pink flowers which appear through most of summer surmount the many stems in plumes. The brightest cultivar called 'Fire Candle' is a very deep rose and 'Robert' is bright pink. 'The Rocket' is deep rose again but a less bright shade than 'Fire Candle'.

Monarda (Bergamot) An aromatic plant that is best in sun, though it will thrive in light shade, but in any soil that is not waterlogged. The curious shaped little flowers appear in circlets in summer and are pink, red or purple according to cultivar. The leaves make a mat over the ground and are very dense in texture, and the stems rise 60 cm to 1 m (2 to 3 ft) according to the position, carrying the flowers at the tips.

Nepeta (Catmint) Aromatic plant that is usually rather rampant in its ordinary form *N. faassenii*, better known as *N. mussinii*. It likes sunshine and well-drained soil, where a single plant will spread to 1 m (3 ft) across in a season, standing about 60 cm (2 ft) high, but it dies back to a central crown in the autumn. The flowers are light violet which tone very well with the greyish mass of foliage. *N. nervosa* is a much more restrained plant, only 1 ft high and half that in spread. The flowers are indigo. Both are in bloom through much of the summer.

Paeonia (Paeony) Splendid plants whose only weakness is a short flowering season. Nevertheless, their foliage is strikingly handsome, often having a reddish tinge. Growing about 75 cm (2½ ft) tall, the plants flower in June, each bloom having a most opulent appearance and silken texture. The flowers can be single or double, while others have a strangely complex centre due to some of the petals being quilled. There are many cultivars, ranging from white through innumerable pinks to deep red. While they flower best in sun, they will grow well in light shade, though all must have rich, deep soil.

Phlox Favourite cottage garden plants that flower in August and have a refreshing if nostalgic spicy scent. The flowers come in rounded clusters at the tips of 1 m (3 ft) stems that rise from a tight clump of foliage. The plants like rather damp soil and the flowers last longest in light shade, as they are often scorched in strong sunshine. Many cultivars ranging from white to purple.

Physostegia (Obedient Flower) Its common name stems from the way in which the individual flowers on the spike stay in any position to which they are pushed. *P. virginiana* has amethyst-coloured flowers on 60 cm (2 ft) stems, but is rather inclined to spread freely. 'Rose Bouquet' is more clump forming and a brighter colour. There is also a white, 'Summer Snow', flowering in late summer. All thrive on any soil, but are best in sunny places.

Polemonium (Jacob's Ladder) The arrangement of the leaflets along the centre leaf rib suggests the common name. The flowers are usually lilac or mauve, saucer shaped, and come in early summer, the stems standing 45 cm (18 in) tall. The foliage makes a tight clump which is very weed resistant. Bed them in sun and in light soil. On heavy ground the plants are inclined to rot away in damp winters.

Polyanthus No matter how long delayed, our chilly springs prove to have no perils for our polyanthus. A few flashes of belated sunshine and out they come with the daffodils. And what a show they give! The lustre of the present day polyanthus's colouring is one of the sophisticated delights of a garden in spring. It is a long way removed from the pale tint of its ancestor, the humble wild Primrose. April is the time of year to look over the polyanthus you have already and mark any especially

Gold-laced polyanthus are enjoying a revival in popularity

good colours for propagating by division. When the flowers are finally over you can lift the clumps on a wet day and simply pull them apart. Then you plant the pieces for the summer on a patch of spare ground where they are going to be shaded perhaps by a row of runner beans. Provided you work in plenty of peat and feed with general fertiliser they will grow into fat clumps for another season.

Personally I do not like the pink and the orangey shades together. In our garden I grow yellow, bright red and orange kinds together in one area, blue in another, pink and soft reds together in yet another enclosed patch. However, I also have a planting of the old gold-laced polyanthus which have a golden edge to each of the flowers and which I divide up every year to preserve the vigour of the strain, as you have to with the rare double primroses.

Polygonum A family of plants which includes some ineradicable weeds so all kinds have to be regarded with reserve. Nevertheless, a few are valuable garden plants for areas where they can be left to spread. One of the best is *P. amplexicaule* 'Atrosanguineum', a 1.2 m (4 ft) plant with dense leafy growth and spires of deep red flowers for many weeks in late summer. Of the same height, *P. campanulatum* has pink flowers through most of the summer and autumn, the self-supporting stems rising from a tight mane of growth, again reaching 1.2 m (4 ft). *P. affine*, in its 'Darjeeling Red' or 'Lowndes' cultivars on the other hand, is a flat-growing plant with little spires of red flowers through the autumn. It is excellent ground cover. All grow in any soil, but flower best and are least rampant in the sun.

Potentilla (Cinquefoil) While this is usually known as a shrub, there are a few herbaceous kinds which flower in the late summer and are sufficiently strong growing and dependable for planting in the forefront of spring-flowering shrubs. Growing to 45 cm (18 in), *P. recta macrantha*, often called 'Warrenii', has bright yellow flowers for many weeks in summer, while another called 'Philosa' has pale yellow flowers for a long time. Both have very pleasing foliage.

Prunella Several plants related to the wild 'self-heal' which invades lawns are good garden plants, largely for ground covering, but flowering in the late spring. The favourite is 'Loveliness' with lilac flowers, and this in turn has both white and pink flowered forms. *Prunella webbiana* has rose flowers. All stand about 20 cm (8 in) tall when in flower, but for the rest of the season are almost flat.

Ranunculus (see also page 164) Though this family includes the buttercup, several kinds can be grown in damp soil beside water. Best is *R. acris* 'Flore-pleno', with double yellow flowers in branched heads standing 60 cm (2 ft) high. *R. bulbosus* 'Speciosus Plenus' is similar, but a little less than 30 cm (12 in) high. Both flower best in sun. Mark carefully when planting as the leaves are very similar to those of the ordinary Creeping Buttercup, and can easily be weeded out in mistake for it.

Rheum (Ornamental Rhubarb) Looked at for its sculptural quality, ordinary culinary rhubarb is highly decorative, but two kinds are worthy of places where their architectural forms stand out in relief. Both have the characteristic foliage. *R. palmatum* 'Rubrum' has reddish leaves and very handsome flower stems 1.5 m (5 ft) high produced in late spring and summer. The earlier flowers of *R. alexandrae* are produced in spires instead of rounded heads as in the other case and they are yellow instead of red. Best in shade and damp soil, but will grow anywhere.

Rodgersia Grown mostly for their handsome foliage, these plants, their flower heads can be very decorative and last for many weeks. They grow to about 60 cm (2 ft). All must be grown in moist soil and shade suits them best, for their fine leaves are inclined to be scorched in the sun. *R. aesculifolia*, *R. pinnata* and *R. podophylla* have roughly similar leaves like those of the horse chestnut tree, but those of *R. tabularis* are large and round.

Rudbeckia (Cone Flower) While most members of this group are too tall for labour-saving gardens and need to be staked, several grow to only 60 cm (2 ft) from a dense clump of foliage and spread well. Best of all is 'Goldsturm', but other good ones are *R. speciosa* and *R. deamii*. All have deep yellow daisy flowers, each with a chocolate coloured cone at the centre. They will flourish in any soil, but are best in sun to be sure of a big crop of flowers through the late summer and autumn.

Salvia (Sage) The ordinary culinary sage is classed as a shrub, but there are several kinds with similarly aromatic leaves and flowers which are actually herbaceous plants. Though most of these are either biennial or need very light soil, *S. superba* lives up to its name. It is a robust perennial that flowers in July and again a few weeks later if its first spent flower spikes are trimmed off. It produces a tight clump of leaves and the stems mostly stand about 60 cm (2 ft) tall. Best is 'East Friesland', a compact grower with violet flowers. 'May Night', not found so often, is an even deeper colour. The plants must have sun and are best on lightish soil.

Saxifraga umbrosa (London Pride) This good-tempered plant is excellent for setting in the forefront of shrubs, even on poor soil and in shade, where it can spread as far as it will. It can cover large areas with evergreen foliage and produce a cloud of pink flowers in the late spring.

Every rosette of leaves pulled off an existing patch can be made to grow into a new plant to build up large colonies.

Scabiosa caucasica (Scabious) Essentially a plant for light soil and sunshine. The cultivar that has survived generations is 'Clive Greaves', producing its mauve flowers on wiry stems, through much of the summer. However, on heavier ground, but still in the sun, you can grow the crimson kind with smaller flowers, *S. rumelica*.

Scrophularia aquatica 'Variegata' One of the few variegated-leaved plants, apart from the reeds, that will do well in damp soil. Grown only for its foliage, in a season it makes a plant almost 1 m (3 ft) high and as much across. The silver leaf colouring is most pronounced in sun, but it will flourish in light shade.

Sedum (Ice Plant) A splendid group of plants for sunny places. Most familiar is the 30 cm (1 ft) high *S. spectabile*, with silvery leaves and flat heads of carmine or bright pink flowers in the late summer, when they prove most attractive to butterflies, which are constantly found on them. Because its leaves are fleshy and silvery, this suggests it has a preference for well-drained soil, and for an open sunny position. In fact the soil doesn't matter, provided it doesn't get waterlogged, but a place in the sun favours flowering and gives the best leaf colouring. These days there are three superior forms of this species, named 'Carmen', 'Brilliant' and 'Meteor', all of which have rich-coloured carmine flowers. A more robust plant is 'Autumn Joy', about 45 cm (18 in) high and with tawny flowers in the late summer.

Sedum maximum 'Atropurpureum' is valuable for its fleshy purple foliage, growing about 13 cm (5 in). This goes well with bronze, copper and yellow flowers. It is rather floppy but is exactly the thing to have to loll about among plants of these other colourings. With these too, one can effectively plant *S. telephium* 'Munstead Dark Red'.

Sidalcea This mallow-like plant makes a tight clump of rounded leaves and in July and August has 1 m (3 ft) stems set for much of the way up with saucer-shaped pink or red flowers. There are many varieties and it is one of the best kinds for making a show of flowers and excluding weeds with its leafy growth. It does not mind damp soil, and will grow almost anywhere, though it has most flowers when in a sunny position. Much to be preferred to hollyhocks, which are unreliable, for a cottage garden effect.

Sisyrinchium striatum One of the few dependable hardy plants with pale yellow flowers. These are produced in spires in early summer on plants with grassy leaves which grow very densely to about 45 cm (18 in).

Sisyrinchium striatum

8
Bulbs for Year-round Interest

Hardly has the year begun before somewhere in the garden there are bulbs on the move, an assurance that nature knows no close season really. And with the first perceptibly lengthening days come the first flowers. Indeed, true gardeners – the highest praise it is possible to bestow in the reckoning of some – make it their ideal that never in the whole year, not on any day, should they step out into the garden and fail to find something in flower. Of course, in January it is the snowdrops, at least in the more sheltered spots under trees and beneath hedges, such places demonstrating their natural warmth by the fact that snow seldom lingers long there. Plant a dozen and in fewer years you can have a thousand.

Spring is proclaimed by the daffodils making an opening of their two months' season. The first are the smallest, as though a little bashful about blaring their trumpets. And the last are the well-loved so-called Poet's Narcissus, the Pheasant-eyes. But in between comes a cavalcade of flowers that change almost with the days, there are so many of them – large trumpets, small-cupped kinds, white, lemon and even pink, some with orange cups, and even some of a rose-tinted buff shade. There are doubles with tousled flowers that suggest old prints, others so stylish that they could hardly have been created by nature. But they surely have an excitement of flowers that seem to join hands in wild celebration that another spring is here, another year of promise only waiting for fulfilment at the gardener's hand.

However, before I get too carried away, let us not forget the practicalities involved in order that we may enjoy the beauty of bulbous and cormous plants, season by season.

Bulbs for spring

Get the holidays over, families off home again or back to school in September, and it's time to plant the bulbs as well as start the autumn clear up in the garden. Nothing to be gained by hanging about.

Bulbs, in truth, are neatly wrapped-up parcels, containing leaves, stem and flower all packed close together and only waiting for the sun, the moisture and the longer days to release them. There is no need to plant in direct sun. Some kinds will flourish and flower without it.

The three chief kinds of plant in shade are snowdrops, winter aconites and narcissi – and that includes daffodils. To specialists narcissi and daffodils are one and the same family of plants, but to gardeners daffodil implies a narcissus with a long trumpet. All the other bulbs you are likely to encounter or want to grow really need sunny places. If they are to flower again another year they must get their bulbs ripened by the sun during the late spring, after they have done flowering. You must remember that they had their origins in places like Turkey and Greece, Spain and Portugal, where they get baked during the summer. Under the right conditions some of the bulbs will seed themselves freely and this, of course, is aided by the sun, though it must be said that snowdrops seem to be able to seed themselves quite well in the shade. In fact, if you notice, they drop their seed pods while they are still green.

An investment One of the important things to realise about bulbs is that when you buy and plant them you are actually making an investment. They increase so readily by making more of themselves each year and thus building up clumps. The bulb season starts in January with the snowdrops and continues until early June with the very last of the tulips, the flamboyant Parrot-type that makes such a strong appeal to flower arrangers. But the really big show comes during March and April, when most of the crocuses come, to be followed by the daffodils. By crocus, most of us mean the large-flowered Dutch type which you see in public parks, but actually there are many more which flower earlier and actually increase more freely that are known, though among them are actually many cultivars.

Perhaps the brightest blue bulb of spring is the little Glory of the Snow, or chionodoxa. The blue is emphasised by the white eye each flower has. Again it is a prolific self-seeder, a handful producing a galaxy in a very few years. You also get especially free seeding from *Anemone blanda* and *A. appenina*, which can always be relied on to increase naturally, provided they are given places where they get the sun and the seeds have the chance to ripen off fully in the late spring. They have starry flowers lying on ground-hugging hummocks of ferny leaves. Sometimes they are mauve, sometimes pink or white. Again they disappear completely soon after their flowering days are over.

In few gardens do you ever see much of the Snakeshead Fritillary, *Fritillaria meleagris*. It gets its common name from the strange regular way in which the flowers are marked with mauve and black, though sometimes you get green and white ones from the self-sown seedlings. It was once a native bulb growing in damp meadows. Now it's almost

Fritillaria meleagris, the Snakeshead Fritillary

died out, though you should experience no difficulty in buying bulbs. Given the damp place it enjoys, it will grow 23 to 38 cm (9 to 15 in) tall with several 4 cm (1½ in) long bells per bulb. Quite a different looking plant, *F. imperialis*, the Crown Imperial, with flowers of orange or yellow, is one of the most dramatic of all bulbous plants and deserves a key spot in the garden where it can make its strongest effect. Since it insists on both sun and well-drained soil, it makes an unusually fine tub plant.

Leucojum vernum, the Spring Snowflake, looks like some giant snowdrop that has strayed out of its season, for it does not flower till April. It grows well between herbaceous plants that come into leaf a little later and is not fussy about the ground in which it is planted. It increases well, too. Erythronium, or Dog's Tooth Violet, comes in several forms. There is one called 'White Beauty', but there are yellow and mauve kinds also. Valuable for shady areas of the garden, preferably a bank where they can be raised up a little to show off their engaging Turk's cap form.

The best value in tulips, if you want kinds that will flower well one year and again and again in the future are two dwarf types, known as the *kaufmanniana* and the *greigii* type. They grow hardly more than 30 cm (1 ft) high and have really lovely colourings. Usually each carries two colours in sharp contrast. The centres of the flowers can be very pretty too, another good reason for planting them in the sun, where they open their flowers wide. However, if you want to build up garden colour schemes the better kinds with the greatest variety are the early-flowering tulips, which come out in April and grow about 45 cm (1½ ft) tall, and the Darwins, which are in bloom in May and grow 60 to 75 cm (2 to 2½ ft) high, thus suiting them for planting in rose beds to get a second display from the same patch of ground.

Planting late The planting time for bulbs can be quite upset by the weather. You can just hear those old gardeners who did everything on time muttering about, 'What it's all coming to' – as though anything ever did come to anything. They would religiously have put in their bulbs by halfway through September, daffodils by early October, tulips soon after. But changes in the weather cause changes to be made in that routine. These days all our springs often seem to be wet, our autumns dry. Often you cannot get a trowel into the ground in September – on some land you would have to use a mattock to make the hole.

Experience shows that you can get away with planting many kinds of bulbs even as late as early November and still get good flowers from them. The limiting factor could be the wetness or dryness. One is disinclined to plant when the soil is sodden. But in truth you can make a hole in wet soil with a trowel, put the bulb in and just lever the soil back over it again. Nature will do the rest. After all, you can grow just about any bulb, can't you, with its roots dangling into water?

I would not, thought, reckon to plant snowdrops as late as October, nor Dog's Tooth Violets. These two will have lost too much of their natural moisture from their miniature bulbs to do much in their first year, if they survive it. To buy a cheap job lot would be taking a chance. But crocuses have it in them to last in good condition, so do daffodils, and as for tulips the Dutch themselves will tell you that November is as good a planting time as any.

I have known daffodil bulbs planted in woodland just by flinging them about like the sower going forth to sow. Never mind whether they fall the right way up or not. Somehow they produce roots and grow. However, good bulbs cost money. They deserve something better than cavalier treatment. If one does just have to plant when the soil is far from right, then it would be well worthwhile making a hole for each and putting a handful of moist peat in the bottom. If you really want to reap the full reward of your investment you want to scatter the ground liberally where you are going to plant them with a slow-acting fertiliser. For this bonemeal is the easiest to come by.

Position for best effect What are the best places for planting bulbs that you are in a hurry to get in? It's best to plant the earliest flowerers close to the house where they can be seen from the windows. Then you will get full value from them. I would even go so far as to say line the path from the road to your front door with the earliest bulbs. Then you really will enjoy them. Don't worry about the after effects. It is in the nature of the earliest arrivals to retire gracefully very soon afterwards, leaving no untidy leafy growth behind them. Not like those April-flowering grape hyacinths whose leaves stay there in the way until well into June. Crocuses of all kinds, but preferably the large Dutch cultivars, will go well in the forefront of borders. I have had some come up year after year at the base of a lavender hedge. Their foliage is soon gone.

I have learned that daffodils and narcissi look best in patches of at least a dozen of one kind, and that they do well between herbaceous plants and shrubs. Though I now regret the many yellow daffodils I once planted between camellias. Even if one did have a munificent win, caution in such matters would be advisable. Now I hate the bright pink of the camellias out with the gold of the daffodils, and hasten to cut the latter. But it would be all right if they were white ones. I don't regret the 200 'Thalia' narcissi that in a wild moment once went in between all those bright pink Japanese azaleas. If they are out together one enhances the other. Another thing experience, the best tutor though you never recognise it early enough in life, has taught me about daffodils: don't plant them in view of a window that the sun strikes directly. It will strike the daffodils too. It will make them all face it; drawn by its compelling force they will turn their backs on your windows, a very important matter when you admit that it is from there that for the most part in the spring the garden is enjoyed.

I have long ago given up growing daffodils in grass. Their leaves go on so long that the grass is growing up, the weeds with it, and seeding well before you can safely dispose of the foliage. This is such an important practical point for the welfare of bulbs: you must give the leaves time to die naturally if you want to see them thrive and flower again.

Tulips – where's the best place for them? Well, if you don't have the formal beds which are changed with the seasons – and a deep enough pocket to pay for a new lot of bulbs every year, the labour too to keep lifting and planting them – I am sure the best places are bays in borders with mixed plantings of hardy plants and shrubs, and in rose beds. Of course, in the latter case you have to be mightily careful not to damage the roots of the roses as you thrust in the trowel or you can start up the vile process of suckering. But here the bulbs can rest year after year, flowering again if they will, or perhaps not, when nothing is lost and you are not disappointed by a bare patch. The dwarf *Tulipa kaufman-niana* and *T. greigii* types will have five or six seasons of flowering life.

Be careful, too, where you plant muscari (Grape Hyacinths). These lovely blue flowers look wonderful in the mass in spring, but their leaves are inclined to persist somewhat embarrassingly into the early summer. However, a position as an edging to a rose bed is a good place for them, especially as they increase well from their own offsets rather than seed far and wide like crocuses and snowdrops do.

Those enchanting little bulbous irises are plants for really well-drained spots in the garden where they can get well and truly ripened. But you could hardly say the same about the scillas. These grow anywhere in the sun, the ordinary *S. siberica* seeding itself very well indeed, its superior cultivar 'Spring Beauty' lasting in flower for six weeks but never producing a seed.

Snowdrops Now snowdrop collecting has become something of a sophisticated gardening cult in recent seasons. Some collectors buy one bulb at a time and increase it in pots of peaty soil in a frame, rather than commit it to the ground right away. But the truth must be told that a snowdrop is a snowdrop, and the points of distinction between those the collectors seek out, paying considerable prices for, and those the rest of us like to enjoy in masses are fine indeed.

Masses – that's how you want to have your snowdrops. Break yourself over it and never buy less than a hundred, even though they may increase so very readily. Then you can spread them about the garden prodigally. At least, within sight of your windows for a start. Later on, as you divide the clumps, you can spread them further and further away until one day the whole garden, as you look out on it on a February morning, seems full of them – and spring will certainly not be very far behind at all.

How deep to plant? If you want to be orthodox you will take a trowel and make a little hole for each one, burying it a few centimetres down, more if it is a snowdrop. Who has the time or the patience? And is it necessary? No! Not at all. In Holland, where their very lives depend upon them, they scatter their small bulbs and then rake them in. After all what happens if you inadvertently leave a few small bulbs on the surface? They grow, don't they? Well then, I reckon a jolly good idea is to place them on the surface, if you cannot believe that they will come the right way up of their own accord, and then cover them with a layer of peat.

Crocus Only in the full sun will crocuses open their flowers fully, even on chilly days, and reveal the brilliant orange organs within. Indeed, they span the whole of the spring weeks, from the time when it seems more like winter to when those premature summery days arrive. There are hundreds of crocuses, if you count the varieties into which the many species have subdivided themselves. Fortunately, to avoid the confusion that results and which experts ponder long over, only a mere handful are available from the average bulb dealer or the local garden centre. The early ones, however, must be clearly distinguished from the more familiar big Dutch type which come out with the daffodils. The others are altogether smaller and often slender in outline.

The most prolific self-seeder is *Crocus tommasinianus*. Every season it sets and ripens seed which is scattered on the four winds to every crevice where it can lodge. Mice may be fond of the corms of crocuses in general but this one defies them by its sheer numbers. In February wherever it is planted the days are surely enlivened by its silver-lilac flowers in great masses. Hardly any leaf enhances the flowers but this makes them seem all the more abundant. Not until the flowers are over do the leaves grow up, and then they are there for very few weeks. Quickly they die away, and then for the rest of the year *C. tommasinianus* leaves no trace of itself. Its deeper coloured cultivar, 'Whitewell Purple', saves its charms until early March.

More bluish in colour, *Crocus sieberi* follows hard on *tommasinianus*, and seeds well, while *C. biflorus*, palest mauve but striped with a deeper colour, accompanies it. For a very early yellow you can go to *C. ancyrensis*, the flowers appearing in tightly packed bunches in February or even January in sheltered places. All these are quickly followed in early March by the cultivars of *C. chrysanthus*, the flowers blue and white in 'Blue Bird', shiny brown and yellow in 'Zwanenburg Bronze', white in 'Snow Bunting', yellow marked with brown in 'E. P. Bowles'. This is the chief one for making clumps. Nobody need hesitate to plant these in grass, since their leaves last such a short time that they do not hamper early mowing as daffodils do.

Daffodils and narcissi The different cultivars and species come out separately between early February and the end of May, many cultivars overlapping. This at once indicates the error of mixing daffodils: you just don't get that good show altogether. Those that are going over mar the effect made by those just opening. If you plant never less than ten bulbs of one cultivar of daffodil and you were planting a hundred bulbs which would mean that by interplanting cultivars you could get daffodils from late February until the end of May.

Now it happens that the earliest daffodils are some of the best kinds for leaving in the ground to increase every season. They are derived from a species growing wild in Spain and Portugal called *Narcissus cyclamineus*, but this does not mean in this case that they want dry, rocky positions. They increase very well under trees in quite heavy soil. The three cultivars generally available are called 'Peeping Tom', 'March Sunshine' and 'February Gold'. They differ only in the degree to which their petals – technically the perianth segments – are swept back, instead of at right angles to the trumpet.

At the other end of the season comes the pheasant-eye type, typified by the robust cultivar 'Actaea', with pure white perianth and reddish cup. In between come a vast number of daffodils and narcissi differing in the size and the colour of their trumpets or cups. Some particularly pleasing ones have pale yellow perianths. The doubles are a growing number, with more cultivars being sold each season. To some they are frankly grotesque. Others regard them as old-fashioned and charming.

A special word must be said for the white daffodils 'Mount Hood' and 'Mrs E. H. Krelage'. 'Ice Follies' is a particularly fine all-white narcissus, while 'Thalia' is one with small flowers in pairs. Most bulb dealers also sell the pink trumpet daffodil, really an apricot colour, 'Mrs R. A. Backhouse'.

When planting daffodils, don't overlook the miniatures among them. They're so delightful. *N. cyclamineus*, mentioned above, is a dainty 10 to 20 cm (4 to 8 in) high with swept back petals and so tiny it needs planting in colonies of 50 or more for a striking show. *N. bulbocodium* and *N. triandrus albus* are the other most commonly planted miniatures, though there are many less familiar ones, mostly worth trying.

The dainty Hoop Petticoat, *Narcissus bulbocodium*

Broken tulips and parrots Tulips make up a vast family, the stems varying from a few centimetres to 1 m (3 ft) tall, the flowers often in proportion. Their colour range is greatest of all bulbs and gardeners can use them as a painter's palette. Broken, breeder, bizarre and bij-bloemen, Rembrandt and parrots – the Dutch have certainly coined some odd names for their groups of tulips. But then there is much that is odd about tulips. No other flower has ever inspired the mania that gripped the Dutch in the century after the first wild tulip was brought from Turkey to Europe.

No other flower has made anything like the same fortunes for its breeders and dealers than the tulip did in the 17th century, when houses were mortgaged and possessions sold to buy the bulbs. One single bulb of one variety is reported to have been sold for 4,600 florins and a coach with two dappled greys.

Now the tulips that aroused the frenzy, this madness that ruined some and enriched others, were actually suffering from a virus that can cause streaks and featherings of a different colour that have led to the so-called 'broken' tulips. Disease it may be, but it does them no harm. However, it was catching in one sense. So much so that it reached the little mining and industrial villages in the vicinity of Derby. There in the early 19th century a mini-tulipomania gripped the artisans of this district who bred broken tulips by the hundred. Half a century ago Sacheverell Sitwell, whose home was one of the great houses of the region and who investigated it, was able to trace relics of this activity but I fear that all the cultivars then raised have since disappeared. They remain a sadly sentimental record in his book *Old Fashioned Flowers*.

Broken tulips have a close affinity with the type known as parrots, for these have flowers that are strangely marked with a contrasting colour, usually green as in their best known variety 'Fantasy'. But they have more than this. The flowers are not only big and composed of waved petals, but at the margins they are deckled as though someone had been at work on them with dressmaker's pinking shears. With the others you have to take what you get in a mixed lot, but each of the parrots has been given a name of its own. There are 'Orange Parrot', 'Black Parrot' and 'Blue Parrot'. There are red and pink cultivars, all with the same strangeness of form and colouring.

But parrot tulips have a secret life of their own. They are sports that have appeared ready grown, as it were, on other tulips. They have been noticed in the tulip fields and propagated from pieces of tissue rather than seeds. Grow them in kitchen garden rows specially for cutting for the house as they are not tulips for massed planting. One of these blooms can inspire a flower decoration, especially as the heaviness of the flower head twists and bends the stems into strange shapes and the looseness of the petals allows them to fall about in that sweet disorder that makes the Old Master flower studies so affecting.

Besides, if you grow them in this way it makes the process of lifting, drying off the bulbs and replanting in autumn after summer storage that goes with tulip growing a much easier business than it would be if they were grown in flower borders with other plants. And once you get to know them you really will want to cherish the bulbs for another year and propagate from them.

Cottage tulips and viridifloras What is a cottage tulip? None can tell you. It's just a group into which a whole lot of tulips are put which flower late in the season, have somewhat pointed petals and which defy classification into any other section just because of their variety. Of course, they are not green all over. They simply have green woven into their colourings. One viridiflora tulip in a tall champagne glass on a dinner table would make a talking point that could far exceed the courses. There is one called 'Artist', perhaps most complex of all, for the salmon and pink colouring merge to make a terra-cotta tint which in turn merges into the green flash that runs through each petal. 'Greenspot' takes my eye too, parti-coloured in green and white, while in 'Groenland' rose takes the place of the white, and in 'Formosa' yellow is combined with the green. Sometimes one catches sight of one called 'Pimpernel', and, yes, it is red and green.

There is a striped group of tulips called Rembrandt type, for they are the kind depicted by the Old Masters. The greigii series of tulips, which grow only 30 cm (1 ft) tall, are notable for the chocolate-coloured markings on the leaves, a direct legacy from their wild ancestors. Unlike many other kinds these can safely be left in the ground to increase and flower again in successive seasons. In the fosteriana series the flowers are tall and especially flamboyant. They can look out of scale in the ground but come into their own when they are grown in outdoor containers, a role which is also well suited to the early double tulips, which have the longest flowering season of the family. The elegant shape of some kinds of tulips has earned them the collective name of the lily-flowered type. These also are especially good for flower arranging. Tulips grown for this purpose are best planted in short rows on a spare plot, perhaps in a small piece of kitchen garden.

Some tulips have double flowers, and these are the best kinds to grow as tub plants to precede the summer-flowering plants like geraniums to be planted in them later. Double-flowered tulips tend to remain in flower longer than any other kinds though they do not offer a wide colour range. Fortunately they are all short growing.

The tulips most commonly available and with the greatest colour range are the so-called single earlies and the 45 to 60 cm (1½ to 2 ft) tall Darwin type, which are the tallest. They follow in succession. While they are not dependable for a second season's flowering if left in the ground the best way of treating them is to snap off the spent heads as soon as flowering is over and lift the bulbs just before the foliage has completely died down and store them for the summer months. Then replant the largest bulbs in the autumn.

An elegant lily-flowered tulip

Summer-flowering bulbs

The main difference between the bulbs that are planted in spring and those put in during the autumn is the rate at which it all happens. You can plant in April and have them in flower a couple of months later – at least some of them. The spring-planted kinds differ, too, from most other summer-flowering plants in that they need hardly any soil preparation. In this, of course, they show their kinship with some spring flowerers. But where do you plant the summer-flowering bulbs when in spring the garden already seems full with fresh new growth? Well, take gladioli for a start. The very best place for these is in rows between vegetables, where you can cut them for the house by the armful.

Next best is patches in the foreground of spring-flowering shrubs or in mixed borders. Here they are of special value to anyone making a new garden, just because in their very first season they will give as good a performance as they ever will. Gladioli are particularly good value because for each corm you plant in spring you will be able to lift two in the autumn to store for another year. Only if you like to grow flowers for show, or if you 'do the flowers' for the church, are you likely to want to use the large-flowered gladioli these days, now that it is possible to get miniatures in such a wide variety of the tall but delicately formed butterfly type. These two are the best for borders and for cutting for the home.

Particularly good for border groups are the Cape hyacinths, or galtonias. They make stately spires of white, hyacinth-like flowers of great beauty and elegance which slip most elegantly, and conveniently, among hardy border flowers in a mixed planting. Of course, given their origin they need a light soil and a sunny place. Indeed, their origin makes it astonishing that they should flourish in our gardens at all. In gardens on light soil they grow again a second year, but elsewhere have to be lifted and stored like gladioli or dahlias.

The acidanthera has white flowers (maroon at the centre) and is an Ethiopian species of exquisite beauty when seen against an evergreen background. No bulb, spring or summer kind, flowers for as long as the Chincherinchee does. Correctly this is called *Ornithogalum thyrsoides*, a close relative of the ordinary Star of Bethlehem, *O. umbellatum*. It has the same white flowers, though on spires a metre tall.

Liking a hot, dry position, are the tigridias, some of the most vivid flowers you could ever grow in your garden. They have somewhat triangular blooms, brightly coloured and sharply zoned with contrasting colourings. In their vividness they are matched by the sparaxis, taller growing to 75 cm (2 ft), while tigridias are only half this height and no good for cutting because they last but a day, to be followed by another show of flowers the next morning. Sparaxis, on the other hand, last for several weeks.

What about the ranunculus, too? These are the rosette-like flowers known from the bunches that appear in florists' shops in spring, having been flown from the south of France. But it is perfectly possible to have them in your own garden in summer, too, if you plant the strange claw-like tubers in spring, giving them sun and soil drainage.

Ixias, or the African Corn Lily, wait until early summer before coming into flower. Their colours are strong and vivid, immediately suggesting the garden position they enjoy – a place in the full sun where the soil is particularly well drained. The bulbs are on the tender side and need a winter covering of leaves or peat.

Have you ever seen a crinum bulb? All 60 cm (2 ft) of it? If you haven't you could hardly believe it existed. It's as big as one of those great leeks vegetable specialists put on show. But when it begins to grow it's even more alarming. The great strap-like leaves reach 1 m (3 ft) long, and there's not just a few of them but a great thicket of lush green. At last, in the late summer comes the flower. It is carried in bunches of half a dozen or more on thick stalks 1 m (3 ft) tall. A majestic trumpet it is, a flourish of trumpets in fact. They can be deep rose pink, or they can be white, always waxen and so surprising.

You would make a mistake though, if you were not very careful about where you would plant it. If you wanted to move it how would you get it up? Nor would you need to for the crinum can indeed stay where it is put. Until not long ago I used to visit the nursery where *C. × powellii* was first planted in this country in 1893. There are other species but this is the only reliably hardy one, a hybrid between two South African species. It was still there, having grown to a clump 2.5 m (8 ft) across. Then it had been planted close to a greenhouse wall. Subsequent experience has established that it needs just a warm spot in the sun with something behind it to keep off the colder winds. Then this handsome great thing will outlive anyone who plants it and delight all who are lucky enough to see it at its supreme moment.

Crinum × powellii

Lilies in shrub borders What effect do you get from a shrub border once the spring is finally over? What more than shapes and leaves while you are waiting for the autumn colour? Even then many of them are evergreen and go on just the same. One answer, perhaps the best of answers, is to add some lilies to them. Most lilies flower in June and July, giving a great burst of astonishingly splendid blooms and equally surprising perfume during the warm months of summer. In every way they are fitted to grow among shrubs. In the first place they are not very good at holding themselves up in open positions. They need something to loll against. Far better that than tying them to stakes. Left to themselves, to use the odd shrub here and there as a prop, they assume positions and outlines of an elegance that matches the delicate pre-Raphaelite quality of the flowers.

They like the soil moist but they like it to be well drained. They like to have their flowers in the sun but the roots in the shade. Which is exactly what positions between shrubs will provide them with. The roots of the shrubs will help to drain away from the soil the surplus moisture that will readily rot them if it lies about them for long.

By their own leaf fall and the layers of humus-forming matter that are wisely put between them from time to time, shrubs help to build up that woodland-like soil round them which is exactly what lilies enjoy most. Without it they can flower and flourish for a year and then appear no more.

Propagating lilies

Once I started with half a dozen bulbs of the tall orange-yellow *Lilium henryi*, then after six or seven seasons when I happened to be forking round them one day I prised some up and discovered I now had a hundred for replanting in what became a really bold colony when all they previously had given was a spotty effect. Of course, when I bought them I could have pulled off several of the outer scales from each bulb (1) and put them in a polythene bag of soilless compost based on peat, closed the top and hung them up in a light window. After about three weeks roots would show through the polythene, and when these are about a couple of centimetres long (2) pot up each new little plant separately (3). In a frame for a season they will become new lily bulbs to be planted out the following spring.

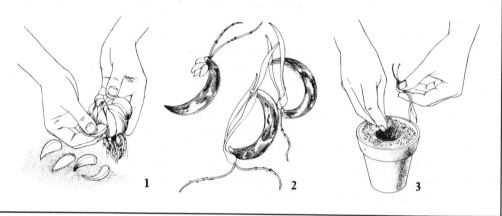

There is much talk about stem-rooters and surface rooters. In truth it is academic, for the Madonna Lily, *Lilium candidum*, is about the only lily you are likely to have to worry about not planting too deeply because it produces its roots from the base. This one you hardly have to cover. But then the late summer is the time for planting it. All the others that you buy in the garden centres and through mail order during January are lilies that do root from their stems, as well as from the base of the bulbs.

Thus you want to give them a covering over the tops of the bulbs of about 10 cm (4 in). More than that if you live on light soil, certainly, but if the ground is on the heavy side you would not be wise to put them any deeper than this for fear of their getting too much moisture. Then increase the depth at which they lie gradually with helpings of peat or leafmould, or perhaps composted bark when you can get hold of it. This technique really will help to build up the right woodsy soil in the shortest possible time.

One of the best kinds is the old and handsome *Lilium regale*, as white as a lily should be save its golden throated and plum-coloured flush, and heavily scented. Both *L. henryi* and the hybrid called 'Maxwell' are reliable, good increasing orange-yellow sorts. And of course, there is a fine tiger lily, *L. tigrinum*, in its various forms, which has orange flowers. All grow around 1.2 m (4 ft) tall.

From these you move up into a higher price range. Exceptionally good value can be had from *L. umbellatum*, a low lily only 75 cm (2 ft) tall, best in its hybrid of close parentage called 'Enchantment'. These give upright-looking orange flowers. If you think these too hectic sounding, then you probably like the pink and crimson-marked kinds of the white *L. speciosum*, a most elegant lily which is often grown in pots.

Of course, they can also be used where herbaceous plants are mainly of those kinds which wait for the early autumn days before they begin to flower. Thus you could compose three-season borders with shrubs for spring, lilies for early summer and hardy border plants for the declining days of summer and autumn.

What is most important about planting is not to leave the bulbs hanging about. They are only too ready to lose much of the moisture content and then fail. Plump, fresh bulbs are the ones that grow readily.

Alliums If for 'allium' you were to read 'onion', you would be doing these beautiful bulbous plants a very poor service. You would be much more just to them if you were to read 'lilies'. For this is what alliums are botanically. But not lilies that are fussy about soil, insisting on lots of humus in the ground. Although they like a well-drained site just the same, with the perverseness that possesses quite a few plants, the alliums actually enjoy the going when it's tough. They would quickly perish on wet soil with their roots perpetually cool and moist. For these are native plants of the Mediterranean region where they are used to growing on soil that has hardly any humus in it, where the sun beats down on them for weeks at a stretch. The wonder is that they thrive in our gardens as easily as they do. Indeed, some seed themselves about freely once you have established them.

One of the things that you should also know about them is that they do take a long period of rest every season. So don't worry if you notice the foliage quickly becoming scruffy at some point. It can wither in a matter of days. But always it leaves behind it the stem with plenty of seeds in the round heads, a little like onions or leeks that have gone to seed. And indeed, these two everyday plants are certainly members of the big allium clan. This disappearance of the foliage means that you can tuck the bulbs in among other plants that come into flower after the alliums, which are usually in bloom in late spring and early summer. The seeds are almost always viable. Catch them before they fall and sow them in a box of light soil compost.

The round heads of the flowers come in various tints of yellow, pink or mauve but there are a great many species and all are different. They range from tight little heads the size of a greengage to great things nearly as big as a beach ball.

As a footnote don't forget the common garden chives. If these were always known by their botanical name of *Allium schoenoprasum* you wouldn't find them in a vegetable garden at all. And if they didn't grow so freely they would be highly prized in flower gardens. As it is all you get nowadays is the odd clump outside the kitchen door. Once upon a time, in the day of big kitchen gardens they were planted as neat little edgings to the vegetable beds. They had to be taken up and replanted every two or three seasons. But what did that matter when labour was so cheap and so abundant? Even so, the idea isn't at all a bad one. The plants are evergreen, staying there the whole year round, and in the late summer you get masses of these charming purplish flowers. Another idea would be to grow them in bays in a flower border, perhaps interplanted with some of the smaller spring bulbs.

Autumn-flowering bulbs

No one who has not already tried them can believe that bulbs which you put in during July or early August really will flower a month or so later. Most of them are dependable flowerers too, the one exception being the sternbergia. It insists on a place in the sun. Give it half shade and it fails to flower, even though it may go on growing. Give it anything but light soil and it may rot off in a wet winter. Plant it later than the middle of August and it may show the same sort of resentment.

Happily sited, though, and planted in time, it is superb. It produces golden goblets that stay there for some weeks in September, not like the fleeting crocuses of spring. For indeed, crocus-like it is, though botanically it is classified with daffodils and is therefore a member of the amaryllis family. All very confusing.

In fact, the whole naming of these autumn-flowering bulbs seems tangled. Two other types, the autumn crocuses and the colchicums, are both referred to commonly as crocuses. The former are crocuses all right and belong to the iris family, while the colchicums in fact belong to the big lily family. Both look much the same, the colchicums seeming simply to be bigger versions of the crocuses.

Colchicums and autumn crocus If you were to look a bit further though, underground in fact, you would find that the true crocuses have corms which last a year, then perish but leave behind them replicas of themselves. On the other hand, a colchicum bulb gets bigger year by year, producing offsets also, which in turn go on season by season.

This behaviour of the bulb has an important practical upshot for gardeners. So many young do the crocuses proper produce after a time, so thick do the patches become, that you have to make sure to plant them only in places where their foliage which lasts from spring till midsummer is not going to be a nuisance, slender though it is. A patch of grass that does not grow too strongly will do, perhaps a rather dry part where the grass always looks a bit pinched. Colchicums, as befits their lily status, want the going rather richer. Their foliage by contrast is lush and broad. You can plant in grass that grows rather strong, but you have to cut round them in early summer, at least until the leaves have half withered.

For my own part I have the crocuses growing in plantations of rhododendrons where because of the leafmould put round them nothing much grows, and I hand weed from time to time. But the colchiums I have in places where I have carpeted the ground with rough and endlessly forebearing ground coverers which do not suffer when the colchicum leaves flop on them. For this purpose I have found the cultivated nettle, *Lamium maculatum*, suitable, also that marvellous evergreen ground coverer with white strawberry flowers in spring called *Potentilla alba*.

No connoisseurs of bulbous plants deny that the colchicum called 'Waterlily' is the most handsome. Its name so well describes the lilac flowers. However, over many years now we have every season enjoyed the flowers of the ordinary *C. autumnale*, which I believe is still wild in some parts of Britain, and which I once bought on a market stall. They are single and mauve too, but produced in great numbers.

One called *Colchicum agrippinum* is especially nice to have for the flowers of white and purple are chequered like a fritillary. If we are voicing flower similes we should say that the handsome 'Lilac Wonder' has flowers like those of a magnolia.

To talk of a yellow colchicum is more academic than practical, for you could go all through your gardening life without ever seeing it. It is called *C. luteum* and when you know of its Kashmir origin, this indicates that it wants careful placing – well-drained soil with enough humus in the ground to encourage it and enough richness to nourish it, the sort of position you would find for some rare lily. As of course it is!

The books will tell you that autumn crocuses are wild plants of Eastern Europe but I have certainly seen them in the Western Alps, not in little patches either but growing in great drifts that from a distance look like a sheet of glistening mauve. I must have started with not more than a dozen corms of the one called *C. zonatus* but actually named by botanists now – and in some bulb catalogues – *C. kotschyanus*. Today whenever I weed anywhere near the spot where they went in I find I lift corms. There must be thousands growing there. And in autumn they really do make a sight. I admit that in the spring when the leaves are there I sometimes think these are a bit of a nuisance, but the foliage doesn't last long above ground and you can be tolerant for a few weeks.

Another kind which I find almost equally prolific and therefore very good value to buy is *Crocus speciosus*, which is a deeper and bluish mauve when in flower. I have heard tell of a white form of this, which would be well worth having, but it can't be such a free grower or it would appear more often in bulb catalogues.

Others wait until October before they open. This is where those with more unpronounceable names come in. There is *Crocus goulimyi* and *C. karduchorum*. Each has a flower of pale lavender. There is even one kind that is so reluctant to bloom that December is here before it opens. This is called *C. laevigatus* 'Fontenayi'. You could say that in this case the colour of the flower almost approaches violet. In view of its tardiness, it is a corm to plant in some sheltered spot where the frost is not going to get it. You want to put it in the shade of an evergreen, within view of your windows.

Amaryllis For a single bulb of *Amaryllis belladonna* – one of the most musical of all plant names! – you may have to pay quite dearly. What do you get for it? A big bulb that will increase year by year so that after a few seasons you have a clump. Flowers in the autumn that have a delicate spring quality as though they are too frail to take what this season may bring. Pale rose pink, they are carried in big clusters on the tips of stems that rise leafless from the ground.

For what happens is that the leaves that have spread over the ground all through the spring and summer wither and shrivel as the autumn approaches, as though they were dying, or at least as though that was that for one season. When they have almost disappeared the flower stems rise, reaching 45 cm (1½ ft) in days. Then the flower, wondrous thing that it is opens.

Where? In a sheltered place and in well-drained soil. Some growers reckon to put the tops of the bulbs 15 cm (6 in) down, right out of the way of frost. Those with a little more understanding of the mysterious ways of plants halve this, knowing that then the bulbs get more of the ripening influence of the sun in summer and flower more certainly. Winter cold may come and freeze the soil deep, the bulbs with it – unless they have a bit of extra covering. But this is easily and effectively provided by a blanket of the autumn's fallen leaves. They may freeze on top, but when have you failed to move them with your foot because they have been been frozen tight to the ground? Not often, and unlikely on the south-facing border in the lee of a wall or fence which the bulb likes.

Cyclamen Late summer is the time when the corms, as they are usually but mistakenly called, of the hardy cyclamen appear in the shops. (In fact they grow from tubers which last from year to year.) Two of these will often bloom soon afterwards. Well, the one species of these that comes out in the autumn is that generally known as *C. neapolitanum*, though correctly it should now be called *C. hederaefolium*. This second name is rather better for it, since it indicates the ivy-like shape of its foliage. But it would have to be variegated ivy, as the leaves are beautifully marked with silver. They appear after the flowers and last through the winter and spring, dying away in summer, so this is a valuable bonus. The other autumn cyclamen is called *C. purpurascens*, but this is a much less reliable plant. It certainly has a scent, which the other lacks, but it does not self-sow in the free way that *C. neapolitanum* does.

When you buy these tubers, always look for the rudiments, leaves and buds at the top of the tuber. They should flower in their first year. Otherwise you may have to wait a season, though this would be well worth it. The position? Plant *Cyclamen neapolitanum* anywhere, even in dry shade, while *C. purpurascens* prefers a place in the sun with moister soil. Given these situations the chances are that they will outlive anyone who plants them, provided the squirrels don't get them!

Nerines Everything about nerines seems a bit unreal. They sell the bulbs in the autumn and the spring, sometimes at intervals through the winter. You plant them and see no more of them for months and months, certainly not until the following autumn if you put them in during say October; taking a couple of seasons to settle down.

They came originally from South Africa but instead of planting them deep so that they are protected from the cold in our climate you have to set the bulbs with the tops poking out through the soil. When they have made up their minds to flower they hold back until the late autumn, and then they go on flowering into the winter. October and early November is nerine time. The leaves come after the flowers have gone and they die away in late spring.

You might think that their place of origin would have made them vulnerable to cold and wet, but the flowers actually have a resilience that enables them to put up with as much as we usually get around that time without suffering damage. So late in flowering, they seem determined to show what they can do then. So do the bulbs themselves. Leave them to increase in their own good time and way and you will soon have a hundred where you planted ten.

And the flowers themselves – they certainly look as though they had been made, not grown. They are just about the nearest thing you could have to artificial flowers raised in the open. As lilies botanically they are trumpet shaped but small and have half a dozen or so bunched together at the top of a 45 cm (1½ ft) stem. The segments that compose the trumpet are divided from one another and turned back, while they are also frilly at the edges. They look as though they had been cut by hand from crepe paper, especially as they glisten as if the frost was lying on them.

As for the brightness of their pink colouring, that looks pretty artificial too. Quite right, then, that nerines should require a position in the shelter of a sunny wall: they would look out of place in anything but a rather formal environment.

We are talking, of course, of *Nerine bowdenii*. For though there are many nerines – the name commemorates a classical sea nymph – this is the only one that is hardy enough for outdoor growing in the less cold parts of the country. It does need a sunny place and one where it is not going to get frosted easily. And that is something that can unfortunately happen unless you take care to cover them over with some fallen leaves or peat some time during the late autumn.

Naturally, as a South African it likes the soil to be well drained, but it's always fun sorting out the places in a garden where this or that will grow. As the nerine in flower has no leaves of its own, you could well carpet the ground around it with some other plant, for this will enhance its appearance and help a bit in the essential winter protection. If you want something that will come out at the same time, try a carpet of the deep blue hardy plumbago, *Ceratostigma plumbaginoides*. Or, spreading more readily is the carpeting bugle called *Ajuga* 'Burgundy Glow'. This has the characteristic shiny foliage and spires of blue flowers of the wild bugle in late spring, but each leaf is a little tapestry of green, silver and pink, making it a highly decorative plant.

Schizostylis Another South African plant which will flower brightly in English gardens on a dull November day is *Schizostylis coccinea*, commonly but less often called the Kaffir Lily. Such is its desire to please, that neither our weather nor our soil can daunt it. A pity, then, that it does not have a more romantic botanical name instead of one that merely derives from the Greek indicating that the column of the flower is divided into three parts. The flowers, which can be pink or terra-cotta red, are like gladioli and the plants themselves grow like clusters of giant chives. The only firm demand they make of you is that they should be given a place in the sun. Otherwise they will grow practically anywhere, though one should resist the idea that they might like a dry spot. In fact, they seem to grow better in damp ground. Here they grow into broad clumps that should be divided up every few years in the early spring to make sure they go on flowering well.

Schizostylis coccinea, the Kaffir Lily

9
Small Gardens and Patios

'The size of a garden has very little to do with its merit. It is merely an accident relating to the circumstances of the owner.' That's about as far as the quotation from Gertrude Jekyll goes when it is repeated, as it often is. But what she went on to say, more significantly though in rather muddly prose for her, is: 'It is the size of his heart and brain and goodwill that will make his garden either delightful or dull, as the case may be, and either leave it at the usual monotonous dead-level, or raise it, in whatever degree may be, towards that of a work of fine art.'

Well, making a really small garden approach a work of art involves much tearing at the heart as the brain has to take over, and if it was goodwill towards all plants that she was referring to, then I'm afraid a great many favourites have to be passed by on the other side. For choosing intelligently for a small garden includes turning your back on many of those you would most like to include. Reticence must rule. One must be reticent in the number of species planted and those that are chosen have to be the more reticent kinds, not the cascaders.

But here's a consoling thought for small-scale gardeners. In the early spring you see so many forsythias in the roadside gardens as you go about, so many flowering cherries, in the summer so many different kinds of roses, in the autumn so much hectic leaf colour ... why, if you can enjoy them there, be so possessive about them? Why not restrict your choice to the kinds of plants you don't see everywhere else?

If you've just moved into a new house that's got only a very small garden or if you find yourself with an old property whose ground falls a long way short of your dreams, forget about the odds against you and think only of the special opportunities it offers.

In the first place you'll be led into thinking up ways of making it attractive – through the whole twelve months of the year. For the scene you create there will be brought very close to your windows and within view the whole time. For another thing, you probably won't have a lawn to mow and to worry about but you'll have the chance of making pleasing patterns with paving to form a garden feature in itself. You'll also be able to grow plants in big pots, tubs and urns. In these you can often be successful with plants that wouldn't have too good a chance in the open ground. Frequently they are kinds that have to be kept out of harm's way from slugs or need sharply draining soil, which is easy to manage in a tub. Because they're so close you will want to make the most of the walls or fences, choosing for them the climbing plants – or those responsive to being trained on them – that will make the most effect either with their flowers or their evergreen foliage.

Making a tiny garden can be a challenging enterprise, largely because you have to choose very much more carefully than you do for a large plot. It calls for a lot of judgement, balancing one idea against another, and for the exercise of some special skill, acquired from observation and practice, in looking after the plants encouraging them in some cases and curbing them in others.

Do away with your lawn

You can tell what's coming from the shamefaced look that spreads over the countenance and the hesitancy that at once says, 'I don't quite know how to tell you this, but ...'

'Very well, then I'll say it for you: you've torn up the lawn and put it all down to concrete. And I don't blame you. You clearly couldn't go on with your ideal of a lawn like a golf green in that little patch. Everything was against you ... the drainage, the surrounding trees, the worms, the moss, the poor soil, the kids bringing in their friends to play. What else could you do in the end but change it all from soft surface to a hard one?'

I've had a conversation like this so many times. I know gardeners of enthusiasm and erudition who have been driven to despair by trying to keep even a tolerable lawn in a 'town garden', as the house agents would describe it. To others it would be a backyard. But even so it can be someone's dream of heaven. And truth to tell often the most suitable plantings for a town garden are the esoteric woodland plants that are rarely seen, if at all, in our famed, flowery country gardens.

Strangely assorted companions though they may be, woodland plants and paving look made for each other when you see them together. I have carried in my heart for long years now the memory of a little garden I once knew in London where the paving would have done credit to a Mediterranean villa and the plants were all lush and cool. And so many of them, all different. Yet it measured only 5×3.3 m (17×11 ft).

Paving can be pretty when it is imaginatively designed and skilfully laid. Just as some gardens are built up on their paths which take the eye on imaginary journeys out into the countryside beyond the boundaries,

so little backyard gardens – 'patios' in the marketing language of house agents – can be built up on their paving. These can be highly decorative features in themselves. Ideas are what go to make good gardens, as well as soil and plants. Imaginative ideas can transform the meanest patch into something that will always draw your gaze to it and away from the despiriting environment made by the backs of other buildings.

The word patio has widened its meaning. From the shady enclosed courtyard with a fountain in the centre surrounded by potted plants, such as you glimpse through the grilles of doors when on holiday in Spain, it has now come to mean any paved area on to which you step from the house. It implies a terrace as well as a courtyard, or even just a small garden. But its features are the same.

Usually it will have three walls, if not four, but they will still be a home for climbing plants which can drape them, even though they may rarely see the sun. For there are climbers for all situations, and some of the kinds most suitable for north – and east-facing walls have the most interesting foliage. Here there is scope for making use of the wide range of climbing roses which flower the summer through and for the even bigger range of clematis which can often be encouraged to grow jointly with the roses.

The paving should be soft and sandy in colour, though perhaps set in panels outlined with hard bricks to help make an attractive pavement. Mixed colours in paving, as well as random sizes, are seldom as smart as when one colour is used with the slabs all the same size. A patio is essentially a place for relaxing in tranquility. The simplest way of making a pleasing pattern with paving is to use the same material in

A 'woodland' corner in a shady town garden

175

different sizes. You could lay perhaps four squares in the centre, then surround the square formed with slabs half the original size, then more square ones, and continue in this fashion until the ultimate surrounding area where the flower beds are to be made is reached. More complicated would be to make panels of reconstituted stone slabs by enclosing each group of four in bricks or some other kind of stone. However, it is always best to work with a module so that you don't have any awkward areas to fill in.

Points to success It's a romantic idea to lay paving stones on a layer of sand overlying soil and 'grow' things between the cracks. This may look nice, but if ease of maintenance is your aim you will not achieve it this way. Much better to lay each slab on a weak cement mix and tamp each level with a log. Underneath the slabs there should be an ample depth of rammed hardcore – 23 cm (9 in) at least – and this should be 'bound' with finer stony refuse. Only then should the paving stones be laid. Each should rest on five blobs of cement, one in the middle and the others at each corner. Then it is easy to tamp them down one by one so that they are all even and, with the hardcore making sound foundations, don't settle so that the area becomes distorted and perhaps dangerous. The cracks can be grouted with more cement.

The paved area should not lie perfectly level, however, but follow a slight tilt so that rain quickly runs away leaving no puddles so it can be used in damp weather. This also serves the purpose of draining surplus water quickly from the big pots, urns and tubs which, will undoubtedly have to be installed as final embellishment.

Ideas for creating interesting paving schemes using several materials can often be gleaned from noting carefully the pavements in pictures of fine works of architecture. There's nothing wrong in copying and adapting. Wren himself took classical buildings as his models and Palladio got his ideas from Greece too! Paving stones, bricks and cobbles can all be woven into the pattern that forms the open area of a patio; when using cobbles try to get flattish ones or bring the cement in which they are set for firmness close to the tops. Otherwise they are most uncomfortable to walk on, even dangerous in wet weather.

Introducing plants Old stableyard setts can be sunk into the soil to make a floor with coarse grass growing between them. A rotary mower set high could then be run over the area from time to time without fouling the blade. I have seen this used to great effect in a small patio associated with weathered boulders, and the odd spreading shrub to soften them, the whole giving a rather Japanese effect. Boulders can be as interesting in outline as the shrubs themselves and will change in colour with the light and dampness of the weather.

The soil in back yards is often poor and badly drained. The best way of dealing with the problem, and at the same time creating a much more interestingly designed overall scheme, is to build low retaining walls where the flower beds are going to come and then fill in with fresh soil bought from a garden centre. It usually comes in polythene sacks that are clean and easy to handle. As you fill in mix in damp peat or Forest Bark to help give the new soil body and hold the moisture, as in their early days raised beds can be too well drained.

Any change of level, however small, adds interest to a tiny garden, so if the site is flat or slopes only very slightly, variation of contour can be achieved by making a platform which is little more than the depth of a brick.

Tubs and containers

Growing plants permanently in pots is a sort of fantasy that derives from gardens in hotter places than our own, which are always embellished by potted plants standing in the open air. The practice here derives from the age of the Grand Tour when noblemen went abroad as part of their education and not only picked up fine pieces of classical sculpture and antique furniture but also ideas for the development of their estates. Soon they were building orangeries like the ones they saw in Italy. Even there it was too cold in winter for the potted lemon trees and orange trees to stand out all the year. They had to be taken in for the chilly winter months.

I suppose that lemon and orange trees growing in pots were a convention of Italian gardens which derived from the pleasure it gave in such a hot land to pick a fruit and suck its refreshing juice. The upshot of this was of course a whole industry in fine terra-cotta pots, as well as buildings to house them.

Of course the other influence which has had a hand in the creation of the convention of standing out potted plants is the paucity of soil in some hot places. In parts of Spain, for instance, there is hardly any soil to be had at all. It is something to be cherished in containers, like water. If you can't find it naturally on the earth all around you, you have to husband little bits in pots and then grow in them whatever you can.

Hence, then, a whole technique of growing plants out of doors in pots has spread across the Continent of Europe, from the barren parts to the more verdant ones. Perhaps it has its most vivid expression in the Spanish city of Cordoba where, though the gulleys of the street may run with unmentionable filth, the flower-filled patios, the balconies and the window boxes are a sight that visitors come from everywhere to see in May. Just then everyone opens their patios for public delight, when everything overflows with geraniums, roses and jasmine. No wonder we wished to import something of this.

Small town gardens or patios are dreary places unless embellished with potted plants stood out in summer. And if you can keep plants indoors or protected during the winter the more interesting your terrace display can be in summer. However, if space is at a premium, and it usually is, you can always plant up tubs to give interest throughout the year.

A succession of colour The soil in a tub is always warmer than that in the ground, hence you get quicker growth. Again, it's easier (and less costly) to refurbish the soil in a tub by adding rotted organic refuse of one kind or another than it is to an open-ground bed.

Once the principle is accepted of using in this way seasonal flowering plants that are customarily changed over from time to time, a whole field of gardening in containers is opened up, with many opportunities of changing the plants much more often than they would be in the open ground in order to maintain a long succession of colour.

The first thing to understand is that you need the largest possible containers your garden will take. This is not as wild as it sounds because tubs placed in position always seem smaller than they do in the garden centre when you buy them. This does not mean either that you can't move them about because of the weight of soil in them. I strongly favour using peat-based composts which are lightweight, and feeding the plants regularly.

It does not imply moving everything and therefore an excessive amount of work. I find that bulbs can stay in place year after year. Their power to rise to the surface from whatever depth they are planted is astonishing. They can actually lie below the level that will be disturbed for other plants later. At least, this goes for hyacinths, daffodils and crocuses, which I find do best in tubs. Indeed, you can interplant the bulbs of all three, making a succession with these for the spring months. As the last of them, the hyacinths, go over, you can then slip between them with the point of your trowel your fuchsia cuttings, plants that develop at a really surprising rate once they get going.

Or, of course, summer bedding plants of many other kinds. Here I am sure it is best to get those which have been raised in small containers of peat-based compost. These suffer the least disturbance and therefore check when they are planted and development is swift, especially with one or two puffs from a sprayer charged with foliar feed. While they are growing away the foliage of the bulbs will be withering and it can be cut right down once it is half browned.

I think this is the answer where the problems of cost and space inhibit growing bedding plants on any scale. Buy them in from garden centres, but only a few so that the outlay is not exorbitant and grow them in big tubs as accent plants in the garden and on terraces, as well as doorways and along paths. In fact, you then appreciate them more, as you are brought in closer acquaintance with them.

When petunias are grown in containers they are much more likely to get their dead heads snipped off than they are in the open ground and performance is then maintained. Sometimes, in spite of all one's efforts, the plants get a bit tired looking. Whip them out, and replace them with something else! You can often find young plants offered for sale when the summer is quite advanced.

Alternatively, as summer comes towards its end, the bedders can be replaced with small plants of pompon chrysanthemums pinched back to make them bushy and brought along in the summer in a large box of peat-based compost. Take what are called a little disrespectfully Irishman's cuttings. These are simply rooted bits pulled off the parent plant, which can then be discarded. In the late autumn, when the season really is over what have by then become real chrysanthemum plants are taken out and laid in a box of soil, which is then left in a sheltered corner for the winter, protected, of course, from slugs. Come the spring and new growth, the cuttings are pulled off and allowed to become small plants in another box, and it is from this that they are transferred to the tubs.

What about the winter? Nothing better than one of the variegated forms of ivy, unless it's the variegated *Vinca major*, the large-growing periwinkle. These can be kept for the rest of the year in small pots plunged in the ground. Both plants need very little soil in their pots, which can be slipped in the top of the tub and only removed when the first signs of bulb growth appear.

Vinca major 'Variegata'

Flamboyance and perfume If you can provide some winter protection, perferably indoors or in a greenhouse, the field is wide open. Small lean-to greenhouses with sliding doors are very reasonably priced and one can be found to fit into all but the tiniest of gardens. With the help of this facility a more varied collection of plants can be kept to bring a continental brilliance to your backyard or patio during the summer months.

Geraniums come first, and this argues the case for growing the plants on from year to year so that they develop woody stems, instead of bringing along a fresh batch from cuttings every year. I find myself that it is much easier to keep over the winter the scented-leaved kinds, as these develop most readily those tough stems. With them I group the so-called Unique series of old-fashioned geraniums, which have distinctly funnel-shaped flowers often blotched with a contrasting shade at the centre.

There's no doubt at all that the best of all flowering plants to make a show of colour is the old Ivy-leaved Geranium. It will trail if you want it to and it will stand up straight if gently staked with a few twigs. It flowers ceaselessly from the time you put it in until the late autumn. Some of the colours are a bit garish for the open ground, but somehow this is a factor that makes them look just right in a tub. Mostly they come in pinks, scarlet and mauve, but if you want yellow or orange try the trailing gazanias. These have silvery leaves and an apparently endless succession of bright daisy flowers.

179

Next in importance come the fuchsias, not the hardy ones, but the great range of cultivars styled greenhouse fuchsias. In truth they do very well out of doors during the summer and have more flamboyance than the hardy kinds. Flamboyance, indeed, is the first thing asked of in a potted plant standing outside. I long to have bottlebrush bushes and Bird-of-paradise Flower plants to stand out but for the moment I am content with other tender plants of Mediterranean and Australasian origin.

Scent is another factor for intimate enjoyment. I have long had several bushes of the lemon-scented lippia and the tender lavender, *Lavandula dentatus*, which I believe is the source of lavender water produced in the South of France, and much more heavily scented than our ordinary Mitcham Lavender. In Spain I have seen carnations and stocks grown as potted plants. It may have been the heat that helped to give them their especially heavy scent, but I suspect that it was also the restriction at the root which assisted too. All aromatic plants are at home in poor soil. Every season I contrive to have a few verbenas and heliotrope stood out in containers hardly big enough for them.

Other kinds of potted plants with silvery leaves that would not be altogether hardy out of doors and which need glasshouse protection to keep the rain off in winter include woolly ballota, artemisias – also aromatic – helichrysums and all the thymes. One must also use tender herbs like basil and tarragon. In fact, a potted herb garden is a much more satisfactory garden proposition than one set in open ground.

There are even water plants that you can grow in pots and stand out. All the cyperus, or Umbrella Plants, look best this way, and so do those miniature water lilies, the white *Nymphaea pygmaea* 'Alba' and its pale yellow cultivar 'Helvola'.

In my garden, small as it is, I cannot grow the splendid cannas, and so have these in pots. Nor can I grow alpines, due to the heavy soil, so I have tried many sempervivums in bowls: they never need any attention. Lately I have added some plants of the blue parochetus and having started on these there can be no end to them. All they need in the winter is the covering of a frame. Here they would be boring in summer, out of doors they become moments of surprise and excitement.

A permanent effect Fuchsia breeding in recent years has resulted in a great many sturdy, large-flowered kinds that will stand the buffetings of the weather out of doors. Since these can be cut right to the ground in the early spring, to make them behave like herbaceous plants, they are very suitable for permanent plantings in association with bulbs, with the fuchsias to follow a little later on. The whole planting can be left undisturbed from year to year.

Shrubs that seem to me excellent as tub plants for permanent effect should of course be evergreen. Apart from the obvious examples of topiary in box and yew, both of which will endure dryness, the golden

Cyperus can be grown successfully in a container provided the soil is kept permanently moist

splashed *Elaeagnus pungens* 'Maculata' makes a splendid tub shrub. So do those forms of *Prunus laurocerasus*, the common Laurel called 'Zabeliana' and 'Otto Luyken', with outstretched branches. I also recommend the aromatic-leaved *Choisya ternata*, the Mexican Orange Blossom, all the hebes, and the scarlet-berried skimmias.

Some of the best plants of lavender I have ever seen have been grown in pots, presumably because it was then possible to shelter them a bit and give them a longer growing season. Myrtle (*Myrtus communis*) is another that likes this treatment, and so does rosemary (*Rosmarinus officinalis* and its cultivars), a plant that in clay soil districts can easily die during the winter.

All the sages, forms of *Salvia officinalis*, are good in tubs, and this includes the so-called Jerusalem Sage or *Phlomis fruticosa*. Cistus can be good in tubs, provided they are kept in the full sun, while other tender kinds that enjoy sharp drainage and a little protection include all the silver-leaved shrubs, palm trees and even the ordinary Bay Laurel, *Laurus nobilis*, which in some areas gets its leaves browned in the open ground.

One gardener I know grows his camellias and rhododendrons in pots, for which he otherwise has to make up special beds, and then treat the plants with sequestrene to prevent the lime harming them. Such plants are best in the light shade, provided they get enough rain, for the one thing that makes them drop their buds and spoil the show is alternate spells of saturation and dryness.

Appendix

What's in a name?

'All those long tongue-twisting names ... Why will they go on using them? ... What's wrong with bluebell or daisy or marigold?' Non-gardeners complain ceaselessly about it. And with some reason, when you remember that even the specialists use common names for birds in their everyday conversation about the subject. But not gardeners. They have to talk of cypripedium, say, when they are discussing orchids, sambucus when it's elders and philadelphus when it's mock orange. 'Why can't they use simple common names that everyone under-stands?' is the familiar cry.

Everyone? By no means. What would daisy mean to someone in, say, Samoa? But nearer home common names apply to different plants in different parts of the country: the bluebells of Scotland are quite different from the bluebells of Sussex. The fact is that there are so many different plants in the natural world – more than a quarter of a million flowering kinds alone – that you've just got to have some system for identifying them individually. Otherwise you could never be sure which one you were talking about. Though there may be close similarities, every single one of that great number has its own individual characteristics. And then you have to add to them the vast accumula-tion of what you might call man-made plants, selected or specially bred by crossing two species.

Tower of Babel We would be in a hopeless tangle without the use of an international tongue, which in this case is Latin for convenience throughout the world, and without the general assent of plant scientists as to which plant should be called what. Anyway, we all use the Latin in everyday gardening talk already without knowing it. Crocus, forsythia and dahlia are Latin botanical terms. Who quarrels with these? If we all know them, why not others too?

Fortunately there is an international assembly of plant scientists which meets from time to time and whose task it is to consider the names of plants and make it all both simple and universal so that everyone who talks about plants is in no doubt about which special kinds they are referring to. This involves dividing them up according to their similarities and their differences.

Differences and similarities, that is, first in the organs of reproduction which every plant has and then in the leaves and finally in the flowers again, subdivision being subdivided. It is this that gives a plant more than one name.

For practical purposes it is first the family into which plants are grouped, like say rose or lily. Each of them can contain many genera (singular *genus*), as both these families do, but basically all do have the same floral characteristics. The generic name is the plant's first one, like *Rhododendron*. Next the members of this are found to form themselves naturally into a number of groups, which are called the species. So now we've got to two names, like *Rhododendron ponticum*, the common mauve one sees everywhere in early summer.

But within the species there can be many variations of colouring, perhaps, or of form. And so a third subdivision is necessary, but this time not into groups. Now it is that an individual is given a name of its own. If it was a variation that had occurred in the wild, as very often happens, it would have a third Latinised name, such as *variegata*, indicating that the leaves bore distinctive markings. Or it may be a special seedling selected in cultivation from a batch and showing a difference from all the rest that someone had considered worth perpetuating with a name of its own. He might give it his own or his wife's or that of the place where it had been noticed originally.

Varieties and cultivars So now we have got all three. In the latter case it would officially be called a cultivar, since it had arisen in cultivation, thus 'Compactum' denotes a form in which a dwarf, compact habit has been favoured by a plant breeder. This term is not so often used in conversation as is the word variety, which should correctly be reserved for special form which had arisen in the wild, perhaps a stronger shade or different colour altogether, a taller grower, one with variegated foliage or a dwarf.

Now just because all this is decided by scientists who spend their days in libraries and laboratories it doesn't mean that it is without romance. In bestowing names on plants they don't do it entirely on a descriptive basis, translating simple terms into the Latin. They often give a plant a name that honours someone important to the world of plants, and sometimes they make up a new name that expresses a likeness to another plant. It may all be a matter of reason but there are always touches of poetry.

Finding out the meanings or origins of plant names can become a fascinating fireside study. And when you begin to learn something about them it makes you look at plants much more closely than you ever did before. You also learn about the people who have brought plants from the wild into cultivation, and about obscure figures who might not otherwise be even names in history books. Far from long names for plants being an encumbrance and hindering the enjoyment of growing them, they actually enhance the joy of gardening, quite apart from the downright usefulness in classifying some of the wonderfully diverse features of the natural world and enabling them to be talked about as individuals – and bought in garden centres under their own pet names!

Change of name But why, you may reasonably ask, do they keep changing them? Why when we've learned that a certain plant is called *Viburnum fragrans* do we wake up one day and find that it's now *Viburnum farreri*, and that what we've always known as *Erica carnea* now has to be called *Erica herbacea*? Yes, the names of plants do change but not just to vex you or satisfy the whims of taxonomists, as those who study the names of plants and decide on them are called.

The set of international rules that governs the deliberations of these strange fellows includes a sort of primogeniture. This declares that the correct name for a plant is the one by which it is first described scientifically. Now scientific literature is extraordinarily diverse. When a new plant is given a name those who are identifying and describing it may not know of some reference to it elsewhere in forgotten libraries or manuscripts, perhaps compiled only from a dried specimen of the plant now before them as a living thing. The early reference may come to light only much later. Well, the rule of priority must apply and the plant must revert to the first name given it. You cannot have two titles for one and the same plant. That's really what it's all about.

Index

The figures in *italics* refer to illustrations